The Truth About

Feeding Your Horse

The Truth About

Feeding Your Horse

CLARE MACLEOD

J.A. ALLEN · LONDON

© Clare MacLeod 2007
First published in Great Britain 2007

ISBN 978 0 85131 918 6

J.A. Allen
Clerkenwell House
Clerkenwell Green
London EC1R 0HT

J.A. Allen is an imprint of Robert Hale Limited

Edited by Martin Diggle
Design and typesetting by Paul Saunders
Line illustrations by the author
Charts and diagrams by Rodney Paull

Photographs on pages 3, 4, 19, 25, 63, 82, 83 (left), 89 (top), 115, 117 (left), 119 (left),
137 (right), 151, 158, 160, 172, 176, 188 (bottom left), 237 (bottom) and 249 courtesy of
www.istockphoto.com; on pages 20, 129 AND 133 (bottom) courtesy of Feedmark; on pages 21, 111,
116, 117 (right), 152, 153 (top), 185, 203, 218, 237 (top) and 246 courtesy of Sally Brett; on pages 100
and 107 courtesy of Equimore (www.equimore.co.uk); on pages 168, 201, 228 and 236 courtesy of
Redwings (www.redwings.co.uk); on pages 170, 188 (top right) and 229 courtesy of
www.dreamstime.com. Photograph on page 73 courtesy of EH Haylage (www.ehhaylage.co.uk);
on page 83 courtesy of SPILLERS® (Effem Equine Ltd; www.spillers-feeds.com); on page 101
courtesy of Rockies (www.rockies.co.uk); on page 125 courtesy of Fort Dodge Animal Health; on
page 133 (top) courtesy of Horseweigh (www.horseweigh.com); on page 146 courtesy of
www.grazingmuzzles.co.uk; on page 188 (bottom) courtesy of West End Photography; on page
217 courtesy of Sue Devereux. Other photographs by, or property of, the author.

Printed by New Era Printing Co. Limited, China

Dedication

To the horses: may they continue to teach and inspire us.

Contents

Acknowledgements xii
List of tables xiii
List of figures xv

1 An Introduction to nutrition and feeding 1

2 The equine digestive tract 5

Comparative notes 5
Features of the digestive tract 6
   The mouth and taste; The teeth; Saliva; The throat, oesophagus
   and stomach; The small intestine; The large intestine; The liver and pancreas

3 Feeding behaviour 15

Normal time budgets 15
Selection of food 17
Appetite 17
Rate of food intake 18
Abnormal behaviour 19
   Can certain types of feed or supplements affect behaviour?

4 Nutrients and nutritional requirements 24

Published requirements 24
Water 25
Energy 27

Carbohydrates 29
    Digestion of sugar and starch; Absorption and use of sugar and starch
Protein 35
    Digestion, absorption and use of protein
Fats and oils (lipids) 37
    Omega-3 fatty acids; Digestion, absorption and use of lipids
Minerals 40
    Macrominerals; Microminerals
Vitamins 49
    Fat-soluble vitamins; Water-soluble vitamins

5 Fibre 56

What is fibre? 56
    Types of fibre in feed; Classifying fibre by analysis
Digestion of fibre 61
Absorption and use of fibre 62
Fibre deficiency¹ 62

6 Feeds and supplements 64

Feeds 65
    Labelling and nutrient declarations; Forages and unprocessed fibre feeds;
    Chopped forage/chaffs; Forage analysis; Cereal grains; Grain by-products; Nutrient
    balancing issues with grain; Protein-rich seeds and their by-products; Root
    vegetables; Other straight feeds; Compound feeds
Supplements 95
    Labelling and nutrient declarations; Vitamin and mineral supplements (broad
    spectrum); Salt and electrolyte supplements; Specific nutrient supplements;
    Supplements for specific problems; Plant antioxidants; Probiotics and prebiotics;
    Herbs and herbal blends; Vegetable oils; Fish oils; Treats

7 Pasture 109

Types of pasture, grass species and productivity 109
    Grass growth
Pasture as feed 112
    Grass feeding values for horses
Pasture maintenance 114

Removal of droppings; Optimal grazing; Weed control; Poisonous plants;
Fertilization and other treatments; Minimizing poaching; Shelter, fencing and
access to water

8 Practical feeding 122

Dental health 122
Internal parasite control 124
Description and life cycle of major parasites in horses; Controlling
internal parasites in horses
Practical Diet Formulation 131
Establishing bodyweight and condition; Formulating the ration; Feeding for
weight gain; Feeding for weight loss; More precise calculations for ration
formulation, using nutrient requirements
Practical Feeding Guidelines 151
Access to water; Storage and hygiene; Design and use of feed containers; Maximum
amounts; Make all changes gradually; When to feed; Feeding-related behavioural
problems; Feeding and transportation

9 Feeding for reproduction and growth 157

Feeding broodmares 157
Prior to conception; The first 8 months of pregnancy; The final 3 months of
pregnancy; During lactation
Feeding Stallions 160
Feeding Youngstock 161
The newborn foal; The first few months; Weaning welfare; From 6 months to 2
years; Avoiding developmental abnormalities; Feeding the orphaned foal

10 Feeding for physical performance 169

Energy supply 169
How energy is extracted from feed; Energy storage in the body; The currency of
energy; How energy is produced; What happens when energy supplies run out
Nutritional requirements for performance horses 177
Water and the electrolyte macrominerals; Protein; Antioxidant nutrients; Micronutrients
Practical diets for performance horses 184
Forage and fibre; Starch and sugar; Fat supplementation; Feeding for specific disciplines;
Effects of exercise on appetite; Practical timing of feeding performance horses; Avoiding
prohibited substances

11 Feeding in old age 194

Nutritional requirements of the older horse 194
Dental function 196
Maintaining healthy weight and coping with weight loss 197
Dealing with Infirmities 199
    Joint mobility problems and osteoarthritis; Cushing's syndrome
Supplements for support 201

12 Feeding more naturally 202

Freedom and forage 202
Natural feeds and supplements 204
    Avoiding artificial additives; A vegetarian diet; Organic feeds
General management 206
    Keeping Horses without Shoes

13 Clinical nutrition 209

Colic 209
Acid gut syndrome 212
Diarrhoea 212
Choke 214
Gastric ulcers 214
Skin, coat and hoof problems 216
Food allergies 217
Allergic respiratory disease 218
Practical aspects of clinical nutrient deficiencies 219
Obesity 220
Feeding horses on box rest 220
Sick and anorexic horses 222
    Feeding horses with grass sickness; Re-introducing feed to the starved horse;
    Feeding the horse with liver disease; Feeding the horse with kidney disease

14 Laminitis 227

What happens during laminitis 227
Signs of laminitis 230
    Animals at risk

Diet-induced laminitis 231
    Grass; Starchy cereals
Feeding management of laminitics 232

15 Tying-up (rhabdomyolysis) 235

The disease process 235
    Polysaccharide storage myopathy (PSSM); Recurrent exertional rhabdomyolysis (RER)
Recognizing and Treating the Condition 238
    Feeding management for affected horses; General management tips

16 Feeding myths 242

Appendix – Nutrient requirements for horses 250
Glossary 252
Useful Contacts 259
Index 264

Acknowledgements

First and foremost, thanks to the horses for their patient and enduring efforts in trying to tell us what they need. We still have so much to learn from them. Special thanks to my three, Tapir, Nedley and Juniper.

This book has been brought alive by the wonderful pictures that were given for it. Special thanks go to Sally Brett for her many pictures, and to Clare Lockyer at Spillers Horse Feeds for her help. Thanks also to Bev Rippon, Claire Wiseman, Helen Whitelegg at Redwings, Nik Barker, Sue Devereux, Sue Meadows, Tanya and Darts, and the teams at Best Friend, Equimore, Horseweigh, Animal Health Highland Ltd, Fort Dodge Animal Health, North Walsham Saddlery in Norfolk, Rockies, and The Millers in Aberdeenshire. A special thank-you also to the vets at Fort Dodge Animal Health for their suggestions about internal parasites, which helped with the writing of Chapter 8.

Thanks to Carolyn Henderson, for encouraging me to take the first step and for introducing me to the team at J. A. Allen. Thanks also to everyone at J. A. Allen, for guiding me through the book-creation process, and I am indebted to Martin Diggle and Paul Saunders for their patient editing and design work. Also thanks to my dear husband Lee, my family and all my friends for tolerating me 'disappearing' for weeks on end, to get all my knowledge and experience down on paper. To all the horse owners, managers and vets I have worked with – thank you for your valuable feedback.

List of tables

CHAPTER 2 **The equine digestive tract**

2.1   Age at which horse's teeth appear 7

2.2   Percentage volume of different gut compartments 10

2.3   Digestive enzymes and their substrates 12

2.4   Sites of nutrient absorption in the horse 14

CHAPTER 3 **Feeding behaviour**

3.1   Number of chews and time taken to eat forage and concentrates ... 17

CHAPTER 4 **Nutrients and nutritional requirements**

4.1   Classification of carbohydrates 30

4.2   Minerals for horses; functions, deficiencies and excesses ... 41

4.3   Vitamins for horses; functions, deficiency and excesses ... 51

CHAPTER 5 **Fibre**

5.1   Fibre constituents of horse feed (percentage of dry matter) ... 60

CHAPTER 6 **Feeds and supplements**

6.1   Feed: analytical constituents 68

6.2   Typical analysis of forages 79

6.3   Nutrient composition of cereals for horses 80

6.4   Nutrient content of 2 kg naked oats compared to regular oats ... 82

6.5   Notes on horse feeds available in the UK 94

6.6   'Problem-solving' supplements and what they are likely to contain ... 103

CHAPTER 7 **Pasture**

7.1   Normal ranges of mineral content of pasture grass in the UK ... 113

CHAPTER 8 **Practical feeding**

8.1   The main horse parasites and their control with anthelmintic drugs ... 128

8.2 A strategic worm control plan   130
8.3 Body condition scoring (0–5 scale)   136
8.4 Suitable body condition scores for horses in different disciplines.   137
8.5 Typical daily feed intakes (appetite)   138
8.6 Dry matter of typical horse feeds.   139
8.7 Recommended forage to concentrate ratios (based on Thorough-
     breds and their crosses)   139
8.8 Typical weights of feeds in one level 2.5 litre plastic 'bowl' scoop   143

CHAPTER 9 **Feeding for reproduction and growth**
9.1 Normal growth patterns for young horses   166

CHAPTER 10 **Feeding for physical performance**
10.1 'Fuel' stored in an average 500 kg horse   171
10.2 Constituents of equine sweat, plus concentrations   178
10.3 Constituents of two different types of compound feeds for
      performance horses   185

CHAPTER 15 **Tying-up (rhabdomyolysis)**
15.1 Typical blood plasma muscle enzyme levels   236

Appendix
A.1 Daily nutrient requirements for working, growing and breeding horses 250

List of figures

CHAPTER 2 **The equine digestive tract**
2.1 The equine digestive tract   6
2.2 Equine teeth   8
2.3 Section through the equine stomach   10

CHAPTER 4 **Nutrients and nutritional requirements**
4.1 Dry matter of some horse feeds.   26
4.2 Diagram to show use of energy in the horse.   28
4.3 Diagram to show the structures of starch and cellulose.   31
4.4 Graph to show measurement of glycaemic index of a food.   34

CHAPTER 6 **Feeds and supplements**
6.1 Water content of hay and haylage   74
6.2 Illustration of a carrot to show water and dry matter content   88

CHAPTER 7 **Pasture**
7.1 Typical grass growth throughout the seasons   111
7.2 Diagram of small redworm life cycle and pasture infection   114

CHAPTER 8 **Practical feeding**
8.1 Transverse section of skull, showing hooks on teeth   123
8.2 Measuring a horse's heart girth and length   134

CHAPTER 10 **Feeding for physical performance**
10.1 Simple diagram of the energy metabolic mill   175

CHAPTER 14 **Laminitis**
14.1 Diagram showing location of the digital artery   230

chapter 1

An introduction to nutrition and feeding

Nowadays, feeding horses is a complex business. The huge variety and number of products available give horse owners a great deal of choice, but can also make feeding horses seem more complicated than it really is. Horses are more difficult to feed than cats or dogs because they have a more complex digestive system and they are rarely fed complete feeds, but usually receive forage plus extra feed and/or supplements. As with most things, getting a good grasp of the basics will help the horse owner to make informed choices, rather than relying on feed packaging and advertising, some of which is rather misleading.

Much practical knowledge of feeding is based on traditional circumstances, when horses worked very hard and a limited number of feed varieties were available. Not only do many horses work less hard nowadays, but a huge number of new feeds are available, which means that even the most hard-working horses can have their nutrient requirements fulfilled in a different way; a way which is more healthy for them.

Correct nutrition is essential for good health and performance in horses, and it depends entirely on correct feeding. Horses are adaptive animals, and can appear to cope with very unnatural management and feeding regimes. However, research in the past twenty years or so has provided evidence to support the view that many of the problems our horses encounter nowadays could be avoided with management and feeding regimes that more closely resemble those that the horse has adapted for over millions of years. This is not to say horses cannot be kept intensively, but that with some novel and lateral thinking, their environments and feeding regimes can help rather than hinder their physical and mental health.

Nutrition is a subject incorporating elements of physiology, biochemistry and species behaviour. While a thorough knowledge of the whole science of feeding is not a requisite for an individual owner to feed horses correctly, it

Many horses are kept for leisure nowadays, and don't work very hard.

remains the case that delving into all these areas will help in the formulation of good feeding practices.

A good place to begin with is a look at the anatomy and physiology of the horse's digestive tract, which helps provide an understanding of how horses eat their feed, how they digest it and how the nutrients are absorbed. Next, gaining knowledge of feeding behaviour will help to ensure good welfare and avoid problems. The theory of feeding would not be complete without an investigation of the essential nutrients, the roles they play in health and the daily requirements of the horse. A separate chapter in this book is devoted to fibre, a much misunderstood nutrient, which is of great importance to the horse.

To be able to put a feed ration together in practice, a good working knowledge of all the different feeds is important, including forages, chaffs, straights and other feed ingredients; compounds; extras, including sugar beet, supplements and pasture. An entire chapter is devoted to pasture, the ultimate feed for horses.

With knowledge of the basics, practical feeding becomes much easier. However, before guidelines on ration formulation –'what to feed' – are given, the importance of attention to dental health and parasite control is stressed and explained. There is little point in giving a horse an ideal feed ration if chewing and absorptive ability are impaired. Practical feeding management such as when to feed, how to feed to support normal behaviour and how to avoid feeding-related problems is explained at this point, building on the information given in earlier chapters.

Horses in their natural environment.

Practical feeding of different classes of horses comes next, including feeding for growth and reproduction, feeding for physical performance (the working horse), and feeding in old age. Research in the past decade has changed views on the best way to feed young, growing horses, which should lead to healthier, more robust adults with longer working lives. The same is true for working horses who, in the past, have sometimes been fed with little regard for their basic behaviour and physical needs. The new feeds available allow horses to be fed for optimum physical performance without compromising their general health. Many horses are living well into their twenties and even thirties and some require specialist feeding. For those who choose to manage and feed their horses more naturally, there is a chapter devoted to this subject, including how to ensure that the diet is truly vegetarian, how to avoid synthetic additives and nutrients and how to ensure optimum nutrition in a horse managed less intensively.

After this, are three chapters on clinical nutrition. A large proportion of veterinary problems in horses are linked to feeding and nutrition. How to feed horses with colic, diarrhoea, gastric ulcers, feed allergies, poor skin, coat and hoof health, respiratory disease, liver and kidney disease are discussed. Further chapters are devoted to both laminitis and tying up (rhabdomyolysis), because appropriate feeding is crucial in the management of these conditions. Finally, a chapter about feeding myths will help to dispel the many beliefs that get in the way of correct feeding. The book concludes with a glossary to help explain scientific terms, and a list of useful contacts.

If the entire book is read cover to cover, some repetition will be noted; this happens because I am aware that readers may sometimes wish to refer to one

A group of alert, healthy horses at pasture.

specific chapter at a time. Ideally, however, the first two chapters should be read before any reference is made to the practical sections, because the knowledge gained will help in applying information supplied in the later chapters.

Conversions

Throughout this book metric measurements, which are the feed industry norm in the UK, are used. The following conversions may be useful for readers more familiar with imperial systems.

Metric units	**Metric/UK Imperial**
1 kg = 1,000 g	1 kg = 2.2 lb: 1lb = 454 g (0.454 kg)
1 g = 1,000 mg	28 g = 1 oz: 1 oz = 28 g
1 litre = 1,000 ml	1 litre = 1.76 pints: 1 pint = 568 ml
	1 litre = 0.22 gallons: 1 gallon = 4.546 litres
US comparisons	
0.473 litres =1 US pint (liquid)	**Other Measurements**
3.785 litres = 1 US gallon	1 part per million (ppm) = 1 mg/kg
	1 teaspoon ~ 5 ml
	1 tablespoon ~ 15 ml
	1 US cup ~ 225 ml

chapter 2

The equine digestive tract

HORSES ARE FED to provide their body with nourishment. In order for the horse's body to use the nutrients in feed, the feed must first be broken down, or digested. Digestion extracts nutrients that can then be absorbed through the digestive tract or gut, for use in the body. Although the basic structure of the digestive tract of all mammals is broadly similar, the fundamentals of how it functions can be quite different. Studying the digestive tract of any animal provides an understanding of the type of feed the animal has evolved to eat, and the manner in which the animal ingests that feed, and thus a study of the horse's digestive tract will reveal information that is very useful when choosing feeds and feeding strategies.

Comparative notes

The horse's digestive tract or system reflects its evolution. The horse is a hoofed herbivore and, like ruminants (cud-chewers) including cows and sheep, gains his nutrients from coarse fibrous forage that cannot be digested by omnivores like humans. Just like ruminants, horses digest their diet via fermentation in an enlarged part of their digestive tract. However, instead of an enlarged stomach full of microbes, the horse has as enlarged hindgut full of microbes where fibre is digested. Horses do not chew the cud as ruminants like cattle and sheep do, therefore they do not chew their feed into such small pieces. Horses digest their natural fibrous diet much less efficiently than ruminants, but eat much more. They have higher feed intakes and higher passage rates through the gut, so they can survive on forage of a lower nutrient content. Horses are classed as 'monogastrics' or simple-stomached animals, a group which includes pigs. They are also classed as grazers, but will also browse, eating not just grass and other herbage, but also trees, hedges and shrubs, if given the opportunity.

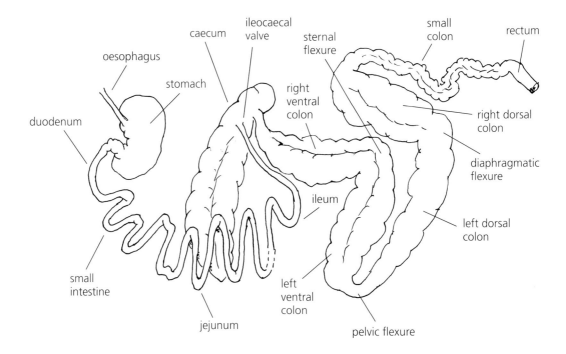

Figure 2.1 The equine digestive tract.

Features of the digestive tract

The mouth and taste

The horse has strong, grasping lips that search out plants of choice, and enable him to pick out desirable and undesirable feeds. The dexterity of lip movement is what allows the horse to eat a feed leaving all the pellets in the bottom of his feed bowl. The muzzle is a very sensitive area, covered with long and short hairs. The tongue forms food into a bolus and passes it to the back of the mouth for chewing. Horses have a good sense of taste, and can be very taste-sensitive to new feed in the diet. Various research trials have investigated food flavour choices by horses, and although foals preferred sweetened solutions (only between 1.25 and 10 g sucrose per litre) most horses show wide individual preferences. Fenugreek, cherry, banana and mint have been proposed as being favourites.

The teeth

Horses have incisors (biting teeth) on both upper and lower jaws, a gap of gum (the interdental space) and large chewing premolars and molars in the back of the mouth. The dental formula of a mature horse is:

Male 2*   (I 3/3, C 1/1, P 3 or 4/3, M 3/3) = 40 or 42

Female 2* (I 3/3, C 0/0, P3 or 4/3, M 3/3) = 36 or 38.

*Each side of the mouth has this number of teeth, hence each must be multiplied by 2.
 I, C, P, M indicate incisors, canines, premolars and molars, respectively.

Male horses have canines or tushes that erupt in the interdental spaces, and small pointed teeth that appear right next to the first upper premolar, called wolf teeth. These are usually removed in young horses because they can interfere with the bit. The molars and premolars may be overlooked because they cannot easily be seen, but they are the grinders that allow the horse to survive on his natural high-fibre diet. All the teeth are hypsodont, which means that, while they first appear as shown in Table 2.1, they are constantly erupting throughout the animal's life. They may grow out and fall out as the animal ages.

Permanent tooth	Age at eruption
1st premolar	5–6 months
1st molar	9–12 months
2nd molar	2 years
2nd premolar	2½ years
1st incisor (centre)	2½ years
3rd premolar	3 years
2nd incisor	3½ years
3rd molar	3½–4 years
4th premolar	4 years
3rd incisor	4½ years
Canine	4–5 years

Table 2.1 Age at which horse's teeth appear.

The incisor teeth look longer and are at a greater slant as the horse grows old, until eventually the teeth appear shorter as they grow out. In addition, the surfaces become more triangular than oval, and look smooth in older horses. Horses' teeth contain different types of dental tissue, which are worn down at different rates, resulting in self-sharpening as the horse chews. The rough surfaces of the chewing teeth (molars) may be worn smooth in old horses whose teeth are growing out. The lower jaw (the mandible) moves both up and down and side to side, to facilitate the grinding of tough, fibrous plant material. The upper jaw (maxilla) is wider than the lower jaw, which aids this lateral grinding process, but leads to the development of sharp edges on the outer edges of the upper teeth and on the inner edges of the lower teeth. If not attended to by a dental technician or vet,

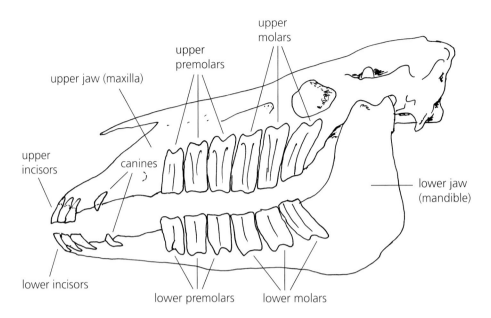

Figure 2.2 Equine teeth.

these sharp edges can cause damage to the soft tissues of the mouth, inability to chew properly, and quidding (dropping half-chewed food from the mouth). Affected horses may show signs of pain or discomfort, especially with the bit. More practical information and advice about dental health is given in Chapter 8.

The wear of the cheek teeth is affected by the diet, with high levels of concentrates fed at head height being most associated with uneven wear and malocclusion (misalignment of the upper and lower teeth). The lower jaw moves forward slightly as the horse lowers his head to the ground, therefore causing a slightly different action on the teeth as the horse chews. Different types of feed require different amounts of chewing, with forages taking many more chews than concentrate feed (see Chapter 3). Ponies tend to chew many more times for the same amount of feed than horses, probably because they have adapted to live on tougher, less nutritious feeds such as hill grasses.

Saliva

Digestion in the mouth is limited to mechanical chewing, or mastication. Food is broken down into smaller pieces and mixed with saliva, ready for swallowing. Saliva helps lubricate the mouth and throat, and helps maintain a healthy stomach environment. Along with food, saliva helps to neutralize stomach acid. Saliva is 99% water, but also contains mucus, a little of the enzyme amylase, and some salts including bicarbonates, making it slightly alkaline. Different types of saliva are produced depending on the diet, with large amounts of watery saliva secreted when dry foods are eaten. Little starch digestion takes place in the horse's mouth, in contrast to that of the human, in which saliva contains relatively high levels of amylase. The action of chewing is necessary for saliva production in the horse, and large amounts are produced as the horse chews. Rarely do horses salivate in anticipation of food, although this is not unknown. As a horse chews, saliva is secreted into the mouth from three pairs of saliva glands: the parotids, situated in front of the ears, the submandibular, situated on each side of the lower jaw, and the sublingual, situated underneath the tongue. Around 10–13 litres of saliva are produced per 24 hours on an average forage diet. Since forage requires more chewing than concentrate feed, a horse fed a high-concentrate diet will produce less saliva than one eating forage. This lower saliva production has a large impact on the horse's health, including an increased risk of stomach ulcers (see Chapter 13).

The throat, oesophagus and stomach

During swallowing, the bolus of food passes into the throat, called the pharynx. The food passes over the trachea (the airway), which is protected by the epiglottis, a flap of cartilage that opens when the horse breathes. The food passes from the throat into the oesophagus, a muscular tube of about 120–150 cm length in the horse, which transports food material, now called digesta, down into the stomach. In some circumstances the oesophagus can become blocked with digesta, which is then called choke.

The lower oesophagus joins the stomach via a strong muscular valve called the cardiac sphincter. This valve does not permit vomiting except very rarely, and stomach rupture may occur if the stomach becomes severely distended. The horse's stomach is relatively small, with a capacity of 9–13 litres (see Table 2.2), and is a J-shaped sac with muscular walls. Stomach or gastric acid production is continuous at variable rates and not dependent on the presence of digesta or eating, except after prolonged periods of fasting. The upper part of the stomach lining (the *saccus caecus*) consists of unprotected tissue (squamous epithelium), which is susceptible to acid damage and gastric ulceration in intensively managed horses (see Chapter 13). The border between the upper and lower parts of the stomach is called the *margo plicatus*, and the area below this is glandular and produces large amounts of mucus. The lower glandular region consists of the fundic and pyloric regions, which have various cells that secrete acid, mucus and pepsinogen (the inactive form of pepsin that digests protein). The pH in this area may be as low as 2.6 (i.e. highly acidic). Bacteria, most of which ferment non-structural carbohydrates such as starch, survive in both areas of the stomach. However, there is little activity of fibre-fermenting bacteria. The hormone gastrin is secreted into the blood from the stomach in response to distention of the stomach wall by feed, and it stimulates the secretion of gastric acid and pepsinogen.

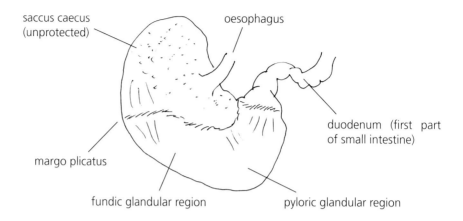

Figure 2.3 Section through the equine stomach.

Most digesta is held in the stomach for a short time – about 20 minutes – but the stomach is rarely empty in a horse with ad lib access to food, and some digesta is retained for several hours. Little digestion actually takes place in the stomach, although some protein is broken down to peptides via the action of pepsin, activated from pepsinogen by hydrochloric acid. Digesta moves out of the stomach via the pyloric sphincter, into the first part of the small intestine, the duodenum.

	% of total gut volume		
	Stomach	Small intestine	Large intestine
Horse	8.5	30.2	61.3
Dog	62.3	23.3	14.4
Cow	70.8	18.5	10.7

Table 2.2 Percentage volume of different gut compartments.

The small intestine

The horse has a relatively short small intestine, at about 21–25 m in a 450 kg animal, and it consists of the duodenum, the jejunum and the ileum. Digesta transit is rapid, with some appearing in the caecum just 45 minutes after a meal.

The horse has no gall bladder; instead bile is secreted continuously, although it ceases after a 48-hour fast. The acidic digesta leaving the stomach is neutralized by bile and bicarbonates secreted from the duodenal glands (Brunner's glands), along with protective mucus. This neutralization is necessary for the action of digestive enzymes and the absorption of nutrients. Digestive enzymes (Table 2.3) are secreted from the pancreas and intestinal lining. Pancreatic juice containing enzymes is secreted continuously in small amounts, and larger amounts are produced in response to the presence of food in the stomach. The small intestine is the site for the digestion and absorption of sugar, starch, amino acids, lipids (oils and fats), minerals and vitamins. The surface area of the small intestine is increased by finger-like projections called villi, aiding absorption. Horses have a limited ability to digest starch, because of relatively low concentrations of the starch-digesting enzyme, amylase (concentrations in the horse are about half in comparison to the pig), but there is wide individual variation. All cereals with the exception of oats should be processed before being fed to horses, to increase starch digestibility. Horses do, however, produce relatively high levels of sugar-digesting enzymes, so they digest dietary sugar well.

Absorption of nutrients takes place by:

1. Passive transport, which involves the simple diffusion of nutrients from an area of low concentration to an area of higher concentration.

2. Facilitative transport, which involves carrier proteins that transfer nutrients into intestinal cells, but still to an area of lower concentration, i.e. down a concentration gradient.

3. Active transport, which involves a large, complex carrier protein that links with the nutrient plus either a sodium or hydrogen ion, and then travels into the cell down a concentration gradient.

4. Pinocytosis, which involves intestinal cells engulfing large molecules, and is most important in newborn mammals who are absorbing immunoglobins present in colostrum.

Products of carbohydrate digestion are absorbed by both facilitative and active transport. The products of most fat digestion are absorbed by passive diffusion after emulsification by bile salts, and medium- and short-chain fatty acids are absorbed by active transport. The products of protein digestion are absorbed by active transport, apart from some proteins, which can be absorbed by pinocytosis, as explained above. Absorption of minerals is not yet fully understood but is believed to be either by simple diffusion, facilitated or active transport. The fat-soluble vitamins (A, D, E and K) are absorbed via passive diffusion along with fats. The water-soluble vitamins are believed to be absorbed via both passive diffusion and active transport.

Enzyme	Substrate	End product
Carbohydrases including sucrase and maltase	Sugars	Simple sugars including glucose, sucrose and maltose
Lactase	Milk sugar (lactose)	Glucose and galactose
Amylase	Starch	Glucose
Proteases pepsin, trypsin, chymotrypsin and carboxypeptidases	Protein, peptones and peptides (breakdown products of protein)	Peptides and amino acids
Lipases	Fat	Fatty acids and monoglycerides

Table 2.3 Digestive enzymes and their substrates.

The large intestine

The large intestine, also called hindgut, consists of the caecum, the large colon, the small colon and the rectum. Digesta reaches the hindgut within around 3 hours after a meal, and by this time all the nutrients digestible by gut enzymes (hydrolysable nutrients) should ideally have been digested and absorbed. Therefore the digesta reaching the hindgut should be of consistent composition, provided that the horse has been fed an appropriate diet. The lining of the large intestine does not produce enzymes, and any digestion here takes place via enzymes which may have been brought down from the small intestine, and by microbial fermentation. Compared to most other mammals, horses have enlarged hindguts (especially the caecum) that accommodate a range of micro-organisms including bacteria, fungi and protozoa, many of which break down dietary fibre. These micro-organisms or microbes break down fibre by a process of fermentation, which produces volatile fatty acids (VFAs), lactate, gases and heat. VFAs are available to the horse and can contribute most of their energy requirements at maintenance level. These short-chain fatty acids are absorbed via active transport. B-complex vitamins and vitamin K are also synthesized by the microbes in the hindgut, and are then available to the horse. If any sugar, starch or soluble fibre reaches the hindgut, it will be rapidly fermented by bacteria that produce lactic acid, another VFA. If large amounts of these feed constituents flow into the hindgut, they will cause disturbance via a rapid drop in acidity. The consequences of this disturbance are explained further in Chapter 4.

The first part of the hindgut is the caecum, a large sac about 1 m long with a capacity of about 25–35 litres, which enters into the right ventral colon. The large colon is about 3–4 m long, and consists of the right and left ventral colon and right and left distal colon, which are joined by narrow bends called flexures. Both the caecum and the colon of the horse have sacculations (pouch-like structures) and these, along with the narrow bends of the colon, separate the hindgut into compartments, aiding microbial fermentation. From the large colon, digesta moves into the small colon, which is about 3.5 m long and spiral in nature. Here, water and some of the minerals, including the electrolytes, phosphorus and a small amount of calcium, are absorbed. Digesta moves from the small colon into the rectum, which is about 30 cm long and holds faeces (droppings), which are eventually voided via the anus.

The movement of digesta through the intestine occurs via peristalsis; wave-like muscular contractions that propel the digesta through, help mix food with digestive juices and enable digestive products to reach the intestine wall for absorption. After a meal, feed waste in the form of faeces begins to be voided after 24 hours and most has passed through by 65 hours, although these rates are variable. Faeces consists of undigested feed residue, water, digestive secretions, cells from the gut wall lining (epithelial cells), salts, bacteria, and products of microbial breakdown of nutrients.

The liver and pancreas

The liver and pancreas are accessory organs, which are involved in digestive processes. The liver produces bile, which is necessary for fat digestion and neutralization of the small intestinal contents, and the pancreas produces digestive enzymes and pancreatic juice, which are necessary for nutrient digestion and neutralization. The liver also has an important role to play in the processing of nutrients after absorption, and absorbed nutrients are carried in a blood vessel (the hepatic portal vein) from the gut directly to the liver. Fats are the exception to this; their breakdown products are released into the lymphatic system (a system of vessels that circulate the body, returning fluid to the cardiovascular system), which allows them to be released gradually into the blood. The liver produces the protein carriers that are required for fat transport from the gut.

Nutrient	Small intestine	Large intestine
Sugars *	Most	Unlikely
Starch	Most (if not overloaded), after digestion to sugars	Bacterial fermentation if small intestine is overloaded, which produces volatile fatty acids (VFAs)
Fibre	A little, depending on source, after fermentation to VFAs	Most, after fermentation by microbes, yielding VFAs
Protein	Most, after digestion to peptides and amino acids	A little
Fats and oils	All	None
Calcium	Yes	A little
Phosphorus	Yes	Yes
Electrolytes	Yes	Yes
Vitamins A and E	Yes	No
B complex vitamins and vitamin K	Yes	Yes, after production by microbes

* Contrary to popular belief, lush temperate grasses are not particularly sugar-rich, but instead may contain high levels of the polysaccharide, fructan. These carbohydrates are not digested by mammalian gut enzymes, but are instead available to lactic acid-producing bacteria. If large amounts are ingested rapidly, the resulting fermentation can alter the pH of the hindgut, causing lactic acidosis, disturbance, and possibly laminitis.

Table 2.4 Sites of nutrient absorption in the horse.

chapter 3

Feeding behaviour

FEEDING HORSES is about more than simply supplying them with the nutrients they require. In the past 20 years or so, research has shown that feeding horses with no regard to their behaviour results in a myriad of problems, from stomach ulcers to abnormal behaviour such as crib-biting to the development of growth problems and colic. Horses spend about 70% of their time looking for food and eating; therefore eating plays a significant role in the day-to-day behaviour patterns of every horse. Knowledge of what drives horses to eat, how they select their food, and how their appetite is regulated helps to provide them with appropriate diets.

As mentioned in Chapter 2, the horse has evolved to survive on low-quality herbage compared to ruminants such as cattle and sheep, but needs to take in large quantities. This entails feeding in such a way as to maintain a high level of gut fill, and if horses are fed high levels of concentrate feed and low levels of fibrous forage, they are at risk of a whole range of health problems, both physical and psychological. The development of abnormal or problematical behaviour is common in horses who are kept in environments and fed in ways that do not allow them to express normal behaviour, therefore it makes sense and improves welfare if horse-keeping takes normal equine behaviour into consideration.

Normal time budgets

Time budgets describe how animals spend their time. Given free choice in a natural environment, horses spend a variable amount of time on eating, playing, resting, moving around, interacting with others, breeding (if applicable) and engaging in other behaviour. Both feral and domesticated horses will spend about 70% of their time eating and in feeding-related behaviour, if given the choice.

Ideally, all horses should have access to forage at all times, allowing them to

Given the choice, horses spend about 70% of their time grazing.

exhibit their natural feeding patterns. In addition, research studies have shown that offering stable-kept horses a variety of different forages encourages them to spend more time foraging in the stable, thus reflecting a more natural eating pattern. Horses who are kept stabled for long periods would benefit from being offered a net of soaked hay or haylage, a trough of quick-dried grass or alfalfa, a bucket of root vegetables and a bucket of hay replacement chaff or high-fibre cubes in a feed-decanting ball.

The need for horses to eat large quantities in order to fulfil their nutritional requirements has produced an intrinsic motivation to search out food and eat. Fulfilling this need to forage and eat is a fundamental aspect of good welfare. Feeding a horse too little forage, for example by feeding a small net of hay at 6 pm and nothing until the morning, enforces an overnight fast that not only will lead to physical distress (see Chapters 8 and 13) but will also cause frustration and mental distress, and a higher risk of abnormal behaviour.

Fibrous forage takes four times as many chews as concentrate feed (Table 3.1); it therefore takes up much more time to eat and is associated with higher saliva production rates. Average saliva production of a forage-fed horse is about 10–13 litres per day.

This horse is playing with a feed ball at pasture, but these balls are particularly useful for keeping stabled horses gainfully occupied.

	Chews per kilo of dry matter	Time taken (minutes)
Hay	3,400	40
Oats	850	10

Table 3.1 Number of chews and time taken to eat forage and concentrates.

Selection of food

Horses are very selective about what they eat and their dextrous lips help them to select what they want. Young, succulent plants tend to be selected first by a horse at pasture, and in the spring horses can be seen browsing on hawthorn and other hedgerow trees as well as grazing. There is no evidence to prove that horses have an innate sense of what is good for them, or what is poisonous. Many poisonous plants will be avoided either because of their unacceptable taste or a past association with a feeling of illness after eating them. If a horse feels ill after eating a specific food, that food is likely to be refused in the future. Horses have a high drive to fulfil their appetite so, if no appropriate or appetizing food is available, they will eat less acceptable plants, including poisonous plants, and both faeces and fencing.

Horses, like most other mammals, do have an appetite for salt (sodium chloride) and will search this mineral out when they require it. There is no evidence to prove that horses have an appetite for any other nutrients, despite what is commonly believed. In research trials, horses preferred more palatable feeds (often including molasses and grain) that were unbalanced, rather than plainer but well-balanced feeds (i.e. those containing all the essential nutrients). Therefore a preference for a specific food should not necessarily be taken as a physiological need for the nutrients it contains. Nevertheless, there is no harm in allowing a horse to choose his preferred plant material at pasture in a way he would do naturally – although at no times should horses have access to poisonous plants. Never assume that horses will avoid poisonous plants – this is a myth.

Appetite

Appetite is the desire for food, which results in what is described as a voluntary intake of food. How much a horse eats per day ranges from 1.8–3% of bodyweight, with most horses eating between 2 and 2.5%. The brain is involved in both the desire to eat and in satiety, which is the feeling of fullness or no desire to eat any more. However, what signals the brain is very complicated and poorly understood. Driving factors for food intake are thought to be a combination of the amount of dry matter consumed, passage rate, the concentration of certain digestive products in the intestine and blood and the derived energy. The process of intake is thought to be different between horses and ponies. Long-term intake is also affected by the hormone leptin, which is produced by fat (adipose tissue) and tends to reduce intake, but further research is necessary to understand its role in horses and ponies.

Food intake in horses is not driven only by energy needs, and horses will continue to look for food even after their energy requirements are met with concentrate feed. Their motivation to forage and chew overrides their energy needs. Horses will even eat droppings (copophragy), woodshavings and start chewing stables if fed low-fibre diets. Horses not in work will, given the choice often overeat in terms of their energy requirements, and will become obese. Conversely, while it used to be thought that horses would compensate for low-energy feedstuffs by consuming more, this is not necessarily true. Horses and ponies given a single forage ad lib will consume less straw than grass or hay, and it has been proposed that this may be relate to a feedback mechanism from the time spent chewing. Practically, this means that straw is ideal for feeding to overweight horses and ponies, providing they have good dental function. It is low in calories (energy) and will fulfil chewing requirements and voluntary intake at lower levels than grass hay. Ponies given ad lib access to high-fibre pelleted complete feed will initially consume very large amounts, but over many weeks they will regulate their intake to more normal levels. One researcher found that it took about 9 weeks for intakes to stabilize. This long adaptation period makes studies of feed intake difficult, and questions studies of voluntary intake to date, which often use only a couple of weeks adaptation period.

Rate of food intake

Chewing rates and food intake rates depends on the individual horse and the type of feedstuff. Research has shown that horses will take between 3,000 and 4,500 chews per kilo of hay (dry matter); the higher values probably relate to higher fibre, more stemmy hays. For concentrate feed, horses will take around 800–850 chews per kilo of dry matter for oats, and 1,400 chews per kilo for mixed concentrates. Horses are thought to generally chew food to a specific particle size before swallowing, so a horse with dental problems and inadequate chewing ability will need to take more chews, and will probably have a reduced intake, i.e. eat less to compensate. Large particles seem to increase the passage rate through the digestive tract in horses, and this may be partly why old horses with reduced chewing ability suffer from sloppy droppings, even when fed adequate dietary fibre.

It used to be thought that chopped forage took longer to eat than unchopped (long) forage, primarily because of the extra time taken to pick up the chopped forage. A horse eating long forage takes fewer bites because the long pieces tend to 'feed in' together. However, more recent research has not confirmed this difference, possibly because a longer period of time was given for the horses to get used to the forage before measurements of intake rate were recorded. Therefore is it possible that, over time, horses may adapt to eating chopped forage as quickly as unchopped.

Horses may eat their concentrate feed very quickly, increasing the risk of choke and overloading the stomach capacity and small intestine digestive capability. There is disagreement between researchers as to whether or not adding chopped forage (chaff) to concentrate feed slows the intake rate. However, adding plenty of chopped forage to a concentrate meal will extend eating time by making the meal larger. Feeding forage before a concentrate meal is perhaps the best method of slowing intake because, being less hungry, the horse has a lower motivation to eat. This pre-feeding with forage also increases the utilization of the concentrate feed – the horse digests it better. Alternatively, concentrates can be replaced with other feeds in horses with moderate energy requirements (see Chapter 8).

A good mouthful!

Abnormal behaviour

Ongoing research studies prove conclusively that stabled horses fed high levels of starchy concentrate and too little forage are more likely to develop abnormal behaviour including wood-chewing and the oral stereotypies crib-biting and wind-sucking, which used to be called vices. Calling such behaviour 'vices' illustrates a human inability to understand equine behaviour and therefore be able to apply strategies to improve equine welfare. It is a relief that the word 'vice' is going out of fashion because it indicates that horse owners are taking responsibility for their domesticated horses' welfare. Wood-chewing, described as a redirected behaviour, is a less fixed, repetitive behaviour than oral stereotypies, but tends to lead to crib-biting. Crib-biting (or 'cribbing') involves the horse grasping a fixed object with his front (incisor) teeth, pulling back and drawing air into his upper throat (oesophagus) while making a characteristic grunt. Wind-sucking involves the horse carrying out the same action without grasping an object. In most cases the air sucked in is not actually swallowed. Crib-biting and wind-sucking tend to become fixed and appear to have no obvious function. It was thought that they simply exhibited frustration, but it is more likely that they have complex causes, which may include a need to replace foraging and chewing activity and to produce saliva, an alkaline substance that buffers stomach acid. A horse may

Crib-biting.

begin wood-chewing in an attempt to obtain dietary fibre. Recent research studies have shown that horses will work to obtain fibre even when their energy requirements have been fulfilled, which illustrates the horse's intrinsic need for dietary fibre.

Feeding high-concentrate diets causes increased acidity in the stomach and hindgut, increases the risk of stomach ulcers and reduces the production of saliva. (In horses saliva is produced only when chewing, therefore a high-concentrate, low-fibre diet will be associated with lower levels of saliva production.) Since saliva buffers stomach acid – which horses produce almost continuously – lower levels lead to higher stomach acid levels. Associated with this acidic stomach and hindgut are increases in abnormal behaviour, and more aggressive behaviour. Researchers have shown that feeding antibiotics which lower hindgut acidity reduces this abnormal behaviour in concentrate-fed horses (although this is not recommended as a regular, ongoing remedy).

Oral stereotypies and wood-chewing may be attempts by horses to cope with acidic guts, as a result of high-concentrate diets. Feeding antacids and feeding a higher fibre, lower starch diet can help to reduce crib-biting and wind-sucking in some horses. Recent research has shown that, although cribbing horses do produce saliva, their stomachs become more acidic during cribbing. This increased acidity probably results from the response of the stomach to an impending meal, indicated by the saliva production.

Crib-biting and wind-sucking are thought to be activities that become remote from their original cause, which means they will persist even after the horse's management is changed and foraging needs are fulfilled. Some horses will crib-bite or wind-suck less when turned out to pasture, but others will not. Controlling wood-chewing, cribbing and wind-sucking is challenging. However, the first steps must be to reduce the starch content of the diet, preferably to zero, and increase fibre supply. Horses should be allowed ad lib access to forage, with the nutrient quality of the forage selected carefully, according to the needs of the horse. Working or breeding horses with higher nutrient requirements should be fed good quality forage such as haylage, and moderate- to high-energy fibre-based feeds including quick-dried grass or alfalfa, sugar beet and highly digestible fibre compounds. Oil should be added if extra energy is required, and maximum amounts can be fed (see Chapter 8). Grain, coarse mixes and any other starchy feeds should be avoided. Antacid supplements can be added to the diet, but should not be used in an attempt to counteract starchy meals. Some horses respond to antacids with a reduction in cribbing, but the response varies with individual horses. Ideally, affected horses should be turned out as much as possible and allowed contact with other horses. There is no evidence that oral stereotypies can be copied by one horse from another. If more than one horse on a yard starts cribbing, it is likely to be rooted in the management of that yard, which increases the likelihood of any susceptible horse to begin. (There *may* also be an effect of stress as horses watch and hear their neighbour cribbing, but this is merely a suggestion and is unproven.)

Crib-biting and wind-sucking have traditionally been controlled with the use of collars that physically prevent the neck arching in the way necessary for the behaviour to be performed. These are inhumane, because affected horses have a very high motivation to crib-bite or wind-suck, and will do so more after collars are removed. Preventing a highly motivated behaviour causes frustration and compromises welfare. Behaviourists and research scientists recommend that a rubber or other surface that will not wear down the teeth is offered to the cribbing horse, to allow him to crib without excessive wear of the incisor teeth.

Cribbing has been associated with some forms of colic, and many owners wish to prevent their horses from cribbing in the belief it will reduce the likelihood of colic. This is unproven, and it is more likely to be the lack of forage and/or time spent cribbing and not eating that increases the risk of colic in cribbers, rather than the act of cribbing itself. Encouraging a cribber to eat forage, especially by turning out to pasture, is recommended.

Even in winter, horses will be happier playing in the snow, rather than standing in their stables.

Why some horses crib-bite or wind-suck and others in the same situation do not is still not fully understood. Research studies following foals from birth have shown that those who spent more time suckling were more likely to develop abnormal oral behaviour. Professor Christine Nicol at the University of Bristol suggests that these foals may have spent more time suckling because they already had stomach problems, or they were hungrier, perhaps because their dams produced less milk. Hungrier foals are more likely to eat concentrate feed, which may predispose them to cribbing. It is evident that, right from birth, attention should be paid to ensuring a high-fibre, relatively low-concentrate diet with the provision of an environment that allows the foal or horse to exhibit normal behaviour.

Can certain types of feed or supplements affect behaviour?

Most horse owners are convinced that certain feeds affect their horse's behaviour, and the most commonly named culprit is oats, which are believed to have a 'heating' or excitable effect. Whether or not a particular food or the total amount of dietary energy can affect a horse's behaviour is as yet scientifically unproven either way. In the author's experience, horses who appear to react to some feeds with excess excitability, respond with a calmer attitude to a reduction in total starch in the diet, rather than a change from oats to other cereals. Of course, good management and training will also help produce a calmer horse, and in no circumstances should the feed only be considered when a horse becomes too lively for his owner.

The story of oats is interesting because many factors may be involved. In the first place, the idea that oats cause excitability does not fit with the cause of excitability being too much dietary energy. Oats are the cereal grain lowest in energy, compared kilo for kilo with barley, wheat and maize. In addition, oats are the grain lowest in starch, although the starch is more digestible than in other cereal grains. Perhaps the traditional use of oats as a 'working horse' feed has furnished them with the tag of causing excess excitability. Working horses tend to be more excitable and may be more challenging to ride, because they are physically fit and tend to be stabled (i.e. not at pasture) for most of their time and therefore have restricted movement. Oats were an ideal food for working horses in the old days because they were high enough in fibre and low enough in starch to be fed in very large quantities without causing gut disturbance, as other cereals would.

Research is starting to indicate that higher starch diets cause horses to be more reactive and/or aggressive, and more physically active than those on lower starch diets (especially those on high-fat, low-starch and high-fibre diets). Weanling foals fed diets high in fat and fibre are less stressed, less active and easier to handle than those fed high-starch diets. During research studies investigating other factors, horses fed high-fat rather than high-starch diets were less reactive, and had lower heart rates during exercise. It is not yet known why starch, fat and fibre affects horses in this way, and much more research is necessary before the interactions are understood. In the meantime, supplying horses with a more natural fibre-based diet, using fat supplementation to help fulfil energy requirements and supplying minimal amounts of starch seems to be the best strategy to help maintain normal behaviour.

Feeding cereals including oats in at attempt to liven horses up can be successful, but only for horses who are susceptible to the 'heating' or 'exuberant' effect, and not all are. Unfortunately there is no legal feed or supplement that can guarantee a more energetic horse (if that horse is already healthy). Cereals should be added to a lazy horse's diet with care, because many such horses tend to be overweight and good doers; therefore the energy in the grain is more likely to be laid down as fat, rather than expressed in more exuberant behaviour. Putting on extra weight is likely to make a lazy horse even slower. (Note that research has shown that starchy feeds may cause a horse to be more reactive and less attentive rather than simply more forward-going, so the inexperienced handler or rider should beware.) The most effective way to give a horse more energy in his behaviour is to get him fitter via a conditioning exercise programme. Effective training, causing a horse to become more responsive, may also help.

A huge variety of supplements that claim to change equine behaviour – usually to calm – are available, but there is little scientific evidence to support their use. A suitable high-fibre, low-starch diet, good training, quiet handling and good management are probably more important. More information about calming supplements is given in Chapter 6.

chapter 4

Nutrients and nutritional requirements

ALL HORSES REQUIRE water and these essential nutrients: carbohydrates (including sugar, starch and fibre), protein (including 11 essential amino acids), fats and oils, vitamins and minerals. The nutrients described in this chapter are known to be essential to avoid disease, but it is possible in the future that other nutrients essential for optimal health might be identified. A balanced diet supplies all the essential nutrients every day in amounts that lead to neither a net gain nor loss for a horse in optimal condition. So, for example, a nutritionist may describe a supplement as 'balancing a diet', which means it makes up the nutrient shortfalls in that diet.

Most feeds are made up of a complex mixture of various nutrients; therefore most unprocessed feeds are a source of more than one nutrient group. Some feeds supply mostly one group (e.g. processed cereal grains that are mainly starch, and straw that is mainly insoluble fibre) and a few supply just one group (e.g. vegetable oil that is almost 100% oil). Some feeds supply different proportions of nutrients depending on their growth stage, e.g. grasses. Nutrients themselves will be covered in this chapter, good sources of each nutrient will be covered in Chapter 6 and later, in Chapter 8, the use of different feeds to supply necessary nutrients will be explored. As mentioned earlier, horses have a fundamental requirement for dietary fibre, a complex feed component that is digested and utilized by the horse in a complex manner. It is also a widely misunderstood feed component, hence the whole of Chapter 5 is devoted to it.

Published requirements

Nutritional requirements for horses were published by the National Research Council (USA) in 1989. Unfortunately, these have not yet been updated, despite the fact that much has been learned from research since then. NRC levels should be taken as the absolute minimum required to avoid deficiencies: some levels for optimal health are higher and most nutritionists use an adapted version of the NRC requirements. Energy requirements can vary widely, depending on the individual horse's temperament and the environment, and are difficult to predict. The published requirements should be used simply as a guide.

Nutritional requirements change according to the activity, growth stage or reproductive status of the horse, which is sometimes called 'class'. Young horses under the age of 2 years, pregnant mares, breeding stallions and horse being exercised have different requirements from adult horses at maintenance (rest), and these can be found in the NRC (1989) publication. Tables of values can be found in the Appendix, and information about micronutrient requirements in Tables 4.1 and 4.2 in this chapter.

Water

Although not strictly classed as a nutrient, water is essential for life and makes up about 65–75% of the mature horse's body, and 80% of the foal's. Horses can survive longer if deprived of feed than if they are deprived of water. Water is necessary to help propel food through the gut, acts as a solute in which nutrients and other substances can be transported around the body and in which excesses and waste products can be excreted via urine and faeces (droppings), acts as a medium for all bodily metabolic processes, and plays an important role in thermoregulation (the regulation of body temperature). Water is lost in faeces, urine, breath and sweat, and losses can be very high in horses subject to strenuous exercise (see Chapter 10). Fluid balance in the body is controlled by hormones, and the kidneys are involved in maintaining overall body fluid balance.

Water is vitally important to all equids.

Water is drunk, ingested in feed and gained from bodily metabolic processes. The water content of horse feed varies widely, from as high as 80% in fresh spring grass to 10% in quick-dried forages. This variation in water content means that comparing nutrient content of fresh feeds can be misleading, and nutrients are usually expressed on a dry matter basis.

A 500 kg adult horse at maintenance in a temperate (moderate to cool) environment, eating a dry diet of hay and concentrate feed, requires about 20–25 litres of water per day (about 5 litres per 100 kg of bodyweight), but voluntary intake can be as high as 35 litres. Horses often drink more than they require. The amount of water drunk will decrease as the moisture content of the diet increases. Horses

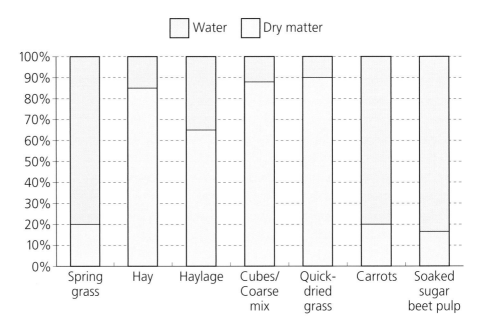

Figure 4.1 Dry matter of some horse feeds.

eating a diet of 40% moisture or more fulfil their water requirements from their feed. Grazing good spring grass, horses do not need any additional water, but will drink if water is available, and ideally water should always be offered. Increasing dietary fibre intake increases faecal moisture and water intake. Lactating mares require more water to support milk production.

The biggest factor that impacts on water intake is the horse's need to cool his body in hot climates, or during exercise. An increase in environmental temperature from 13 to 21°C increases the horse's water requirements by 15–20%. Dehydration is common in exercising horses, as a result of high sweat losses, and more information about this and the water requirements of such horses can be found in Chapter 10. Diarrhoea is another cause of excess water loss leading to dehydration, and more information can be found in Chapter 13.

During eating, water moves into the gut in the form of saliva, which may total over 12 litres per day in a 500 kg horse. The water content in the gut of horses fed grass hay is greater than that in concentrate-fed horses, and this water reserve can be useful to horses performing prolonged moderate intensity exercise, or any exercise in hot, humid environments.

A lack of water is harmful, ranging from unhealthy to lethal. Water deprivation for 24 hours causes a 4% loss in bodyweight through dehydration. One of the first signs of dehydration (decreased body water) is reduced skin elasticity, which can be assessed from taking a pinch of skin on the base of the neck, and measuring how long it takes to return to normal. In fully hydrated horses, this is instant, and if the pinch mark stays longer than 1 second, it indicates dehydration of around 6% or greater. At 8% dehydration, the skin pinch takes even longer to return to normal and capillary refill time is increased to 2–3 seconds (instead of the normal 1.5–2 seconds). Capillary refill can also be assessed by pressing a finger or thumb onto the horse's gums and watching the colour return. At 8% dehydration, the mucous membranes of the mouth will be dry.

At 10% dehydration, the horse will be weak, have a high resting heart rate and have tight skin and a capillary refill time of more than 3 seconds. If no water is given, and the horse becomes more dehydrated, death is imminent. It should be noted that water deficiency increases the risk of impactive colic and reduces performance in athletic horses, and physical performance is detrimentally affected before the signs of dehydration can be seen.

Water replenishment is made more efficient by offering an electrolyte solution of a specific concentration, which is called an isotonic oral rehydration solution. These solutions are absorbed into the body more quickly than plain water. However, plain water must also be given because plain water is better for a dehydrated horse than no fluids at all. In severe cases, fluids may have to be given via a nasogastric tube, directly into the stomach.

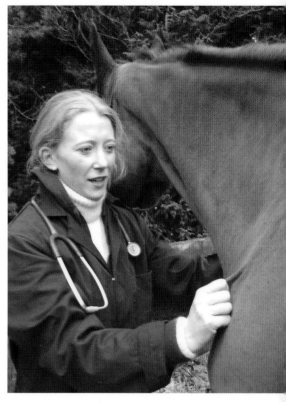

Taking a skin pinch to check for dehydration.

Energy

Energy is not classed as a nutrient, but is an essential derivative of feed nutrients including carbohydrates, fats and oils and, to a lesser extent, protein. The chemical energy bound in feed is extracted by the body via digestion and then either stored or used immediately in the body's metabolic mills. Energy is fuel, which is measured in calories, and it drives every bodily process, including what can be seen (e.g. movement) and what cannot be seen (e.g. recycling of red blood cells). Thus, even when a horse is standing still, resting, energy continues to be used. Dietary energy should not be confused with a horse's temperament, or how intrinsically energetic he is.

Fibre is an important source of energy for horses, unlike humans who rely primarily on non-structural carbohydrates, e.g. sugar and starch, for their carbohydrate energy. Protein is used for energy to a much lesser extent, although some amino acids are used as a source of energy by some body cells. There is more information about how energy is extracted from nutrients and used in the body in Chapter 10.

We tend to talk about the potential energy of a feed as 'calories'. A calorie is the amount of heat energy required to raise the temperature of 1 gram of water by 1°C. In the UK, we describe the energy in horse feed in megajoules (MJ) whereas in the USA the energy is measured in megacalories (Mcal). 1 MJ equals 1,000 kilojoules (KJ) or 1,000,000 joules.

To convert between Mcal and MJ: 1 MJ = 4.184 Mcal

1 Mcal = 1MJ ÷ 4.184

In human food, energy is generally measured in kilocalories (kcal), yet described as calories. Horses require so much more energy per day than humans that their requirements are measured in megajoules rather than just joules. An average horse at maintenance has an energy requirement of about 69 MJ per day, whereas an average human requires 2,900 kcal, equivalent to about 12 MJ.

Feed has a gross energy, which can be measured with a bomb calorimeter. The feed is burnt in oxygen, releasing heat energy from the chemical energy, and the increase in the temperature of water is measured to get a reading. However, gross energy is not a particularly useful measurement, because the horse cannot use all the energy available. Some energy is lost in the faeces, and the remainder is described as 'digestible energy' (DE). More energy is lost in the urine and through the production of gas such as methane, and the remaining energy is described as 'metabolizable energy' (ME). Finally, more energy is lost in the form of heat, and what remains is described as 'net energy' (NE). In the UK, the USA and Australasia, feed energy is usually given in the form of digestible energy (DE), so a feed may have an energy measurement of 9 MJ DE/kg.

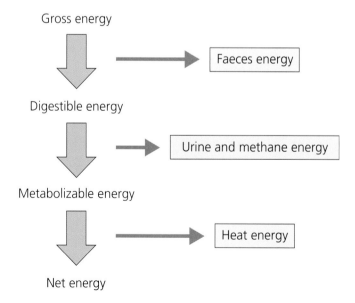

Figure 4.2 Diagram to show use of energy in the horse (losses shown in boxes).

Digestible energy of a feed can be calculated by either:

- Digestibility trial – where horses are given a feed of known gross energy, and the energy lost in faeces is measured.

- Chemical analysis – where predictive equations are used to measure DE with reference to the chemical composition of the feed, i.e. various nutrient levels including protein, oil, ash and fibre.

- Tables of DE value – tables of established DE values for feed ingredients for horses are available, and can be used to calculate the DE of a compound (mixture of ingredients), according to the percentage inclusion of the ingredients.

When the energy of feeds is compared, this must be done on a like for like basis. For example, sugar beet is a medium-energy feed, supplying about 11 MJ DE per kilo of dry matter, similar to good grass. However, sugar beet is usually fed soaked, in 4 times its volume of water. Soaking in this way brings the energy level down to just over 2 MJ per kilo.

Carbohydrates

Carbohydrates are a wide group of compounds that includes sugar, starch, fibre (both soluble and insoluble) and glycogen – the energy storage compound in equine muscle and liver. The topic of carbohydrates can be confusing, especially as the term is often used by horse owners to describe just the type that can be digested by enzymes produced in the horse's gut (non-structural carbohydrates). To create further confusion, fructans – water-soluble and non-structural carbohydrates found in grass, are often included in this description, despite the fact that

Forage and cereal grains. Both feeds are rich in carbohydrate; hay is rich in fibre and cereal grains are rich in starch.

they cannot be digested by gut enzymes, and are instead broken down by microbial fermentation, in both the fore and hindgut.

To understand more about carbohydrates, see Table 4.1 below.

Sugars	Monosaccharides	Glucose, fructose, mannose, galactose, xylose, ribose, ribulose	
	Oligosaccharides	Sucrose, lactose, maltose, cellobiose, raffinose	
Non-sugars	Polysaccharides	Homoglycans	Starch, glycogen, cellulose fructan, mannans
		Heteroglycans	Pectins, hemicellulose, gums, mucilages
	Complex carbohydrates	Glycolipids Glycoproteins	

Table 4.1 Classification of carbohydrates.

Adapted from P. MacDonald et al (2002), *Animal Nutrition*, 6th ed., Pearson Prentice Hall.

All carbohydrates are formed from saccharide units, and named accordingly. Sugars are called monosaccharides, because they consist of one unit. The term oligosaccharide is used to describe a carbohydrate that consists of more than one unit (monosaccharide), including disaccharides (two units) such as table sugar (sucrose) but usually, in fact, it refers to those that contain more than ten units. The term polysaccharide is used to describe carbohydrates that contain many units, and these tend to be large molecules or 'polymers'. Starch and plant fibre such as cellulose and glycogen are polysaccharides. The type of carbohydrate tends to be used in its description, with starch often being called 'non-structural polysaccharide'. Many types of fibre have structural roles in plants, however other fibres do not, therefore fibre does not tend to be called 'structural polysaccharide'. Instead, fibre is sometimes referred to as 'non-starch polysaccharide'. The nomenclature is rather confusing because many different polysaccharides exist, all with different features, so it is difficult to group them clearly.

Carbohydrates are primarily used in the body for energy supply, and the monosaccharide glucose is the body's most important fuel. Glucose is the subunit of starch, cellulose, and glycogen. Horse's diets contain variable levels of starch and cellulose and, under normal circumstances, no glycogen.

The fate of carbohydrates in the horse's body depends on whether or not they can be broken down by digestive enzymes. Sugars (mono- and oligosaccharides) and starch (a non-structural polysaccharide) are digested by enzymes, which produce simple sugars including glucose. Carbohydrates that cannot be digested by gut enzymes include fibre and other non-starch polysaccharides including fructan (the major grass carbohydrate storage substance). There is some debate over the use of the term 'fibre' because, although it is used to describe carbohydrate fractions that cannot be digested by gut enzymes, this makes it very difficult to analyse in a laboratory. Laboratory analysis is an important method of characterizing feedstuffs; therefore, terminology needs to correspond to what analytical techniques are capable of. For ease of reference, the term fibre will be used in this book to describe plant cell wall material (lignin, cellulose, hemicellulose and pectins) and the more soluble non-cell wall polysaccharide constituents (gums and mucilages), but not fructans.

Comparing starch and cellulose in diagrammatic form (see Figure 4.3) shows how they differ in just one aspect – the link between the glucose units. Gut enzymes can break the starch link (an alpha-1, 4 linkage), but not the cellulose link (a beta-1, 4 link). Fibre-degrading bacteria can break this bond, and this takes place by a fermentation process. The digestion of fibre and other non-starch polysaccharides will be investigated in the Chapter 5.

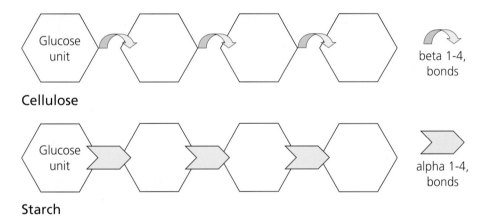

Figure 4.3 Diagram to show the structures of starch and cellulose, showing the glucose unit linked by different types of bonds.

Digestion of sugar and starch

The breakdown of sugar and starch in the horse's gut takes place via enzyme hydrolysis in the small intestine. Digestive products of the non-simple sugars are their monosaccharide constituents, which are absorbed efficiently by the horse. Digestion of starch produces its monosaccharide sub-unit, glucose. Two forms of starch exist; amylose and amylopectin, both of which consist of large numbers of glucose molecules. Amylose consists of a linear unbranched structure and amylopectin has many branches. The ratio of each in feed varies, but most cereals contain 3 amylopectin to 1 amylase.

The activity of starch-digesting enzymes (amylases) in the horse's small intestine is much lower than other animals and humans; therefore their capacity to digest starch is limited. Coupled with a fast passage rate, this means that if horses are overfed starch, some will flow undigested into the hindgut. Here, the starch is not acted upon by digestive enzymes, but is available as a foodstuff for specific types of bacteria in the microbial population. Starch-loving bacteria ferment the starch, producing propionic acid and large amounts of lactic acid rather than glucose. Contrary to popular belief, lactic acid is not inevitably a 'baddy'. It can be absorbed and utilized by the horse and is a useful energy source. Only when present in very large concentrations (whether in the gut or muscles), which overwhelms the body's ability to recycle it, is it undesirable. However, if production does overload the absorptive capacity, as is the case when plenty of starch is available, it builds up in the hindgut and produces an acidic environment. Hindgut acidity from the proliferation of lactic acid bacteria has unhealthy or even dangerous consequences for the horse and the excess acidity can either directly or indirectly cause discomfort, diarrhoea, colic, laminitis and a range of other health problems. The mechanisms that cause these changes are not yet understood, but disruptions include a huge overgrowth of lactic acid bacteria and consequential loss of fibre-loving bacteria, a leaky gut wall, and the release of various active substances into the blood, including endotoxins and amines.

For a healthy digestive system, starch should be digested and absorbed in the small intestine. Horses fed high-starch diets produce higher levels of propionic acid in the hindgut than horses fed forage diets. High levels of propionic acid in the blood suppress the appetite in farm animals, and might also do so in horses, which may help to partly explain why working horses on large amounts of grain or coarse mix tend to go off their feed. Practical feeding guidelines to help avoid starch overload are given in Chapter 8.

Absorption and use of sugar and starch

The products of sugar and starch digestion are absorbed through the gut wall and carried in the portal circulation, which takes them directly to the liver for further processing. Fructose is taken up more slowly than glucose, which is taken up relatively rapidly. In the liver, most of the simple sugars are converted to glucose derivatives, which can then be stored as liver glycogen or transported for use elsewhere in the body, including to the muscles where glucose is stored as glycogen. Glucose is used by almost all body cells as a source of energy, and its levels in the blood are strictly controlled. In response to an influx of glucose, i.e. after a meal, insulin is produced, which cause the body cells to take up glucose via glucose transporters. The liver – and to a lesser extent the muscles – take up extra glucose and convert it to glycogen in a process called glycogenesis. When blood glucose levels drop, the release of glucagons is triggered, along with a decrease in insulin, which stimulates glucose release from liver stores in a process called glycogen-olysis. The rate and extent to which feeds cause an increase in blood glucose is called the 'glycaemic response' or 'index'.

The glycaemic index

The glycaemic index of a food is widely used in human nutrition, and is just starting to be applied to horses. The glycaemic index (GI) of a food is a measure of the rate of digestion and conversion into glucose (sugar). The faster a food causes a rise in blood sugar, the higher its GI. In humans, the GI of a food is calculated by an area under a curve on a graph, so it reflects not only the peak blood glucose, but also how long the blood glucose stays elevated. So, for example, a specific amount of a single food based on its carbohydrate content is eaten, and blood sugar values tested every 15 minutes are plotted on a graph. The value is usually expressed as a percentage, compared to the blood sugar response of the same amount of a reference food such as glucose. The GI of hundreds of human foods is known. Unfortunately, mixing foods in a meal does not always give an expected GI, and much research is necessary before the GI of a variety of horse feeds is known. In addition, horses seem to have a wide individual variation in their glycaemic response to feeds, further complicating the issue. However, in general, refined starchy foods such as grain and sugary foods such as molasses will have a high GI index, whereas high-fibre foods tend to have a lower GI. Knowing the GI of foods and avoiding high GI foods might be useful to help control unwanted excitable behaviour in some horses, although there is no scientific evidence for this yet. More importantly, horses with certain diseases including laminitis and Cushing's syndrome are likely to benefit from low GI foods, because of their higher likelihood of insulin resistance. See Figure 4.4 page 34.

Insulin resistance

If the effectiveness of insulin in transporting glucose out of the blood into body tissues in impaired, the horse (or human) is said to be insulin-resistant or insulin-insensitive. It is thought that, as is the case in humans, if a horse has high blood sugar over long periods because of a diet with high GI, and therefore elevated levels of insulin over long periods, this can lead to insulin resistance. The problem is compounded by a lack of exercise, because exercise helps to boost insulin action and the uptake of sugar by body cells. Insulin resistance appears to be more common in ponies than horses.

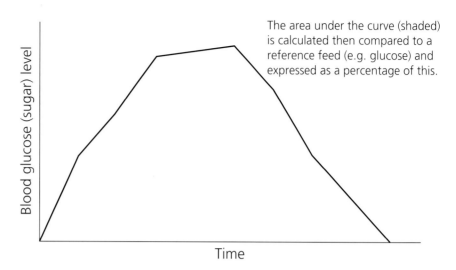

Figure 4.4 Graph to show measurement of glycaemic index of a food.

Despite the fact that glucose is such an important fuel for the body, it also has damaging effects if not taken up and processed normally, as is the case with human diabetes. Fortunately, horses and ponies do not seem to develop type 2 diabetes (where the pancreas cannot produce enough insulin), because they seem able to keep producing high levels of insulin in response to high GI diets.

Insulin resistance is often associated with high body fat or obesity, which could develop after years of a high GI diet coupled with overload of dietary energy (calories). In humans, the combination of a high-fat, high GI diet combined with low levels of exercise and development of obesity has led to a disorder called 'metabolic syndrome'. This syndrome is characterized by obesity, insulin resistance, hypertension, increased risk of heart disease and diabetes. It is believed to be linked to high body fat levels, which contribute to the insulin resistance via hormone activity. Fat (adipose tissue) is known to be an active body tissue that secretes hormones and affects the entire body. Some vets and researchers have proposed a similar syndrome in horses and ponies, called 'equine metabolic syndrome'. This condition is characterized by obesity, insulin resistance and a higher risk of laminitis. Horses and ponies have evolved to lay down fat stores over the abundant summer months, but then lose this extra fat during the winter. Just like humans, a continuous and plentiful diet combined with low activity/exercise levels leads to a higher risk of ill health. Horses' bodies cope well with fluctuations in blood sugar, but research is starting to show that continuously elevated levels lead to all sorts of problems. For more information on how insulin resistance has been implicated in the development of laminitis, especially in obese horses and ponies, see Chapter 14.

Protein

Protein comes from the Greek word meaning 'primary', which reflects its importance to the body as a source of amino acids. Proteins are complex compounds made up of amino acids linked together like a string of pearls, and the horse has a dietary requirement for actual amino acids rather than protein *per se*. The digestive process frees amino acids from dietary protein.

Horses, like other animals, cannot make their own amino acids in order to build body protein, but they can make some amino acids from others. There are 20 amino acids found in the protein in food, but 10 of these are essential for the horse, because they cannot be synthesized within the body and must be supplied by the diet. The essential amino acids for the horse are: lysine, methionine, threonine, valine, leucine, isoleucine, arginine, tryptophan, histidine and phenylalanine. The amino acids that can be made within the horse's body from the essential amino acids are termed non-essential. The process of producing them, called transamination, takes place in the liver, which continuously processes the products of protein digestion to ensure that the body receives the specific amino acids it needs.

The quality of dietary protein refers to its composition of essential amino acids. High-quality proteins are complete, i.e. they supply all the essential amino acids, and examples are foods of animal origin including meat, eggs, fish and cheese, most of which are unlikely to be used in horse feeds. Plant foods tend to have low-quality protein, i.e. too little of one or more of the essential amino acids. The essential amino acid present in the lowest quantity in feeds is often called the 'limiting' amino acid, and in many equine feeds this is lysine, followed by threonine then methionine. Therefore feeds that do supply plenty of lysine, such as soya bean meal, sunflower seeds and linseed, should be included in equine diets to ensure that the body receives all the essential amino acids, without which its ability to produce its own proteins will be impaired.

Although protein is not used to any great extent for the production of energy in the healthy horse, some amino acids are important sources of energy for specific body cells. Not only dietary protein is available for use in the horse's body – endogenous proteins, or those from inside the body including sloughed gut lining cells, digestive enzymes and mucus are also digested.

Protein makes up about 17–19% of the body, and is found in almost every cell. It occurs in a wide variety of forms and has a wide variety of roles in the body. These roles can be classified by function:

- Structural, which make up muscle, skin, hair, cartilage and other connective tissue.

- Enzymes, which act as catalysts affecting the rate of reactions within the body.

- Hormones, which are chemical messengers that generally regulate metabolic processes.

- Immune compounds, which are carried in the blood and help fight foreign substances such as bacteria and viruses.

- Transport compounds, many of which transport nutrients within the blood and include haemoglobin, which transports oxygen in the blood.

Digestion, absorption and use of protein

Digestion of protein begins in the stomach with the action of hydrochloric acid, which starts to break down the protein structure. The enzyme pepsin is produced in the stomach, and starts to break protein bonds and to produce polypeptides, oligopeptides and some free amino acids, which empty into the small intestine. Most protein digestion takes place in the first part of the small intestine, the duodenum. Various enzymes produced by the pancreas break down the protein peptides and two main end products result: dipeptides and tripeptides, and amino acids. These end products are absorbed into intestinal cells (enterocytes), where some of them (e.g. glutamine) are used, but most are transformed to the basic building block amino acids. Uptake occurs throughout the small intestine. (Whether or not the horse can absorb amino acids from the hindgut is not known, but some researchers have proposed that some may be taken up, but are not transported out into the body.)

The amino acids absorbed in the small intestine are then transported in the portal circulation blood to the liver. The liver has the important role of monitoring the amino acids and adjusting the rates of their metabolism to suit the requirements of the body. The liver also synthesizes the amino acids required by the body – although some amino acids are not metabolized by the liver, but released into the blood as they are. Most of these are the branched chain amino acids (BCAAs), which can be used by the muscles and tissues such as brain, heart and kidneys, for energy.

After the amino group has been removed from amino acids in the liver, the remainder of the molecule, which is called its 'carbon skeleton' can be used to produce energy, glucose, cholesterol and fatty acids, depending on the amino acid being broken down and the nutritional state of the body. The waste nitrogen from excess amino acids is removed as ammonia, which is converted to urea, which is then excreted via the kidneys in urine. In cases of liver disease, the ammonia cannot be converted efficiently and builds up, causing toxicity symptoms including mental abnormalities (see Chapter 13). Because the liver and kidneys play important roles in excreting compounds resulting from excess protein intake, in cases of liver or kidney disease dietary protein should be kept low.

Fats and oils (lipids)

Fats and oils are more correctly termed lipids – a large group of compounds that are hydrophobic, or water-repelling. The water-repelling nature of lipids makes them a challenge for the horse's body, which consists of around 70% water and uses water as a solute for all sorts of compounds. Lipids need to be dispersed in the gut if they are to be broken down and absorbed, and are then bound to proteins once in the blood to enable them to be transported to where they are required. Simple fats are called triglycerides, and consist of fatty acids joined to a glycerol 'backbone'. Certain types of fatty acids are essential in the diet because they cannot be synthesized within the body. These essential fatty acids are linoleic acid and alpha (α) linolenic acid. Fats are necessary in the diet for the absorption of the fat-soluble vitamins A, D, E and K. However, only a small number of lipids are important as sources of dietary energy.

Fats and oils are the most common lipids in plant-based horse feeds. Oils are liquid at room temperature, and fats are solid – but the term 'fat' tends to be used as a general description of both.

The sources of lipids in the typical equine diet are vegetable oils, and in some cases, fish oils and/or animal fat are given. However, horses have evolved eating a vegetarian diet and the practice of feeding fish or animal products is questionable. Fatty acids are rich sources of energy for the body, and supply over two times the amount of energy per gram compared to carbohydrates. If the calorific intake of the body is greater than required, the extra energy is stored in the form of triacylglyceride fat in adipose tissue – which also has an important role as an insulator. If the stored energy is required, fatty acids are mobilized as a response to hormones. However, lipids are not used just for energy; many have hormone-like actions in the body and are described as 'bioactive'. (For example, eicosanoids are bioactive derivatives of fatty acids that are involved in various regulatory actions in the body, including inflammation and immunological processes.) Adipose tissue itself is also a storage organ for certain hormones. It produces a hormone called leptin, which affects appetite and, in healthy individuals, helps to regulate body fat levels – although more research is necessary to understand precisely what effects leptin has in the horse.

Apart from the essential fatty acids, fats and oils– although they are suppliers of high levels of energy – are not *essential* in themselves. Horses appear to thrive on low levels of dietary fat of around 3%. A high-fat diet for a horse would be over about 7%, whereas this would be a very low-fat diet for a human, whose normal diet is around 30% fat. Despite the fact that the natural equine diet of plant material is very low in fat, horse do digest and absorb fat efficiently, provided it is introduced gradually. Providing energy from dietary fat gives the benefit of a reduced heat burden for exercising horses, when compared to providing that energy from starch, since the body's utilization of the products of starch digestion produces more heat. Exercising horses produce large amounts of heat from muscle metabolism and fat supplementation can help to reduce this, as well as helping to avoid the detrimental effects of high dietary starch levels.

Fatty acids are named according to their chain length, or the number of carbon atoms they contain. The number ranges from 2 to 24, and these chains can either contain all single carbon-carbon bonds (saturated), one double carbon-carbon bond (unsaturated), or two or more carbon-carbon bonds (polyunsaturated). The short-chain fatty acids with between 2 and 6 carbons are commonly called volatile fatty acids (VFAs) and are very important in equine nutrition, because they are the products of microbial fermentation, primarily in the hindgut. Fatty acids are also named in note form according to their chain length and the sites of any double carbon-carbon bonds. For example, omega-3 is used to describe fatty acids with a double carbon bond at the third carbon. The essential α linolenic acid is an omega-3 fatty acid, and the essential linoleic acid is an omega-6 fatty acid. Vegetable oils usually consist of a mixture of different fatty acids, although some are rich sources of particular fatty acids. Linseed (flaxseed) oil is the richest plant source of α linolenic acid, and rapeseed oil is also relatively high. Corn and sunflower oils are rich in linoleic acid.

Omega-3 fatty acids

Much interest has been shown in the omega-3 fatty acids in recent years because of their health-promoting effects. Increasing dietary levels in humans have balancing effects on blood lipid, beneficial effects on the blood vessels, and anti-inflammatory actions. In animals, increasing dietary levels has beneficial effects on the skin and coat. Because grass is higher in omega-3 than omega-6, the grazing horse receives more omega-3; whereas cereal grains are higher in omega-6 than in omega-3, so the horse on a grain-based diet will receive a higher proportion of omega-6. A substantial intake of omega-3 fatty acids helps to balance the effects of omega-6 fatty acids, which on their own tend to aggravate inflammatory responses in the body. This balancing effect on omega-6 fatty acids explains many of the anti-inflammatory effects of the omega-3 fatty acids.

Fish oils are a rich source of the very long chain omega-3 fatty acids EPA (eicosapentaenoic acid) and DHA (docosahexaenoic acid), which are transformed from α linolenic acid in the body. Although not classed as essential, these are thought to have more profound anti-inflammatory effects than α linolenic acid, from which they would be made in the body. However, many horse owners prefer to feed a vegetarian diet; for them, linseed oil, the richest vegetable source of omega-3 fatty acids, would be preferable to fish oil.

Unprocessed linseeds.

Digestion, absorption and use of lipids

Fats must be emulsified before digestive enzymes can access their surfaces, and this is done via bile salts. Horses do not have a bile duct, and instead they produce small amounts of bile from the liver almost continuously. Fat breakdown occurs in the small intestine, primarily by enzymes called lipases, which produce a mixture of diacylglycerides, monoacylglycerides and free fatty acids. These combine with bile salts into molecules called micelles, which can be absorbed into the gut wall cells called enterocytes. Within the gut wall, the lipid molecules are further processed into chylomicrons, compounds consisting of lipid combined with protein and carbohydrate, to allow them to be transferred into the lymphatic system. The chylomicrons then gradually enter the blood from the lymphatics, thus not overflowing the blood with lipids. Some free fatty acids may be absorbed and enter the blood, travelling to the liver directly in the portal circulation. The liver plays an important role in fat metabolism, by producing the lipoproteins that act as carriers for fat that has been made in the liver from excess glucose. The chylomicrons of fat from dietary sources are transported throughout the body in the blood. Fatty acids can be freed and used by body cells, and the remainder of the fat is taken up and stored by adipose tissue cells. Fat tends to be cleared out of the blood within a few hours after a meal.

Minerals

A whole range of minerals are found in the body, some of which are there through their presence in the feed, regardless of whether they have a specific role to play. Essential minerals are those that have been proven to have essential roles in body processes, and they make up about 4% of the horse's bodyweight. They have a wide range of functions including giving hardness to the bones and teeth, balancing body fluid, involvement in many enzymes and basic cell activity. Minerals can be categorized by the amount required per day – macrominerals are needed in grams and microminerals (also called trace elements) are needed in milligrams per day.

The macrominerals sodium, chloride and potassium are important in the maintenance of fluid balance in the body and are classed as electrolytes. (In nutritional terminology, while sodium and potassium are referred to in their elemental form, the ionic form 'chloride' is used, since the substance appears in the body in this form, rather than in the elemental form, chlorine.) Sulphur is a macromineral but is not used by the body alone as a nutrient, instead being incorporated into various minerals and as part of the sulphur-containing amino acids, many of which make up structural proteins found in skin, hair and hooves. Some minerals may interfere with the absorption of others, and they interact in very complex ways. Some are toxic in excess, and supplementation of minerals should always be carried out with care. The link between body mineral status and mineral content of horse hair is complex and not understood; therefore analysis of hair cannot be used to assess deficiencies or excesses of minerals.

Macrominerals

Calcium

Calcium is the most abundant element in the body and, along with phosphorus, makes up 70% of the mineral content of the horse's body. Bones and teeth contain about 99% of the calcium, with the remainder distributed in fluids both inside and outside body cells. In addition to its role in bone mineralization, calcium is important for muscle contraction, nerve conduction, enzymes and blood clotting. Calcium absorption occurs in the small intestine of the horse. Absorption is affected by many factors, because calcium can form complexes with other minerals or dietary substances, reducing their bioavailability.

Vitamin D improves the absorption of calcium, whereas phytates, which occur in high-fibre plants and feeds including legumes and cereal grains, bind calcium and reduce its absorption. Oxalates, found in tropical grasses, also inhibit calcium absorption. Magnesium competes with calcium and excess magnesium intake reduces calcium uptake. High intakes of phosphorus also inhibit calcium

Mineral	Functions in body	RDA	Deficiency	Excess	Notes
Macrominerals					
Calcium	Bone and teeth structure; muscle contraction; nerve conduction; enzymes; blood clotting	25–30 g	Skeletal abnormalities including fracture; lameness; DOD*; big head syndrome; weight loss	Large excesses can cause skeletal abnormalities if phosphorus is low	Calcium to phosphorus ratio must be no less than 1.7:1; high magnesium inhibits uptake
Phosphorus	Bone and teeth structure; genetic material and cell membrane constituents; energy production	18 g	Similar to calcium	Calcium deficiency	See above; high magnesium and calcium inhibit uptake; excesses likely in high bran or grain diet
Magnesium	Bone and teeth structure; cell membranes and genetic material constituent; energy metabolism; enzymes	9.4–10 g	Impaired muscle and nerve function; appetite loss; muscle tremors; impaired balance; long term – heart and skeletal abnormalities	No known but high intake inhibits calcium uptake	High phosphorus inhibits uptake
Potassium	Electrolyte; muscle contraction; nerve function	31 g	Unlikely because of abundance in feed; possible from excess sweating/ diarrhoea – fatigue, muscle weakness, nerve irritability, mental disorientation and appetite loss	Unlikely, because of excretion of excess	Large amounts can be lost in sweat and diarrhoea – electrolyte supplementation is required in these cases (should also include sodium and chloride)
Sodium	Electrolyte; nerve and muscle function	30 g	Decreased exercise performance and sweating; muscle and nerve dysfunction; dehydration; reduced appetite; licking behaviour	Colic, diarrhoea and muscle weakness	Huge losses possible during intense or prolonged exercise (via sweating); most horse feeds are deficient and salt should be supplemented

table continues

Mineral	Functions in body	RDA	Deficiency	Excess	Notes
Macrominerals (cont.)					
Chloride	Electrolyte; stomach acid	50 g	Unknown	Unknown	Is replaced along with sodium in salt
Sulphur	Structural role in skin, hair and hooves	Unknown	Unknown	Inhibits uptake of microminerals including copper, selenium and cobalt	
Microminerals					
Zinc	Enzyme activation; immune function; hormones, growth; skin integrity and wound healing; genetic material constituent; protein synthesis	400–625 mg	Poor appetite; poor growth rate; DOD*, skin lesions; poor fertility; interruption of vitamin A use	Not known to arise from feed; industrial contamination of pasture can inhibit uptake of other nutrients including calcium and iron	Ratio of 4:1 with copper recommended; little is stored in the body so ongoing supply necessary
Copper	Enzyme constituent; immune and nerve function; connective tissue structure; hair colour; growth; utilization of iron in red blood cells	100 mg	Anaemia; bone and joint disorders; DOD*; poor growth; infertility; hair depigmentation; gut disturbances	Not known; very high levels probably cause liver and kidney damage	See above
Iron	Oxygen uptake and storage in blood and muscles; enzymes	400–500 mg	Rare in healthy horse because of abundance in feed; anaemia (usually through blood loss or chronic inflammation); poor performance	Liver damage; gut disturbances and other mineral deficiencies; oxidative stress; reduced infection resistance	Iron should not be supplemented in very large doses
Selenium	Antioxidant; immune function; enzymes; pancreatic function	1–2mg	Weakness; muscle dysfunction; poor performance; skin and hair pigmentation loss; poor growth	Fatigue; hair and hoof loss; inhibition of protein synthesis	Lower threshold for toxicity than other nutrients of 10 times recommended amounts

table continues

Mineral	Functions in body	RDA	Deficiency	Excess	Notes
Microminerals (cont.)					
Chromium	Insulin function	Not known	Could result in insulin insensitivity (further research necessary to confirm)	Damage of genetic material	Not permitted as a feed additive
Iodine	Thyroid hormones	1–6 mg	Goitre (enlarged thyroid gland); impaired growth and development in youngsters	Infertility and abortions in mares and abnormal growth in their foals	Seaweed is rich in iodine and should be given to pregnant mares with care
Manganese	Enzyme component; joint tissues	400 mg	Unlikely because of abundance in feed; joint abnormalities and lameness in youngsters	No information (not reported)	
Cobalt	Component of vitamin B12	1mg	Unlikely because of abundance in feed	Toxicity with very large intakes	

*DOD: developmental orthopaedic disease in young growing horses

RDA (recommended daily amounts) are for 500 kg horse in light work, eating 10 kg (dry matter) per day. Lower amounts are published requirements (from 1989); higher are updated recommendations.

Table 4.2 Minerals for horses; functions, deficiencies and excesses.

absorption, and ratios of dietary calcium to phosphorus should be no less than 1.7:1. Calcium is transported in the blood bound to protein, free (ionized) and complexed with other substances. Body calcium levels are carefully controlled and if dietary intake is too low, calcium is released from the bones to meet body requirements. In practice, actual dietary calcium shortages are less common in horses than unbalanced mineral intake that reduces calcium absorption. Calcium shortages (deficiencies) cause skeletal abnormalities, lameness, developmental orthopaedic disease (DOD) in young growing horses, and big head syndrome. Large excesses of calcium can cause skeletal abnormalities if dietary phosphorus is very low.

Phosphorus

Phosphorus is the second most abundant element in the body, and the bones and teeth contain about 85% of the total. The remainder is found in the blood, body fluids and soft tissues including the muscles. In addition to its structural role, phosphorus is an important constituent of genetic material and cell membranes, and plays a vital role in energy production in the body. Phosphorus is absorbed in both the small and large intestine (the colon) of the horse. Its bioavailability is reduced by high levels of dietary magnesium and calcium, and by phytates. Phosphorus shortages cause skeletal abnormalities similar to those caused by calcium shortages. An excess of phosphorus causes a calcium deficiency, and associated problems. In the past, high concentrations of calcium were thought to be harmless, as long as adequate phosphorus was present, but ideally the ratio should not be higher than 2.5 calcium: 1 phosphorus.

Magnesium

Of the magnesium in the horse's body, 55–60% is found in the bone, with the remainder in the muscles, soft tissues and extracellular fluid. In addition to its structural role, magnesium is an integral part of cell membranes, plays a part in hundreds of enzyme reactions, is involved in energy metabolism and is associated with genetic material. Magnesium is absorbed in the small intestine, and also in the large intestine. Magnesium and calcium absorption and utilization compete, and intakes should always be balanced. Excess phosphorus inhibits magnesium absorption. There is also a close interaction between magnesium and potassium. Magnesium deficiencies are associated with impaired muscle and nerve function, with a loss of appetite, muscular tremors and impaired balance. Long-term shortages cause heart and skeletal abnormalities. High intakes of magnesium do not cause toxicity and it is considered a relatively safe mineral. However, magnesium and calcium intake should be balanced in order to avoid competition, i.e. high magnesium intakes must be matched with high calcium intakes.

Potassium

Potassium is an important electrolyte mineral, most of which is found inside the body cells. It maintains electrolyte and pH (acid/base) balance, influences the contraction of all types of muscle –smooth, skeletal and cardiac (heart) – and affects nerve function. Potassium is absorbed efficiently in both the small and large intestine. Potassium is controlled within a narrow range in the body, and deficiency or toxicity are almost impossible from dietary intake, on the one hand because of the abundance of potassium in feeds, and on the other, because of the ability of the body to excrete excess. However, hypokalaemia (too low a concentration of potassium) can result from excessive sweating during prolonged exercise, or severe diarrhoea, and is associated with muscle weakness, mental disorientation and nervous irritability. Potassium deficiency will also cause a poor appetite.

Sodium

Sodium is another electrolyte mineral, although 30% of it is deposited on the bone surfaces, from where it can be released into the blood if the blood sodium level drops too low. The remainder of sodium in the body is found in extracellular fluid, primarily blood plasma, and in muscle and nerve tissue. (It is involved with nerve and muscle function as well as fulfilling its electrolyte role.) Sodium is absorbed efficiently throughout both the small and large intestine. Excess sodium is excreted via the kidneys. Sodium deficiency causes decreased exercise performance and sweating, muscle and nerve dysfunction, licking behaviour and reduced appetite. Most equine diets are low in sodium, even if compound feeds are given, and these do not supply enough sodium to exercising horses. Large amounts of sodium can be lost in sweat in exercising horses, and exercise directly affects daily sodium requirements. Salt (sodium chloride) should be added to the diet of all exercising horses, and to those fed just forage. The amount should be adjusted each day according to the workload of the horse (see Chapter 10). Excess sodium can cause colic, diarrhoea and muscle weakness.

Chloride

Chloride, the ionic form of the element chlorine, is the third electrolyte mineral, which balances the positive charge of sodium. In addition to its electrolyte role, it is required for the production of stomach acid. Absorption of chloride, like sodium, is efficient. Also like sodium, large amounts of chloride can be lost in sweat in exercising horses. Using salt to replace lost sodium also replaces chloride.

Sulphur

Sulphur is an important component of several amino acids, including the essential amino acid methionine. The sulphur-containing amino acids make up structural proteins found in skin, hair and hooves, and sulphur is also found in the B-vitamins biotin and thiamine, in haemoglobin, insulin, bile salts and cartilage. It is not known how much sulphur is required by horses, and excessive supplementation is not recommended because sulphur may inhibit the uptake of microminerals including copper, selenium and cobalt.

Microminerals

The micromineral (trace element) content of unfortified plant-sourced horse feeds depends on the soil in which they were grown. Pasture grass alone rarely supplies all the microminerals required by horses, although grazing horses may consume some microminerals from soil intake. Nevertheless, most horses in the UK receive either fortified feed or supplements, and do not rely on just forage or straights for their micromineral intake.

Zinc

Zinc is widely distributed throughout the horse's body, with high concentrations in the bones, skin and hair. Zinc has a wide variety of functions in the body, including involvement in enzyme activation, immune function, hormones, cell and tissue growth, skin integrity and wound healing, genetic material, and protein synthesis. Zinc is digested and absorbed in the small intestine, and absorption is more efficient with low intakes. Zinc availability is reduced with excessive antacid ingestion in humans, because of a binding of the mineral, and the same is likely to be true in horses. Transport in the blood involves a protein or amino acid carrier. Interactions exist between vitamin A and zinc, with zinc deficiency causing interrupted utilization of vitamin A. In humans, high intake of zinc, along with moderate copper intake, inhibits the uptake of copper into the blood, and a ratio of 4:1 zinc to copper is recommended. It would be prudent to use this ratio for horses – a point examined further under 'Copper' below. Zinc deficiency is associated with poor appetite, poor growth rate and developmental orthopaedic disease (DOD), skin lesions and poor fertility. Little storage of zinc occurs in the body, so an ongoing supply is always required. In excess, zinc is not particularly toxic, and only industrially contaminated pasture has been shown to cause problems in horses. However, very high levels may interfere with the uptake of other nutrients including calcium; therefore these are not to be recommended.

Copper

Copper is stored primarily in the liver but is also found in small quantities throughout the body. The most important role of copper in the body is as a component in enzymes, but its other roles, including immune function and nerve and connective tissue structure, are not well understood. It acts as a pro-oxidant in the body. Copper is an essential component of hair pigmentation. Adequate copper is essential for the healthy growth of young horses, and particularly for the development of strong, healthy cartilage. It is absorbed through the small intestine, but its uptake may be inhibited by large amounts of zinc, iron, or the macrominerals, and, like zinc, its availability in humans is reduced with excessive antacid ingestion. High levels of zinc supplementation should be balanced with copper in a ratio of 4:1. Although there is a lack of evidence that excess zinc inhibits copper uptake in horses as it does in humans, adequate copper levels are crucial; therefore the zinc to copper ratio should be adhered to. Copper and iron have a close interaction because copper is essential for the use of iron in the blood. Copper is transported to the liver in the blood bound to protein or amino acids and the liver is the main storage area for copper. Deficiency causes a wide variety of symptoms including anaemia, bone and joint disorders, poor growth, infertility, hair depigmentation and gastrointestinal disturbance. Excessive intakes of copper are dangerous for sheep and, to a lesser extent, cattle – unlike horses who can tolerate much higher intakes; therefore supplementation to horses in the presence of ruminants should be done with care. High levels of dietary copper leading to high liver levels have not been shown to cause toxicity problems in horses.

Iron

Three-quarters of the iron in a horse's body is found in the haemoglobin in red blood cells and the myoglobin in muscle, both of which are the oxygen carriers of these tissues. Other iron is incorporated in enzymes and is found in the blood and in storage within the liver and bone marrow. The principal function of iron in the horse's body is a factor in oxygen uptake and transport and storage in the muscles. Iron is absorbed in the small intestine and various factors can either enhance or limit its uptake in humans, although it is not known whether this occurs in horses. In humans, sugar and vitamin C enhance uptake, and calcium, phosphorus and large intakes of zinc inhibit uptake. Transportation of iron in the blood is by a protein carrier, which relies on copper for its function. Copper is also essential for the incorporation of iron into the haemoglobin molecule. Excessive intake of iron by horses is toxic, and creates substantial oxidative stress, since iron acts as a pro-oxidant. Toxicity involves liver damage, and may cause gastrointestinal disturbances and other mineral deficiencies. Iron deficiency in horses is rare because of the widespread distribution of iron in horse feed, particularly in forage, and the fact that iron is efficiently recycled within the body, rather than being lost when old red blood cells are destroyed and new ones created. Although iron deficiency does cause anaemia, anaemia is not the same as an iron deficiency; it simply describes a shortage of haemoglobin in the blood. This may arise from a reduced red blood cell count, reduced red blood cell haemoglobin content, or a combination of both. Anaemia can, for example, be caused by either acute or chronic blood loss, which may, in turn, be a consequence of such things as a high worm burden. Therefore, although iron deficiency does cause anaemia, iron supplements should not be used indiscriminately for the treatment of anaemia in horses. Instead, the cause of the anaemia should be diagnosed and treated, and a good broad-spectrum vitamin and mineral supplement containing useful levels of iron, copper and zinc should be fed. Dietary iron alone will not increase red blood cells, or increase the concentration of haemoglobin.

Selenium

Selenium is found throughout the horse's body, and its principal role is as a component of the antioxidant compound glutathione peroxidase. Other functions include an involvement in iodine metabolism, immune function, pancreatic function and enzyme activation. Selenium is chemically similar to sulphur, and can exist within the sulphur-containing amino acids including methionine, cystine and cysteine. The distribution of selenium in feed is highly variable because of its variable concentration in soil, and it appears in forages and seeds as seleno-cystine, selenocysteine and selenomethionine. Selenium-deficient soils are known to occur in parts of Scotland, but there may not be sufficient selenium for grazing horses in pasture grass in specific areas throughout the UK. Selenium is absorbed efficiently in the small intestine, and uptake in humans is enhanced by vitamins A, E and C. However, it is not known whether the same happens in horses.

Like the other microminerals, selenium is transported in the blood by a protein carrier, and excess is stored in the liver. Selenium is toxic in excess, and has a lower toxicity threshold than other micronutrients – continuous intake of 2 mg/kg diet per day (20 mg for a 500 kg horse eating 10 kg feed, which is 10–20 times recommended amounts) results in fatigue, hair and hoof loss, interference in sulphur use and inhibition of protein synthesis. On the other hand, deficiency of selenium causes weakness, muscle dysfunction, poor athletic performance, skin and hair pigmentation loss and poor growth.

Chromium

Chromium is an often-forgotten nutrient, but plays an important role in the function of insulin via a chromium-containing compound called glucose toler-ance factor (GTF). It is therefore essential for normal carbohydrate metabolism. Chromium increases insulin sensitivity, but exactly how it functions is not yet fully understood. Absorption takes place throughout the small intestine, and transportation in the blood takes place via binding to the iron protein carrier, to protein and as free chromium. Brewers' yeast is a good source of chromium, but it is present in many foods including cereal fibre. Chromium deficiency could result in insulin insensitivity, but further research in the horse is necessary before this is confirmed. Stress appears to increase the requirement in humans, but it is not known whether this is the case for horses. Excess intake causes toxicity asso-ciated with damage of genetic material, but certain sources of chromium are more toxic at high levels than others. Chromium is not recognized as an additive for horse feed in Europe, so products offered commercially are not permitted to contain it.

Iodine

The principal role of iodine in the horse's body is for the synthesis of thyroid hor-mones by the thyroid gland, and this tissue takes up most of the circulating iodine. Iodine exists and functions in the body in its ionic form, iodide, which is absorbed in the small intestine. Thyroid hormones are involved in many body functions, including regulation of basal metabolic rate, oxygen consumption and heat production. They are essential for growth and normal nervous system devel-opment. Deficiency results in goitre, which involves an enlargement of the thyroid gland and, in growing youngsters, causes a wide variety of disorders including impaired growth and development. Most horse pasture in the UK is short of iodine; therefore it should be supplemented. Seaweed is a good source of iodine for horses, although total iodine intake for breeding mares should be limited to a daily maximum of 40 mg in total for a 500 kg mare (generally, lower levels would be given). Very high levels of iodine can cause infertility and abortions in mares, and abnormal growth and development in their foals.

Manganese

Manganese occurs in small quantities throughout the horse's body and, like most other microminerals, is a component of enzymes and involved in enzymes reactions. It is important for the formation of healthy joint tissues, especially cartilage. Absorption takes place in the small intestine and there is little knowledge about how this is affected by other nutrients. Manganese is widely distributed in feed and deficiency is unlikely. If occurring, deficiencies in young, growing horses could lead to joint abnormalities and lameness. Toxicity through excess intake is, in theory, possible, but large amounts would have to be fed, and no information on toxicity in horses is available.

Cobalt

Cobalt forms part of vitamin B_{12} (cobalamin), and is necessary for synthesis of this vitamin by gut micro-organisms. It is believed to have other functions including involvement in enzyme reactions. Deficiency and excess are unlikely because most feed contains some cobalt, and most forages contain adequate amounts for horses. Cobalt is likely to be toxic in excess, but very large amounts would need to be fed.

Molybdenum

Molybdenum is considered an essential micromineral, but little is known about its absorption and transport in the body. It is distributed widely in feed, therefore deficiency is very unlikely. Molybdenum, like most other microminerals, is involved the function of various enzymes. In farm animals, particularly ruminants, a high intake of molybdenum inhibits the uptake of copper and can cause deficiencies. In horses no such relationship has been found.

Vitamins

Vitamins are required by the body in relatively small amounts, hence they are called micronutrients, but they are absolutely essential for life and are involved in fundamental processes in the body. Deficiency results in disturbed body function and eventually disease. The name 'vitamin' originated from a 'vital amine' discovered after scientists realized that the body could not survive on a purified diet of carbohydrate, protein, fat, minerals and water. As each vitamin was discovered, the 'e' of 'amine' was dropped when scientists realized that not all vitamins were indeed amine compounds. Initially it was thought that each vitamin was a specific substance with a specific function, but over time it was found that vitamins have a variety of functions and vitamin activity can be found in a variety of related substances.

Vitamins are generally split into two categories: water-soluble and fat-soluble. This division is not related to their structure or function, but to the way they are handled by the body. Water-soluble vitamin C and the B-complex vitamins are absorbed into the blood and are not retained by the body but excreted once their level reaches a certain threshold. The exception is vitamin B_{12}, which is stored mainly in the liver. The fat-soluble vitamins – A, E, D and K – are absorbed in association with fat, rely on adequate bile action and are transported in association with chylomicrons (blood fat transporter molecules).

Vitamin requirements are calculated according to the amount that is necessary to avoid symptoms of deficiency, but requirements for optimal health may be higher. Relatively safe vitamins including water-soluble vitamins and vitamin E should be fed at higher than basic recommendations, especially for certain classes of horses under stress, such as breeding horses, performance horses and those in stressful environments, e.g. long-distance travelling and weaning.

Fat-soluble Vitamins

Vitamin E

Vitamin E consists of several different compounds that are synthesized by plants, including tocopherols and tocotrienols. Oils from plants are considered the richest sources of vitamin E, but green, leafy plant parts are also good sources. Vitamin E is not stored in the horse's body in adequate amounts; therefore a regular dietary supply is necessary. The vitamin E content of unfortified feed tends to be stated in terms of international units (iu), where 1 iu of the vitamin is equivalent to the activity of 1 mg of a synthetic alpha tocopheral acetate.

Vitamin E functions mainly as an antioxidant nutrient in the horse's body, protecting cells against free radical damage, therefore maintaining the integrity of all body cell membranes. Free radicals are reactive substances produced in the normal everyday metabolic function of the body. Body tissues, especially cell membranes, the genetic material DNA and cell proteins are vulnerable to free radical damage. This applies particularly to the highly active muscle cells, and the damage tends to occur in a chain reaction. Antioxidants, including vitamins and enzymes containing microminerals, interrupt the chain by scavenging the free radicals and thus deactivating them. Vitamin E is the most important antioxidant

Vitamin	Functions in body	RDA*	Deficiency	Excess	Notes
Fat-soluble					
Vitamin A	Vision; growth; bone development; reproduction; immune function	22,000–30,000 iu	Weight loss; respiratory and gut dysfunction; poor fertility; anaemia; weepy eyes; poor night vision	Very toxic – bone fragility; skin lesions; reduced blood clotting; internal haemorrhages	Carotenes (provitamin A) are not toxic and are present in very high amounts in green forages
Vitamin D	Regulates calcium and phosphorus balance	3,000 mg	Poor appetite; reduced growth rate; skeletal abnormalities	Toxic if excessive synthetic supplementation; similar to excess vitamin A symptoms	Produced via sunlight on the skin – in this case excesses not toxic
Vitamin E	Antioxidant; immune function; muscle function	800–2,000 mg	Muscle dysfunction; cardiovascular disruption; poor immunity	Least toxic of the fat-soluble vitamins	Slight over-supplementation for performance, breeding and ill horses is recommended
Vitamin K	Blood clotting; protein synthesis	10 mg – no published requirement	Unknown	Colic and kidney failure (excessive synthetic supplementation)	Hindgut bacteria supply vitamin K to the horse
Water-soluble					
Vitamin C	Antioxidant; connective tissue integrity; iron metabolism	None for healthy horses (10 g for horse with respiratory disease)	Unknown, but possibly oxidative stress	Unknown; can be excreted but may cause diarrhoea as in humans	Horse produces own vitamin C; only ill horses, those with respiratory disease and those under intense stress require dietary source
B-complex vitamins	Enzyme components; energy metabolism; nerve conduction	Thiamine (B$_1$):50 mg Riboflavin (B$_2$); 20–30 mg; others unknown	Thiamine: poor appetite; fatigue; mental depression, lack of balance Others: unknown	Excesses are excreted so if in doubt supplementation is safe	Not necessary to supplement in healthy horse on forage-rich diet because of hind-gut production by bacterial fermentation

Recommended daily amounts are for a 500 kg horse in light work, eating 10 kg (dry matter) per day. The lower amounts are published requirements (from 1989); higher are updated recommendations.

Table 4.3 Vitamins for horses; functions, deficiency and excesses.

in cells, and functions along with vitamin C (which helps to regenerate 'used' vitamin E) and carotenoids (provitamin A). Vitamin E functions in close association with another antioxidant compound called glutathione peroxidase, which contains selenium. Immune system development and function relies on vitamin E, and research in mares and foals has shown that passive transfer of immunity is better in mares with high vitamin E intakes. Vitamin E deficiency in horses leads to muscle dysfunction and cardiovascular disruption. Vitamin E is the least toxic fat-soluble vitamin and slightly over-supplementing is recommended, especially for performance horses, breeding horses and ill horses.

Vitamin A

Vitamin A is the term used to describe retinol and retinal, which are found primarily in food of animal origin. Animals that eat plants, including horses, obtain their vitamin A from carotenoids, which are converted in the body to retinol, and are called provitamin A. Absorption depends on dietary fat, and very low levels of fat will result in relatively low uptake of provitamin A. Only certain carotenoids can be converted to vitamin A, and the one with most vitamin A activity is called betacarotene. Fresh grass contains high levels of betacarotene. It is estimated that, in the horse, 8 mg of betacarotene is needed to produce the equivalent vitamin A activity of 1 mg of retinol. 0.3 µg of retinol is equivalent to 1iu (international unit) of vitamin A, so about 1 mg of betacarotene is equivalent to 400 iu of vitamin A. Both vitamin A and betacarotenes can be stored in the liver for later use. While excess vitamin A causes toxicity, excess intake of carotenoids does not.

Vitamin A performs a variety of functions in the horse's body and is involved in vision, growth and bone development, reproduction and immune function. Carotenoids act as antioxidants, suppressing free radical damage in the body. Deficiency of vitamin A causes weight loss, respiratory and intestinal dysfunction, poor fertility, anaemia, weepy eyes and poor night vision. The toxic effects of excess vitamin A are bone fragility, skin lesions and reduced blood clotting, which could cause internal haemorrhages. Care should be taken when adding specialized supplements to a diet containing compound feed, because the safe upper limit of vitamin A may be reached.

Vitamin D

Vitamin D is associated with bone strength and development via its role in regulating calcium and phosphorus balance. There are two main types – vitamin D_2 and vitamin D_3. D vitamins are generally not found in plant material, although some may be present in dead leaves on growing plants, and sun-dried forages. Provitamin D is produced within the skin, and is converted to vitamin D by ultraviolet light. Therefore horses kept outdoors will produce their own internal supplies of vitamin D. Dietary vitamin D is absorbed with fat, just like the other fat-soluble vitamins. It is ultimately converted to calcitriol, which is a compound that is involved in calcium and phosphorus absorption in the intestine. Calcitriol is also involved in kidney function, whole-body calcium status (balance), and cell growth and development. Vitamin D shortages are possible in horses kept indoors and on an unsupplemented diet, and cause poor appetite, reduced growth rate and skeletal abnormalities. Excess dietary vitamin D intake could lead to toxicity, which can cause problems similar to vitamin A toxicity, but overproduction of vitamin D via synthesis in the skin from exposure to sunlight is not thought to be toxic.

Vitamin K

Several different compounds exhibit vitamin K activity, and dietary vitamin K for horses comes from leafy plants including grass, and vegetable oils. Hindgut bacteria also supply vitamin K to the horse. Like the other fat-soluble vitamins, vitamin K is taken via the fat transporters, chylomicrons, which deliver vitamin K to the liver for distribution to other tissues. Vitamin K is necessary for blood clotting and for the formation of specific proteins found in the bones and kidneys. Excess vitamin A intake interferes with vitamin K absorption, and there are interactions between vitamin E and vitamin K, although further research is necessary to fully understand these interactions. Vitamin K deficiency has not been reported in horses, and it is thought that hindgut microbial production fulfils requirements. Excess of synthetic vitamin K causes kidney failure and colic.

Water-soluble vitamins

Vitamin C

Vitamin C can be synthesized within the horse's body, in the liver (unlike humans, who require a dietary source because of a lack of the enzyme required to manufacture the vitamin). Thus healthy horses have no dietary requirement of vitamin C. However, the requirement of ill horses or those under intense stress (for example, from transport or athletic performance) may be greater than normal body synthesis supplies and in such cases dietary supplementation may be necessary. Recent research in horses with airway disease has shown that the ascorbic acid levels within their lung lining is lower than optimum. Supplementary vitamin C has been shown to increase these levels and is recommended for horses affected by airway disease, including recurrent airway obstruction (RAO), previously called COPD (chronic obstructive pulmonary disease). Research has shown that supplementing horses with ascorbyl palmitate rather than ascorbic acid is more effective in increasing body status of the vitamin.

The chemical name for vitamin C is ascorbic acid, and it plays an important role as an antioxidant nutrient in the body, along with vitamin E and enzymes containing microminerals. Vitamin C is an important extracellular (outside body cells) antioxidant and it is also involved in regenerating vitamin E. It is important for connective tissue integrity (hence the reason why lemon juice helps the gum damage of the human disease, scurvy) and iron metabolism. In humans, absorption decreases with increasing intakes of vitamin C (that is, the more humans take in, the less they absorb). Horses absorb dietary vitamin C by passive diffusion in the small intestine.

B-complex vitamins

The B-complex vitamins must be supplied regularly as (with the exception of vitamin B_{12}, which is stored mainly in the liver) they are not stored in the body. Most B-vitamins function in the body as components of enzymes, which are involved in energy metabolism, nerve conduction and, to a lesser extent, metabolism of amino acids. Horses have an internal supply of B-vitamins from microbial fermentation within their hindguts, which meets the requirements of healthy adults. However, if the microbial population is disturbed as a result of an inappropriate diet (for example, sudden change, fibre deficiency, overload of starch), the supply of B-vitamins may be inadequate. Research to date has not been able to ascertain requirements for horses, but the B-vitamins are relatively safe, because of the action of excretion so, if in doubt, these vitamins should be supplemented.

Vitamin B_1 is also called *thiamine*, and is particularly important for energy production in the body. Intake is proportional to energy utilization, therefore exercising horses have higher requirements than horses at maintenance. Thiamine deficiencies cause poor appetite, fatigue, mental depression and, in severe cases, lack of balance and coordination. High levels can be fed without signs of toxicity.

Deficiencies of *vitamin B_2* (*riboflavin*), *vitamin B_3* (*niacin, nicotinic acid* and *nicotinamide*), *vitamin B_6* (*pyridoxine*) and *vitamin B_5* (*pantothenic acid*) are unknown in the horse, but excessive intake is not harmful.

Biotin is a B-vitamin that is involved in energy production and, like the other B-vitamins, deficiencies are unknown in healthy horses. However, supplementary levels of 20 mg per day (in contrast to the 1 or 2 mg per day dietary requirement) have been shown to help hoof problems in some horses. These therapeutic doses need to be fed long term (2 years plus) for best effect; see Chapter 13 for more information.

Vitamin B_{12} (*cobalamin*) contains the micromineral cobalt, and is only available via microbial fermentation. It is absorbed via the large intestine of the horse, and stored in the liver. This vitamin is involved in energy production, red blood cell formation and in the use of folic acid in the body. It is also required for the use of propionate, a volatile fatty acid produced from microbial fermentation in the gut, which can be used directly for energy or converted into glucose. If adequate levels of dietary cobalt are available, there is no need for vitamin B_{12} in the diet. There is no proof that injections of this vitamin can 'cure' anaemia, and they are likely to be a waste of time. Horses with heavy worm burdens can respond to vitamin injections, but are better treated for the worms and fed a high-quality diet instead. Vitamin B_{12} supplementation increases the appetite in some horses fed high grain rations, since such diets produce high levels of propionate. Ideally, however, horses with poor appetites should be fed a reduced amount of grain, because this could help to stimulate the appetite without supplementing with vitamins.

Folic acid, like the other B vitamins, is obtained via microbial fermentation in the gut, and there is no recommended amount available for horses. This vitamin is involved in cell formation, including red blood cell formation. Grass is rich in folic acid, and no deficiencies have been confirmed in horses. Horse being intensively exercised have lower levels of blood folate, and supplementation is recommended for those with limited access to fresh green forage.

chapter 5

Fibre

FIBRE HAS A DEDICATED chapter because it is an often misunderstood component of horse feeds and also a very complex one. In addition, research in the past decade has helped to increase the understanding of how horses digest and use dietary fibre. Fibre used to be considered simply as bulk, which helped a horse to feel full. Whilst fibre does play a role in giving horses gut fill, adequate supplies are also necessary for the health of the hindgut microbes, and therefore the stability of the hindgut environment. In addition, horses at maintenance and even some in light work can extract all the energy they need from fibrous forage. As explained in Chapter 3, horses have a dietary requirement for fibre, and recent research studies have shown that horses will work to obtain fibre even when their energy requirements have been fulfilled. All horses should be fed no less than 1% of their bodyweight per day in fibrous forage; preferably unprocessed, e.g. long hay or haylage.

What is fibre?

Fibre is a type of carbohydrate, and like starch it is a polysaccharide, made up from many units of simple sugars (saccharides). It can be either soluble or insoluble in water. Fibre occurs mainly as the cell walls of plants, where it plays a structural role, holding the plant up. However, other forms of fibre do exist in plants, including various soluble gums and gel-forming substances. Since many different types of fibre exist, it is difficult to classify and describe definitively. The general description of fibre is plant material that cannot be broken down by gut enzymes but, as explained in Chapter 4, this is difficult to quantify with laboratory analysis. (As explained in Chapter 2, dietary fibre is broken down by microbes within the horse's gut, primarily in the hindgut.)

Dietary fibre has also been described as 'non-starch polysaccharides' or NSP, but this classification also includes fructans. Fructans are the primary energy storage of temperate grasses, such as grasses found in the UK. Some species of grass, including ryegrass, are particularly rich in fructans. Fructans, in theory, should be classified as fibre, because they are not digested by gut enzymes, instead being available for gut microbes. However, they are handled in the horse's gut in a very different way from structural fibres such as those listed below under Types of Fibre in Feed.). Therefore, in equine nutrition, fructans are not classed as fibre, but tend to be classed as 'non-structural carbohydrate' along with starch and sugar, because all can cause health problems if eaten in very large quantities. Fructans are also included in the 'water-soluble carbohydrate' (WSC) fraction of plants such as grass. The WSC in plants include sugars as well as fructans.

right A seedhead of ryegrass can be seen in this hay.

below Lush grasses can be rich in fructans.

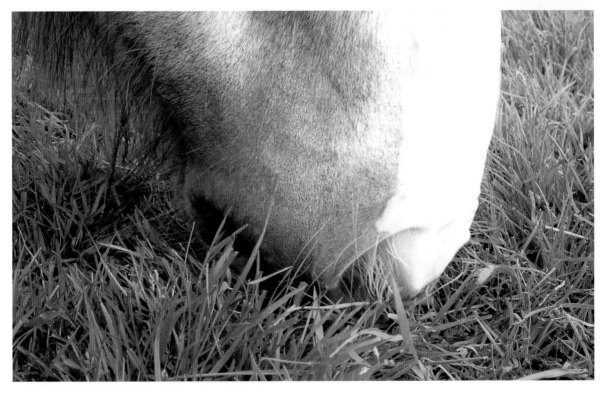

Some fructan in the horse's diet, especially the relatively short-chain type, is beneficial, promoting the growth of beneficial bacteria and appearing to have beneficial effects on the gut wall. However, if very large quantities of fructan are ingested over short periods, there is a huge proliferation of the bacteria that feed on fructan, and the result is a situation similar to that which occurs in starch over-load (see Carbohydrates in Chapter 4). More information on fructans can be found under Causes of Laminitis in Chapter 14.

Because of the complexities surrounding a precise definition of the term 'fibre', for ease of reading, the term will be used to describe plant cell wall material (lignin, cellulose, hemicellulose and pectins) and the more soluble non-cell wall constituents (gums and mucilages), but not fructans.

Types of fibre in feed

Cellulose

Cellulose is the most abundant fibre in plants, and is made up of repeating units of the sugar glucose held together by 1,4 beta bonds. Cellulose is insoluble in water and its degradation in the hindgut by bacterial fermentation varies, but is generally low, i.e. it is a less digestible fibre than others. Grasses contain between 20 and 30% cellulose, and more as they mature. Feeds rich in cellulose include mature grass hay and straw.

Hemicellulose

This is made up of many different sugar units, which give it variable characteristics. Some are more soluble than others, and some are more fermentable than others. It is found in close association with cellulose but despite the name it is not a precursor to cellulose, but a completely different compound. Grasses contain between 10 and 30% hemicellulose, and more as they mature. Bran and the fibre in grains are relatively high in hemicellulose.

Pectin

Pectin is a complex type of fibre that consists of a chain of galacturonic acid units, with other sugars attached. It is soluble, forms a gel in water and is almost completely digestible (fermentable) by gut bacteria. Sugar beet and apples are high in pectin.

Lignin

Lignin is classed as a fibre but is not a carbohydrate, although it is found in close association with cellulose and hemicellulose. It is rigid and gives structure to plants, therefore is found in higher quantities in the stems. Mature plants such as cereals have high lignin levels in their stems, also called straw. Lignin is insoluble in water and indigestible i.e. it is not fermented by gut bacteria.

Gums and mucilages

These are soluble fibres that form a thick, gel-like consistency. They are almost completely digestible (fermentable) by gut bacteria. Gums are excreted at sites of plant injury and exist in relatively high quantities in oats. Linseed is rich in mucilages. Seaweed is high in a unique type of mucilage, widely used in the human food industry, which can be fermented by the horse's gut bacteria.

Since plant cell walls consist of over 95% fibre, which take the form of cellulose, hemicellulose, lignin and pectins, most whole plants are rich in fibre. In contrast, plant seeds, e.g. cereal grains, are rich in starch, giving them a store of energy for new growth. The species and maturity of whole plants influence the composition of each type of fibre, and the total fibre content. As plants mature, the total fibre content increases, and the content of lignin also increases, which helps to keep the plant standing as it grows tall. This lignin decreases the digestibility of the fibre. Generally, the more mature a plant, the higher in fibre and lower in energy it becomes. Fibrous whole plant feeds tend to be called forages (hay, haylage, straw, fresh grass and quick-dried alfalfa and grass). Note that some spring grass can be relatively low in fibre, and high in water-soluble carbohydrates (fructan and sugar).

Classifying fibre by analysis

Understanding the composition and feed value of feeds relies on accurate methods of analysis. As mentioned, analysis of fibre creates a challenge because of the variable forms it takes. Originally, the composition of human and animal feeds was analysed using 'proximate analysis', which described the crude fibre, crude protein, ash and oil contents. Table 6.1 in Chapter 6 (page 63) describes the methods used. These methods are not particularly accurate, and the resulting crude fibre measurement does not include all the cellulose, hemicellulose and lignin in the feed. Nor does this measurement include soluble fibres such as pectin and gums. Therefore crude fibre analysis tends to underestimate the total fibre content of a feed.

Newer methods of analysis are more accurate, but have been developed to analyse feed for ruminants. Fibre is analysed in two different ways, giving readings for neutral-detergent fibre (NDF) and acid-detergent fibre (ADF). NDF consists mainly of lignin, cellulose and hemicellulose, and is a measure of the plant cell wall material. ADF consists of lignin and cellulose (these substances being both neutral-detergent and acid-detergent), and is a useful measurement for forages, because there is a link between ADF and the digestibility of feeds by ruminants. A mature grass hay or straw would be very high in ADF, and would be a useful high-fibre, low-calorie feed for horses because it is relatively indigestible (see Table 5.1). In the UK a modified acid-detergent fibre technique (MADF) is often used to calculate ADF. Although these methods of analysis cannot be considered *ideal* for horses, because they have not been fully validated for the species, they are currently the best available.

In human (and occasionally equine) nutrition the term 'non-starch polysaccharide' (NSP) is often used to describe fibre (including soluble fibre). Soluble fibre is known to lower blood cholesterol in humans, and insoluble fibre increases the rate of transit through the large intestine, helping to preventing a range of diseases including bowel cancer. As explained above, NSP is a less helpful term for equine nutrition, since fructans would be included, and in large amounts these have very different effects on the gut from other fibre. It is not known what effect large amounts of other soluble fibres such as pectin or gums would have on the digestive process or health of the horse, because in practice large amounts are not eaten.

	Crude fibre	NDF	ADF	Lignin
Mature grass hay (mixed species)	38	74	45	11
Early cut grass hay	30	65	36	5
Grass meal	21	72	39	4
Barley straw	39	81	51	12
Quick-dried alfalfa	25	46	34	11
Quick-dried grass	21	54	28	–
Sugar beet pulp	20	49	28	6
Barley	5	20	6	–
Oats	10	31	15	3

(— not available)

Table 5.1 Fibre constituents of horse feed (percentage of dry matter).

Adapted from McDonald et al (2002) *Animal Nutrition*, Pearson Prentice Hall.

Digestion of fibre

As explained earlier, fibre is not digested by gut enzymes produced by the horse, but it is available to the microbes in the gut. Horses have a variety of microbes throughout their digestive tracts, including those that digest fibre and those that digest starch and sugar. Each type of microbe has a preferred food source. Foals, just like humans and other animals, are born with sterile guts. Contact with their dam and the environment leads to establishment of the gut microbes, also collectively called 'microflora'. Most of the microbes reside in the large intestine or hindgut, and the largest proportion are fibre-digesting bacteria. Some bacteria occur in the stomach and small intestine, although numbers in the small intestine are limited as a consequence of the fast passage rate, and most are associated with the gut wall. Many of the microbes in the small intestine play important roles in protecting the gut, and therefore the animal, from invasion by disease-causing (pathogenic) bacteria.

The enlarged hindgut of the horse has been described as a 'fermentation vat' because the resident microbes ferment fibre in order to digest it. Microbial fermentation yields vitamins and large quantities of volatile fatty acids (VFAs), which are a source of energy for the horse. VFAs are also thought to stimulate gut cell proliferation, helping to boost gut health.

The total amount of published research studies into the normal gut microflora of a healthy horse is surprisingly small, and much more knowledge is needed. What is certain is that populations of microbes are dynamic, and although a general balance (homeostasis) is present, numbers of individual types of bacteria or fungi are constantly fluctuating. These fluctuations depend largely on the carbohydrate feed components that enter the hindgut. Such changes are most evident in meal-fed horses. As yet, there is no proven method of assessing the balance of gut microflora from the inspection of faeces (droppings), primarily because the optimum balance is unknown. Such a technique would also be complicated by the dynamic nature of the gut microflora and the fact that many are attached to the gut wall.

Different types of fibre are digested at different rates and to different extents, and some are partially fermented in the small intestine. Plants rich in soluble fibre including gums and pectin and some types of hemicellulose are more digestible, fermented partially in the foregut, and more completely fermented in the hindgut, so the total yield of nutrients to the horse is more than from plants rich in relatively undigestible cellulose fibre. (Note that few foods – even the most mature plants – contain nothing but fibre, and most are a mixture of different nutrients.)

The more fermentable it is, the higher in energy the fibre will be for the horse. Nowadays, manufacturers are more aware of the different types of fibre components of plants, which has led to the development of 'superfibres' in compound feed. Sugar beet and soya hulls are both particularly fermentable and therefore higher in energy than traditional fibre feeds such as hay and straw, both of which are rich in cellulose and not particularly fermentable. Bran used to be thought of as a low-energy bulky fibre feed, but it is actually moderately fermentable because of its relatively high level of hemicellulose and it is well-digested by the gut bacteria.

Absorption and use of fibre

The end products of fibre fermentation by microbes are mainly volatile fatty acids (VFAs), and other substances, including vitamins. The VFAs produced from fibre breakdown are acetic acid, butyric acid and propionic acid. Acetic and butyric acid can enter the metabolic energy pathways directly, in the same way as fatty acids from oil digestion, but propionic acid is transported to the liver where it is converted into glucose. Lactic acid is produced when starch and sugar are fermented, and this can also be absorbed and used for energy production. However, lactic acid causes problems in the horse's hindgut when very large amounts are produced rapidly and absorption rates cannot match production rates.

Lactic acid is produced by specific microbes that ferment starch and sugar. As explained in Chapter 4, when plenty of starch is available, these microbes proliferate rapidly, overloading the hindgut with lactic acid and causing a cascade of effects that result in death of the fibre-fermenting bacteria, production of toxins and other substances, and a leaky gut wall. These changes can lead to diarrhoea, colic, or laminitis. Ensuring an adequate supply of fibre to 'feed' the fibre-fermenting microbes is almost as important as avoiding large meals of starch, which overflow undigested into the hindgut.

Fibre deficiency

Fibre must be supplied to the gut microbes continuously to support their populations and keep them healthy. As mentioned in Chapter 3, horses have a dietary requirement for fibre, without which they will suffer health problems. The main consequence of underfeeding fibre is a disturbance of the gut microbial balance. However, there are also other psychological and physiological effects, because horses have evolved to eat large quantities of high-fibre, low-nutrient feed, and will seek out such material if not fed sufficient. Fibre-deficient horses tend to chew wood and eat faeces, and are at an increased risk of gastric ulcers and the development of oral stereotypies such as crib-biting. These problems are exacerbated if the horse is fed a relatively high level of starch as well as low fibre.

The reliance of hindgut fibre-digesting microbes on a consistent food supply to keep their populations healthy is the main reason why horse's diets should be

All horses should be fed adequate quantities of fibrous forage.

changed gradually. (Another is to allow time for the production of enzymes and nutrient transporter substances to be increased). Even changes in fibre sources should be made gradually, in order to allow the microbial populations to adjust. Changing feeds too quickly may cause gut disturbance, diarrhoea and/or colic.

Ideally, a source of long forage should always be offered, such as grass, hay, haylage and straw. For horses who cannot eat such feeds, chopped forages may be fed instead. For horses who are not able to eat even chopped forages, ground forage can be fed in the form of grass or alfalfa nuts and/or high-fibre compound cubed feeds soaked to a mash. Horses can survive on a diet without long forage, but care must be taken to fulfil their need to forage and to keep them occupied. Many small meals of soaked nuts and/or cubes and sugar beet can be fed, and cubes can be placed into a feed-decanting ball to help.

chapter 6

Feeds and supplements

A HUGE VARIETY OF FEEDS and supplements are available for horses nowadays, compared with many years ago when horses tended to be fed hay, oats, bran and straw chaff. More choice can allow more suitable diets to be formulated, but also causes much confusion. Not only are a huge variety of single feeds available, but a huge number of branded compound feeds are on sale. Clever marketing and packaging can make some similar formulations appear very different. Learning more about single feeds or feed ingredients will help more informed choices about the compound feed to be made, even if the horse owner is not interested in buying single feeds and combining them to make a balanced diet.

Before studying the variety of feeds and feed ingredients available, I recommend that the information about the horse's ideal or natural diet given in Chapter 2 should be read (or perhaps revisited). Equines have evolved over millions of years to survive on a diet of relatively low-quality fibrous feeds and such feeds remain the most suitable for the horse. In some cases it is not possible to feed horses just these high-fibre plant materials, either because they do not meet nutritional requirements (perhaps in the case of an eventer or racehorse) or because such feeds are not available, but at all times the natural diet of the horse should be borne in mind.

Horses were traditionally fed concentrate feed for two reasons; because they were worked hard enough to warrant the extra calories and protein, and because they often did not have access to pasture grass or any other type of feed for hours at a time. This tradition of feeding

There is a wide variety of feed products commercially available nowadays.

concentrates to working horses has remained prevalent to the present day, despite the fact many horses do not work particularly hard, and some of those who do have access to nutrient-rich grass and high-quality preserved forages.

The list of single feeds suitable for horses is very long, but can probably be subdivided into the following groups: forages (grass, legumes and cereal straws, both field-cut and dried and quick-dried or dehydrated), cereals and their by-products, oilseeds and their by-products, roots (including sugar and fodder beet, carrots and turnips), and others such as certain herbs. Each type of feed has specific nutritional characteristics that make it useful in formulating a ration. For example oilseeds are rich in good-quality protein, whereas cereals are rich in energy. By-products should not be rejected for horses because the vegetable material that is left over after food processing for human consumption is, in many cases, more suitable for horses than the whole material. The husk or hull of both oats and wheat are useful horse feeds, yet the whole grain may not be necessary because of its high energy level. In recent years new parts of feeds that have been used for years have been found to be useful for horses. For example, soya bean hulls (the fibrous coat of the bean) are full of highly digestible fibre that makes an excellent feed for horses.

Feeds

Labelling and nutrient declarations

In the UK, there are legal requirements for labelling of horse feed and supplements, which are the same as for farm animals produced for food. Horses are still currently classed by the regulators as being 'farmed food-producing animals' and, despite the fact that horsemeat is not eaten in the UK, some UK horses are exported for meat, which is eaten in other European countries. The information that must appear by law is called the 'statutory statement', which is often found on a separate small white label on a sack of feed or tub of supplement, in addition to the main colour labelling on the packaging. The information must be clear to see, in English and separate from other information. For a complementary feed (i.e. compound feeds and supplements) the following information must be included on the statutory statement:

1. The name and address or registered office of the person responsible for the accuracy of the information on the statement.

2. A description, e.g. 'complementary feeding stuff' and the species of animal the feed is made for.

3. Directions for use.

4. 'Best before' or 'use by' date'

5. Net weight.

6. Batch number.

7. The approval or registration number allocated to the establishment that manufactured the product.

8. All ingredients in descending order of weight.

9. Analytical constituents (protein, oil, fibre, ash, calcium if greater than 5%, phosphorus if greater than 2%).

10. Moisture, if greater than 14%, or if the information is requested by the purchaser.

11. The following additives, and the amount and form added:

   • Antioxidants, colours and preservatives.

   • Vitamins A, E and D, whether naturally present or added.
     – Vitamins A and D must include the name of the vitamin and the active substance level.
     – Vitamin E must include the alpha-tocopherol level as acetate.

   • Copper: the name of the additive and the total level (mg/kg) whether naturally present or added.

   • Enzymes: more information must be available if required.

   • Micro-organisms: the ID and file number of the strains, the number of colony-forming units (CFU/kg), EC registration number, indication of period during which the colony-forming units will remain present, any other information as specified in the authorization concerned.

If a compound feed or supplement contains protein derived from mammalian tissue but containing no mammalian meat and bone meal, the statutory statement must include the statement: 'This compound feeding stuff contains protein derived from mammalian tissue the feeding of which to ruminants is prohibited.'

Other information is allowed on the packaging, but it must not be misleading, is not allowed to make a claim of preventing, treating or curing a disease, and is not allowed to mention a particular disease, unless the product is stated to be a dietetic. Other rules apply for other types of feed including straight feeds, mineral supplements and feed materials (feed ingredients). The rules are published in a

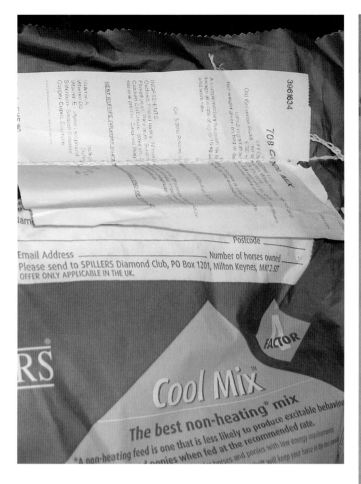

Statutory statements on bags of feed.

document called The FeedingStuffs (England/ Scotland/Wales) Regulations 2005 (published by TSO; www.tso.co.uk) and more about the general rules and regulations governing feed and supplement manufacture can be found on the Food Standards Agency website at www.foodstandards.gov.uk.

The analytical constituents of feed and supplements can cause confusion. These are not *ingredients*, i.e. horse feed does not contain ash. These values are obtained from analysis of the finished feed, and give an idea of the nutrients available to the animal. For example, the ash value is gained from burning the feed at very high temperatures, to give a mineral residue (see Table 6.1, next page). Originally, the composition of food and feed was analysed using 'proximate analysis', which described the crude fibre, crude protein, ash and oil contents of a feed. Although this type of analysis is now known to be rather inaccurate, it is still used for the statutory declaration.

Feed analytical constituent	Method of analysis
Crude fibre	After ether extraction to remove oil, the food is boiled in alkali and acid to give an organic residue that includes cellulose, hemicellulose and lignin, but not necessarily all of those that are contained in the food
Crude protein	Calculated from nitrogen content; actually includes nitrogen from free amino acids, amines and nucleic acids
Ash	The residue left after burning the food at very high temperatures; includes the inorganic material including minerals
Oil	Calculated by ether extraction; actually includes all lipids, alcohol and organic acids

Table 6.1 Feed: analytical constituents.

Forages and unprocessed fibre feeds

Many years ago, 'forage' was used to describe all horse feed. Nowadays the word tends to be used to describe unprocessed fibrous feed including grass, hay (both grass and legume), haylage and straw. As explained in Chapter 3, horses have a psychological need to search out feed and chew, so unprocessed forages provide more than just nutrients. Forages are the group of feeds that may be considered as complete feeds, i.e. they provide a balanced diet if fed solely to a horse; however, this assumes that the forage contains adequate levels of micronutrients, which many do not. Forages are ideal horse feeds because they are of low enough nutritional quality to be fed ad lib, allowing the horse to adopt a more natural feeding pattern and thus helping to promote digestive and behavioural health. Chopped forages can also be included in this category, although a whole range is available, including plain chopped hay, chopped quick-dried grass and alfalfa, chopped hay replacer chaffs and compound feeds made from chopped forages plus concentrates, fortified with vitamins and minerals. Indeed, some of the latter could be fed as complete feeds, although they would be very costly.

Pasture grass

Pasture grass is a bit of an anomaly because its nutrient content can vary so widely. Grass can be the equivalent of a high-protein, high-energy and low-fibre concentrate feed, or a low-protein, low-energy high-fibre forage depending on the time of year, the treatment and the weather conditions. However, in most cases grass should be considered forage. Grass supplies most of the nutritional requirements of most horses in the UK throughout the spring, summer and autumn. More information about grass is given in the next chapter.

Hay

In the UK grass stops growing over the winter months, when the soil temperature drops below about 5 °C. The grass is usually replaced with preserved forage, such as hay or haylage. Hay is grass or other plant material that is cut, dried in the sun, then collected and baled for use at a later date. It may also be barn-dried. In the UK, most hay consists of dried grass, but some legume hay is available, most of which is alfalfa, with some clover. Grass hay can be made from mixed species meadows that are grazed in addition to being cut for hay, and this is described as meadow hay. Seed hay traditionally describes grass straw, which is left after a crop of grass has been grown for the seeds. Nowadays, single-species grass hay is grown, e.g. ryegrass hay, and this is often confused with seed hay. Meadow hay is leafy and contains seed heads, since different grass species mature at different times, whereas seed hay is stalky and may contain empty seed heads. Single species hay can be recognized from its uniformity, and ryegrass or timothy will look stalky, with some seed heads.

Hay can vary widely in nutrient content, but it is generally a high-fibre, moderate-protein feed with low to moderate water-soluble carbohydrate content. Early-cut single species hay and early-cut meadow hay may be very nutritious, whereas late-cut meadow hay, which will look more stalky, is lower in feed value. Seed hay is of relatively low nutritional quality because it is mature, and the nutritious seeds have been removed.

Hay is a good winter horse feed from a nutritional point of view, but unfortunately it is usually of poor hygienic quality. The process of drying hay on the field in the UK, where there are often high moisture levels and rain, results in a product that contains mould spores and dust. Leafy meadow hay tends to be the dustiest, and may also contain high levels of mould spores if not dried properly before baling. Since hay is generally fed to housed animals with restricted air space, the mould and dust content becomes a big issue. Researchers have found that up to half of stabled horses have inflammatory airway disease, although many do not show obvious symptoms (see Chapter 13 for more information). One research study showed that stabling horses after keeping them at pasture caused them all to have upper and lower airway inflammation. Vets now recommend that all hay fed to horses is first soaked or steamed to reduce the mould spore and dust content. Even hay fed out in the field should be treated before being fed. At least 10 minutes soaking is recommended, and no longer than 30 minutes, after which time nutrients will become leached out and the hay will

above A field of timothy grass, ready for hay-making.

Stemmy mature hay.

eventually start to rot. (Although soaking hay for an hour or two is a useful way of lowering the water-soluble carbohydrate for overweight horses or ponies, or those prone to laminitis.) Soaking hay overnight is not recommended. The water left after soaking hay should be disposed of with care because it is considered a contaminant.

Hay is better fed from the ground than from nets. Haynets reduce wastage and, if they have a small mesh, can slow the rate of intake for greedy horses, but they cause an unnatural eating posture and pose a risk of injury if a horse gets a foot caught.

In some countries, particularly the USA, hay cubes or wafers are available; these are chopped hay that has been compressed into small blocks. These are easier to store than bales, and are ideal to soak down for horses with poor chewing ability. Manufacturers in the UK do not seem to have followed the lead on such products.

Hay is better fed from the ground than from nets.

A growing crop of alfalfa.

Non-grass hays, primarily alfalfa (also called lucerne), are becoming more available in the UK. Alfalfa hay is made in a similar way to grass hay, but is more reliant on good weather conditions to dry out the large leaves of the plant. Greater care is necessary in the making of alfalfa hay, because the large leaves may shatter, reducing the nutritive value of the crop. This shattering can also occur when the leaves become brittle after drying, giving the appearance of the hay being quite dusty (although this is a 'cosmetic' dustiness as distinct from the dust/spores in grass hay). Alfalfa hay is quite different from grass hay from a nutritional perspective. It contains much higher protein and calcium levels, similar or higher fibre levels, but lower water-soluble carbohydrate levels. It is a useful feed for youngstock and pregnant mares but should not, ideally, be fed as the sole forage because it would overload most horses with protein. Although not damaging, protein excess is wasteful, and provides an extra heat burden for exercising horses.

Wholecrop cereal hay is not widely fed in the UK, but is popular elsewhere. Cereal hays are made from the whole crop in a green stage, and the nutritive value depends on how ripe the grains are; the more grain in the hay, the more nutritious it is. Oat hay, made from the whole oat plant, is a useful horse feed that is equivalent to grass hay cut mid-season.

Haylage

The difficulties in making hay of a good hygienic quality have prompted more and more producers to turn to making haylage. Haylage is grass or other plant material that is cut, wilted in the sun until a specific level of dry matter is reached, then baled and wrapped in several layers of plastic, or sealed in a plastic bag, excluding air. Producing good haylage requires a high level of expertise from the manufacturer. The naturally occurring bacteria on the grass ferment water-soluble carbohydrates in the forage, producing short-chain fatty acids, which preserve the grass as long as it remains air-free. The manufacturing process ensures a dust-free product with little or no mould spores, which makes a more suitable feed for stabled horses than hay. Haylage is an ideal feed for performance horses, because it is hygienically superior to hay, therefore supporting respiratory health, and because it is usually has a higher nutritive value than hay, meaning less compound feed will be necessary.

After a bale of haylage is opened, it will last several days before it goes off. Haylage is a similar product to silage, which was developed originally for feeding to ruminant animals. The process is the same, but haylage tends to be made from more mature grass, which is dried to a higher level of dry matter than silage. The result is a higher fibre feed, but with lower energy and protein content, that is more suitable for horses. Haylage for horses should have a dry matter of over 55%, protein of less than 12%, crude fibre of around 30% or more, and a pH of under 6. Ideally, haylage with a dry matter of 60% and fibre of 35–40% is best for horses because it can be fed in high quantities. Ponies and horses at maintenance can be

Large and (*below*) small bales of haylage.

fed haylage, but a relatively low-nutrient version should be chosen so that plenty can be fed. Early versions of haylage were over-nutritious for horses, and too low in fibre. The high energy and protein content meant that people fed too little in order to avoid weight gain and therefore their horses became fibre-deficient. Haylage should be fed in *greater quantities* than hay, because more of its weight is water; therefore less is fibre. The dry matter should be taken into account when planning the feed quantity, and if such a quantity would oversupply protein and energy, then either a less nutritious haylage should be sourced, or a less nutritious forage such as stalky hay or straw should be mixed in, provided that it was first soaked.

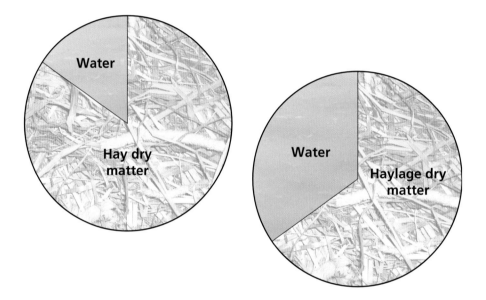

Figure 6.1 Water content of hay and haylage.

Haylage should never be made from hay that has been rained on and, after several days drying, is still too wet to bale. Such material is not suitable for baling for haylage, primarily because it will have lost much of its water-soluble carbohydrate content and therefore may not undergo sufficient fermentation. The safety of haylage for horses depends on a good fermentation. A variety of microbes are normally present on grass, and more may be added in the form of a 'fermentation additive' during the haylage-making process. In well-made haylage there is a large proliferation of bacteria that produce lactic acid by fermenting water-soluble carbohydrates and a good haylage contains a high proportion of lactic acid compared to butyric or acetic acid. However, some clostridia bacteria are present on grass (although most come from soil contamination in the cut grass). If these proliferate, they can cause botulism in the horse eating the haylage. Clostridia require a lot of moisture and will not proliferate in haylage with dry matter of over 50%. They also require a relatively high pH of 7–7.4, and pH of around 4 is required to inhibit their growth. Haylage for horses is rarely as acidic as this because of the restricted fermentation as compared to silage, but provided it is very dry and is not contaminated with soil, the risk of botulism is almost nil. Clostridia bacteria produce butyric acid, so haylages with high butyric acid contents, and specifically those with higher butyric than lactic acid contents, must be avoided.

Good fermentation also depends on the haylage being well packed with as little air as possible in the bale, so the wrapping should be tight around the grass, and the grass inside the bale well compacted. Some manufacturers make large (300–400 kg) bales of haylage, then after the fermentation process has taken place, repackage them into smaller, more easily handled bags, of around 20 kg. Haylage made in this way is perfectly safe for horses and is often of a more consistent quality as a result of better fermentation in the large bale than could be obtained in a small, individually produced 30 kg bale. However, the repackaging process should be carried out with care, with the large bales opened and exposed to the air for as short a time as possible.

Punctured bales of haylage should not be fed because they will have started to deteriorate as a result of the entry of air. Haylages are particularly susceptible to moulding after opening or when a bale is punctured and the resulting mould and the mycotoxins it produces may be dangerous to horses and the people handling the product. A white, creamy substance on the haylage will not harm the horse eating it – it is simply an overgrowth of yeast. If a wrapped bale (rather than a repackaged bagged bale) from one batch smells or looks significantly different from the others, it should not be fed because this could indicate poor fermentation. Bales that contain soil should not be fed because of the risk of contamination with unwanted bacteria, and such bales should be returned to the manufacturer to alert them to the soil problem.

Haylage can be a safe feed for laminitis-prone horses and ponies, but a high dry matter, high-fibre, low-protein haylage with low residual sugars should be selected. The horse must be monitored carefully for weight gain, and if the haylage has to be restricted to avoid weight gain, another forage such as straw should be offered to fulfil the horse's forage requirements.

With reference to the analysis sheet, look for the following in a good haylage for horses:

- High dry matter 55% plus (but no higher than 70%).

- Low pH under 5.5 but 6 is suitable if associated with high dry matter.

- Higher lactic acid than butyric or acetic acid; the lower the latter two and the higher the first, the better.

- Low ammonia; ideally less than 10g/kg total nitrogen.

- No soil contamination.

- High fibre of over 30%.

Straw

Barley straw.

Straw is the highly lignified stems and leaves of the cereal plant. Cereal straws are very high-fibre, low-energy feeds; a by-product of cereal production. Oat, barley and wheat straw are suitable feeds for horses, with oat straw the most palatable. Horses and ponies will eat less straw than hay when offered them separately ad lib; therefore straw is an ideal feed for obese animals, keeping them busy chewing without supplying them with many calories. Since straw is a poor source of minerals, the diet of horses and ponies fed straw as their main source of forage must be supplemented with a broad-spectrum vitamin and mineral supplement plus extra macrominerals.

Straw should always be introduced to the diet gradually because if it is offered ad lib suddenly, it may cause impactions in the gut. Horses and ponies fed straw must always have free access to clean, fresh water, and must have efficient dental function.

Chopped forage/chaffs

Forages such as grass, alfalfa, hay and straw can be chopped and in some cases mixed with other feed ingredients to produce chaff or chop. Chaff describes the husk, awns and other waste material left after threshing cereal from straw, and was ideal for horses in years gone by because it provided good levels of fibre. Nowadays the words chaff and chop are used for any chopped forages. These can be made from fresh grass or alfalfa that has been quick-dried or dehydrated, or sun-dried hay or straw. Chaffs were traditionally used to increase fibre intake, to 'bulk' out the diet. But, of course, horses can extract nutrients from even the driest, stalkiest straw, and chaffs can provide good nutrition.

Quick-dried forages are excellent medium-energy feeds, and can be used to replace part of the long forage (e.g. hay or haylage) or the concentrates (weight for weight) in a diet and are also used in combination chaff products and in compound feeds. Generally, they are made by cutting the grass or alfalfa crop, sometimes crushing it, then drying it quickly at very high temperatures. This process seals in the nutrients and the result is a nutritious feed of much higher quality than traditional forages. Nevertheless, they are so dry that they can shatter, causing dust to form and some companies add either molasses, vegetable oil, or a combination of both, to reduce the dust. The important factor to bear in mind when feeding these forages is that they tend to be very light (low density); therefore much bigger volumes need to be fed than of the compound feed they can replace. For example, one regular bowl scoop of medium-energy coarse mix (1.4 kg) would need to be replaced with about five scoops or a heaped regular bucket full of quick-dried grass to provide the same weight.

Gone are the days of choosing between one basic chaff and another. Nowadays, a whole range of chaffs are available, including the quick-dried forages just mentioned, molassed chaffs (that generally contain about 30% molasses on 70%

Quick-dried (dehydrated) grass.

Quick-dried alfalfa.

A low-calorie 'compound' chaff.

straw), hay replacer chaffs that generally contain either a mixture of alfalfa or grass and straw, with a little molasses and/or oil added, and compound feed-type chaffs that are designed to replace traditional coarse mixes or cubes. The last usually have a concentrate pellet containing good-quality protein, vitamins and minerals added, and are usually marketed as low-calorie feeds. Molassed chaffs are useful for tempting a horse to eat supplements because of the sweet, palatable taste of molasses – especially if the horse does not require much extra feed. However, there is little other use for heavily molassed chaffs, which should never be used to replace forage for a horse with limited chewing ability. The hay replacers or quick-dried forages should be used for these cases. These can be fed safely ad lib, and are sometimes marketed as 'lite' chaffs.

Chaffs are useful to add to the bucket feed for horses who eat too quickly (bolt their feed), and the low-energy hay replacers, or straight chopped hay or straw, are useful to give as a feed to good doers while other horses are being fed. The hay replacer chaffs, quick-dried forages or complete feed chaffs can also provide an alternative to unprocessed forage when it is not available or when it is contra-indicated, for example in a horse with severe recurrent airway obstruction (RAO, formally called COPD).

Forage analysis

Forages can vary widely in nutrient content, and having a sample analysed gives some useful information that will help in the choice of the remainder of the daily ration. Independent nutritionists can offer analysis with a full interpretation. Some feed manufacturers also offer forage analysis, or laboratories can help (see Useful Contacts). The analysis should be interpreted by an equine nutritionist, so if the laboratory does not offer this service, an independent nutritionist should be contacted.

Forage analysis can include the following:

- dry matter

- crude protein

- estimated energy (digestible energy (DE) for horses)

- crude fibre or NDF

- mould and dust

- mould identification

- minerals

- vitamins.

Forage	Crude fibre %	Crude protein %	Estimated energy MJ DE/kg
Mixed grass hay, early cut	30	8–11	9
Haylage, early cut ryegrass	30–35	9–12	9–11
Alfalfa hay	30	22.5	9.5
Straw	40	3.5	6.8
Pasture grass, young	13–17	16	11

Table 6.2 Typical analysis of forages.

Cereal grains

Cereal grains including oats, barley, wheat, and maize (corn) are traditional horse feeds that are good sources of energy. Many years ago these feeds were essential to support the intense levels of work that horses carried out, when the only forages available were relatively low-energy hay and chaff. Nowadays, a whole range of horse feeds is available, and it is possible to support intense exercise without the use of grain in the diet. Cereal grains are often called 'straights'.

Cereal grains are the storage vessel of plants, which support the growth of a new plant. They tend to be packed with starch – up to 73% in maize (see Table 6.3). They are not particularly good sources of protein because they are low in essential amino acids, particularly lysine. Oats have the highest lysine of the cereals. Cereal grains are all very low in calcium, with an unbalanced calcium to phosphorus ratio. This shortage must be balanced out, otherwise health problems will result.

	Crude fibre %	Starch %	Oil %	DE (MJ/kg)	Crude protein %	Lysine %
Oats (white)	10.5	47	4.9	13.4	10.9	0.45
Naked oats	4.5	59	10.0	14.4	13.5	0.6
Barley	5.3	56	1.7	15.4	10.8	0.38
Wheat	2.6	67.4	1.9	16.2	12.4	0.31
Maize	2.4	73	4.2	16.1	9.8	0.25

Table 6.3 Nutrient composition of cereals for horses.

A warning at this point about potential dangers associated with high levels of starch. The high starch content of grains means that they must be fed to horses with care. Overfeeding can lead to undigested starch flowing into the hindgut where it causes disturbance and damage to the microbial populations, which may result in colic, laminitis and diarrhoea, and depressed fibre digestion. (Refer back to Chapter 4 for more information.) Starch should be fed at a maximum rate of 2 g per kg of bodyweight per meal; which is 1 kg starch for a 500 kg horse. 1 kg of starch is found in 2 kg oats, 1.7 kg naked oats, 1.79 kg barley, 1.5 kg wheat or about 1.4 kg maize. In addition, all cereal grains apart from oats should be processed before feeding to increase the digestibility of starch, thus reducing the risk of undigested starch reaching the hindgut.

Cereal grains have a high glycaemic index (GI) compared to forages, and processing them will increase the GI even further. The glycaemic index is a reflection of the rate and total amount of blood glucose increase in response to a meal. Feeding large starchy meals with a high glycaemic index over time may eventually increase the risk of insulin resistance, particularly in sedentary horses and ponies. Insulin resistance has been linked to obesity, colic, laminitis and developmental orthopaedic disease (DOD). Cereal grains should not be fed to sedentary horses, overweight ponies, or horses prone to tying up (rhabdomyolysis) and should be fed in limited quantities to growing horses. In all cases, this is because of the starch content.

Oats

Oats are without doubt the most suitable cereal grain for horses, because they contain lower levels of starch and higher levels of fibre and lysine than other cereals. The starch in oats is more easily digested than other cereal starch, and more oats as opposed to other cereals would have to be fed before a horse would suffer from starch overload and/or laminitis. Oats also tend to be the most palatable cereal. Oats contain soluble fibre, which is known to have health benefits for humans, and may also have health benefits for horses. Oats do not need to be processed before feeding to horses with good dental function. However, the fibrous husk of oats is rather lignified, making it relatively indigestible, and if a horse has poor teeth and cannot chew efficiently, whole oat husks may be seen in the faeces (droppings). Some people assume that their horse has digestive problems if husks are seen in the faeces, but the husks are not digestible and their form does not alter after chewing.

A type of oat that loses its husk during harvesting is available. These oats, called 'naked oats' should be fed with care because they lose the relatively high-fibre and low-starch benefits of regular oats. However, they are high in oil and can provide good nutrition if fed in limited quantities. Naked oats should not replace regular oats directly (i.e. weight for weight) because this would provide a meal with much higher energy and starch, but lower fibre content (see Table 6.4 page 82).

Oats.

Nutrient	Naked oats 2 kg	Regular oats 2 kg
Energy MJ	28.8	26.8
Crude protein g	27	21.8
Crude fibre g	9	21
Starch g	118	94
Oil g	20	9.8

Table 6.4 Nutrient content of 2 kg naked oats compared to regular oats.

Barley

Barley, like oat grain, has a fibrous husk, but contains half the fibre of oats. The husk is more tightly attached than the oat husk, and the grain must be processed (by rolling, crushing or other means) before feeding to horses to allow access to the starch inside. Boiling barley increases the digestibility of the starch, therefore reducing the risk of hindgut disturbance, but will also increase the GI, so boiled barley should not ideally be fed to sedentary horses or those prone to laminitis. Barley has traditionally been used as a fattener for horses, which makes sense because it is higher in energy than oats.

A field of barley.

Wheat

Wheat grains do not have a husk and are rather small, so can easily escape chewing. Wheat should never be fed whole and unprocessed to horses, but both processed wheat and wheat by-products are widely used in compound feed.

Maize

Maize grains are large but very hard, and difficult for horses to chew unless they are cracked. Maize is the cereal grain highest in energy and starch. Processing with heat (steam -flaking, micronizing, extruding or popping) increases the digestibility of the starch, making it safer to feed, but it should be fed in limited quantities. Steam-flaked maize is often added to coarse mixes, even to low-energy varieties, simply to give them colour.

Other grains

Other less commonly fed grains include sorghum, millet and rice. All can be fed to horses but they are not widely available and have no advantages over the other cereal grains.

Cereal grain processing

As mentioned, all cereal grains except oats should be processed before feeding to horses, to increase the digestibility of the starch, thus slightly reducing the risk of starch overflow into the hindgut and the associated disturbance, colic and/ or laminitis. Grains can be ground, rolled, or cooked with steam-flaking, micro- nization (microwaving), extrusion (a high-pressure expansion process) or irradiation. Grinding causes a dusty powder, and can make grain unpalatable; in

A whole grain (maize) and three processed grains *top left* steamed flaked maize; *right* wheatbran; *bottom left* micronized barley.

addition it does not significantly increase digestibility. Simple rolling does give more access to the starch in barley, but is not enough to increase the digestibility of starch significantly. However, cooking grains with moisture and/or heat causes a disruption of the starch granules, making them more digestible.

Grain by-products

By-products of wheat and oat milling are popular feeds for horses, both straight and used in horse feed manufacture.

Oatfeed, wheatfeed and wheatbran

These terms describe the fibrous leftovers from flour manufacture. Oatfeed is a very high-fibre mix of oat husks and hairs that is most often used as an ingredient in low-energy cubes and coarse mixes. Oatfeed is often handled as pellets, rather than in its original form. Wheatfeed is a term used for different combinations or grades of the fibrous coating and germ of wheat. The term 'middling' comes from the stage of manufacture at which this product used to be extracted, and middlings tend to be higher in fibre and of a lower feed value than wheatfeed, but higher in feed value than wheatbran. Wheat middlings may also be called 'thirds' or 'shorts'. Wheatfeed is commonly used in compound horse feeds.

Wheatbran (also called bran) is a well-known horse feed, which contains a moderate fibre level (a little higher than oats), moderate to high starch, moderate protein level of poor quality and moderately high energy (a little higher than oats but less than barley). Bran, like all the cereal grains and grain by-products, is very low in calcium and high in phosphorus; therefore it must be added to the daily diet with care and balanced carefully. Bran is a relatively safe feed for horses but it should, like all horse feeds, be fed every day and not occasionally as is sometimes done. A bran mash fed once a week is unhealthy and should be avoided. Any new feed introduced suddenly causes disturbance to the gut microbial balance and this is probably why a bran mash acts as a laxative. Bran does hold many times its own weight in water, but soaked sugar beet pulp (particularly molassed, which holds water, is palatable and supplies soluble carbohydrate) is a much more suitable and healthy feed for a tired horse after a strenuous day's exercise.

Rice bran

Rice bran consists of the outer fibrous coating of rice (but not much of the husk) and is a useful horse feed that contains high levels of oil, and moderate levels of protein and energy. It is high in unsaturated fatty acids, and is sometimes available extracted – however, much of the oil is lost in this case, and the energy is therefore lower. Stabilized rice bran is also available, and is often used as a supplementary feed for weight gain.

Maize gluten feed

This by-product of the manufacture of glucose and starch from maize consists of the oil-extracted germ, gluten and bran. Used in the manufacture of horse feed, maize gluten feed is high in protein and energy for horses.

Other less widely used by-products of the brewing and distilling industry are available as horse feeds, but have little advantage over other more widely available feeds.

Nutrient balancing issues with grain

Commercial compounds are more expensive than grain. However, a straight grain or grain by-product and grass forage diet is unbalanced and will eventually cause health problems, because grain is a poor source of lysine, has a very unbalanced calcium to phosphorus ratio, supplies high starch levels and the total diet may not supply enough vitamins and minerals. Alfalfa, sugar beet and limestone flour (calcium carbonate) may help balance a grain and grass forage diet, but balancing grain and ensuring adequately low starch intakes can be challenging. Ideally, the grain should be analysed and advice taken from a nutritionist on how to ensure it is included in a balanced diet.

Protein-rich seeds and their by-products

Seeds of certain plants, including soya beans, sunflowers, rape, flax (yielding linseed), field beans and peas are, unlike the cereals, rich in good-quality protein. The first four mentioned are also rich in oil, and tend to be grown primarily for vegetable oil production. The meal or 'cake' that is left over is used as a rich source of good-quality protein in animal feed. Oil can be extracted from seeds in two ways: either by pressing (expelling) or solvent extraction. Some of these seeds, especially soya and linseed, are also useful feeds for horses when given entire, with their natural oil content, but they must be processed before feeding because they contain toxic 'antinutritional factors' (ANF). Like cereal grains, many oilseeds and their meals are high in phosphorus and low in calcium, hence they must be incorporated into the diet with care. They are, however, lower in starch than the cereals and therefore generally safer to feed.

Soya beans

These contain the best-quality protein, with all the essential amino acids, and good levels of lysine but rather poor levels of methionine. However, because, in their raw state, they contain toxic substances they must be heat-treated before being fed to horses. Their oil is usually solvent extracted, and the resulting by-product is called soya bean meal. Full fat soya, which consists of the whole processed bean, is usually available ground and is therefore higher in oil and energy but lower in protein per kilo than the meal. It is also much more expensive than the meal. Soya bean meal is a useful addition to the diet of young, growing horses who do not require large amounts of compound feed.

Soya hulls are the fibrous outer husk of the soya bean (not the pod) and are a useful highly digestible fibre source for horses. They are very high in fibre but low in lignin; making their fibre more digestible than that of forages such as hay. Soya hulls are used in compound horse feeds, especially the medium-energy, low-starch varieties marketed for endurance horses or for 'slow release' energy.

Sunflower seeds

Sunflower seeds have a thick, fibrous coating or husk (also called hull), which is generally removed either partly or entirely before processing, in a process called decortication. The meal is high in fibre and protein, and is very high in the amino acid methionine, although rather low in lysine. Sunflower meal is most often used in horse feed manufacture rather than as a straight fed by horse owners.

A field of sunflowers.

Linseeds

Linseeds (also called flaxseeds) are a well-known horse feed that can help to promote a shiny coat. This is because whole linseed is the best vegetable source of omega-3 fatty acids, which have beneficial effects on the skin and coat (and are also processed in the body into anti-inflammatory compounds). Note that, to obtain full benefit to the coat, the whole (processed seed) rather than just the oil-extracted meal should be fed. Linseeds also contain antinutritional factors (ANF) and can poison via hydrogen cyanide if fed unprocessed and wet. Traditionally, the seeds were boiled to remove the ANF, but nowadays heat-treated (micronized) seeds can be purchased; these are a useful feed for horses with chronic gut problems. In fact, linseed also contains high levels of mucilage, soluble fibre that is available to the gut microflora but cannot be digested by enzymes in the small intestine. This fibre absorbs large amounts of water and appears to have a beneficial effect on the gut lining.

Other seeds and their meals

Rapeseeds (commonly used in cattle feed) contain a variety of antinutritional factors (ANF) and some may still be present after the processing of meal. Recently developed varieties have much lower levels of ANF but do not tend to be widely used in horse feed.

Other oilseed meals include groundnut, cottonseed, palm kernel and coconut (copra) meal but these are not often used in horse feed in the UK. Groundnuts are commonly contaminated with the mould mycotoxin aflatoxin and should not be fed to horses. Coconut and palm kernel meals absorb large amounts of molasses and are sometimes used as bases for molasses to allow it to be mixed with compound feeds.

Peas and beans are protein-rich legume seeds with good levels of lysine, therefore good quality protein. However, both contain ANF, and should be heat-treated before being fed to horses. Steam-flaked peas are often included in coarse mixes to give them a colourful green flake. Both peas and beans are high in energy and contain high levels of starch and thus should be fed to horses in limited quantities.

Root vegetables

The root vegetables carrots, turnips, swedes, fodder beet and mangols are useful horse feeds that are often under-utilized. They are a useful source of a more natural moisture-containing feed during the winter months, when many horses are fed unnaturally dry diets of hay and grain or compound feed. Dried pieces have been used in compound feeds to tempt the owner, and are available as a supplement, although many owners prefer simply to add the fresh variety to the feed.

Root vegetables do contain a high level of water and therefore tend to be given in smaller quantities than are useful. For example, carrots are about 80% water, so for every 5 carrots fed, 4 represent the water content and only 1 represents pure 'carrot' (carrot dry matter). Following on from this although, on a dry matter basis, carrots are relatively high in sugar, on a fresh weight basis they are low in sugar.

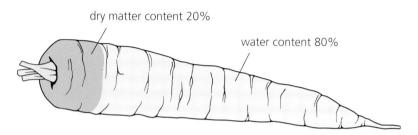

dry matter content 20%

water content 80%

Figure 6.2 Illustration of a carrot to show water and dry matter content.

Sugar beet

Sugar beet is a root vegetable that is an excellent medium-energy feed for horses. The pulp, a by-product of sugar production, is dried (sometimes mixed with molasses), and is usually soaked before being fed. The reason for soaking before feeding relates to its ability to absorb large quantities of water, and therefore possibly cause choke and/or distended stomach and colic. Shreds are usually soaked for 12 hours, and pellets/cubes for 24 hours. Versions that can be soaked more quickly are available nowadays, consisting of micronized flakes of beet that soak down in 10 minutes. All soaked sugar beet should be fed within 24 hours, particularly in the summer when the heat can cause it to ferment and go off. The practice of soaking several days worth and scooping out a little every day is definitely not good practice.

Some compound feeds contain sugar beet, but in small enough quantities that they do not have to be soaked prior to feeding.

Sugar beet pulp contains high levels of soluble fibre, including pectins, which are highly fermentable, thus it is termed 'highly digestible fibre'. Even the unmolassed varieties contain some sugar and therefore produce a relatively high glycaemic response. Sugar beet can successfully replace cereal grains in the diet and it is a more balanced, much higher-fibre, healthier alternative. It has a calcium to phosphorus ratio of about 6:1 and can help to balance the incorrect calcium to phosphorus ratio of cereals and seeds. Molassed sugar beet is useful for working horses and those with fussy appetites, and the unmolassed version is useful for weight gain in sedentary horses and for general use.

Whole sugar beets.

Sugar beet in three forms: *left* soaked; *top right* pellets; *bottom right* micronized flakes.

Other straight feeds

Straight feeds used to a lesser extent for horses in the UK include locust beans, bakery waste, citrus and olive pulp. Locust beans are used in coarse mixes to give a sweet taste, but are not particularly nutritious.

Compound feeds

Compound feeds, traditionally known as concentrate, short or hard feed, are made from a variety of ingredients, and formulated to supply nutrients missing from the forage portion of the diet. Nowadays defining compound feed is less easy because some packaged compounds are not concentrates. There is a wide crossover in forages and 'bucket' feeds, and defining different manufactured feeds is difficult. Because compounds were traditionally fed to balance forage, they usually contained high levels of good-quality protein and energy from non-structural carbohydrates, as well as vitamins and minerals. They were called concentrates because of their high energy density. Note that compounds are not complete feeds, and even some manufacturers make this mistake. A complete feed can replace both regular compounds and forage and must have a crude fibre content of at least about 18%, and ideally a protein level of no more than 8–9% for mature horses.

Three types of compound feed (*top left*) low-energy coarse mix; (*top right*) medium-energy veteran coarse mix; (*bottom*) low-energy 'cubes'.

The first compound feeds for horses were cubes, also called nuts, developed by Spillers Horse Feeds in 1948. Such cubes contain a variety of processed grain,

grain by-products, protein-rich seeds and their by-products, vitamins and minerals, forages, molasses and/or vegetable oil. Following cubes came coarse mixes, which are very appealing to owners, but less useful to sedentary mature horses. Originally, coarse mixes generally contained pellets of good-quality protein and micronutrients, fibre-based cubes and processed grain, peas and beans, all blended with molasses to bind dust. Many were marketed for horses in no or light work, despite the fact that they contained grain; most horses in no or light work do not need grain, peas or beans in their diets. Cubes are usually a better choice for horses because they are formulated just for their nutritional value, rather than for what they look like to the horse owner, and they tend to be higher in fibre and lower in starch. There is no need to worry about what cubed feeds contain because there are strict rules about the ingredients allowed for use in horse feeds, and floor sweepings are not one of them. For those concerned about the ingredients in compound feeds, there are plenty of alternatives (see Chapter 12). Horses do not need compound feeds, and many can be fed home-formulated rations successfully. Nevertheless, compounds do make life much easier and take away the worry of supplying all the necessary nutrients to your horse.

Meeting micronutrient requirements

The vitamin and mineral content of compound feeds is a misunderstood area. Compounds usually contain a broad spectrum of these micronutrients, but they are included at a set rate, and this is reflected in the recommended amount on the feed bag. However, these products are all formulated to balance an average forage diet in an average horse. Since many horses will require less than the recommended amount of a compound to maintain weight and condition, they will not receive the full complement of vitamins and minerals that feed is designed to supply. The answer is not to increase the amount fed – this would cause weight gain – but to look elsewhere for the extra vitamins and minerals. In this case, add a broad-spectrum vitamin and mineral supplement – one formulated by the same company that makes the feed is ideal because it should be compatible.

Different types of compound

A compound feed to suit every different type of horse that could be imagined is available. Despite the fact that just one or two compounds are probably all that is needed for most horses, manufacturers have taken advantage of horse owners' urge to buy the best for their horse and feeds are marketed cleverly with a description of the horse's lifestage, problem, or even a perceived problem.

Probably the most useful compound feeds available are any low-energy, low-starch, high-fibre cubed feeds. These can be fed in low quantities to horses in no or light work to fulfil the need of the owner to feed something from a sack, or fed in relatively high quantities to working horses or those in need of weight gain. With a fibre level of 18% or over, and the correct balance of protein and micronutrients, these can be fed as complete diets. These low-energy fibrous cubes are the safest 'concentrate' feed for horses.

Low-energy coarse mixes, if they contain any cereals, are made for the owner rather than the horse. Unless fed very poor forage, horses in no or light work do not need cereals in their diets. Many of these mixes are described as 'non-heating', which means they will not cause excess excitability when fed as recommended. However, there is no guarantee of this because any cereals may 'fizz' a horse, so a low-energy coarse mix containing barley but no oats would not be a suitable feed for a horse who tended to get excitable.

If more energy is required, other very useful compound feeds contain high levels of digestible fibre and oil, and low starch levels. These are the most versatile compounds because they can be fed in relatively large amounts as conditioning feeds or for hard-working horses, while not overloading the horse with starch. Many are marketed for endurance horses or those who tie up (suffer from azoturia, correctly called rhabdomyolysis), but they have much wider uses than that. These feeds are usually based on soya hulls and sugar beet pulp, both sources of highly digestible fibre.

Low-calorie compounds for good doers or for weight loss are contradictions in terms. The whole point of a compound feed is to make up for nutrient shortfalls in forage; therefore if a horse maintains condition on forage alone, there is no need to add a compound; a broad-spectrum or bespoke vitamin and mineral supplement or balancer should be fed instead. Low-calorie compounds have been developed to fulfil the need of the horse owner to feed something in a bucket and much money is made by manufacturers on these feeds. Such compounds tend to be based on chopped forage with micronutrient pellets, some grains (for visual appeal) and other ingredients such as herbs added. These compounds are most useful for horses who don't require extra feed, but are fed in a group with other horses (either stabled or at pasture) – although sliced carrots or several handfuls of (cheaper) chaff would be just as suitable.

Most manufacturers offer a veteran feed for older horses. However, not all old horses require the high nutrient levels in most veteran feeds (see Chapter 11). Clever companies name their veteran feeds with a particular age, so that horse owners are convinced their horse must swap to such a feed as soon as reaches he that age, regardless of his condition or nutritional needs. Recently, a forward-thinking feed company has launched two types of veteran feeds; a conditioning type and a maintenance type. This choice is sensible, because although many old horses may not require the high energy and protein of a regular conditioning veteran feed, they will still need enhanced micronutrients levels, not found in regular low-energy compounds.

Performance horses, breeding stock and growing youngstock all have significantly increased nutrient requirements compared to sedentary adult horses or those in light work. Compound feeds are useful for these classes of horse although, again, care should be taken to choose the best type. Ideally, the overall type of feed should be considered, rather than just the name on the label. Some manufacturers convince horse owners that their hard-working horse must need a competition feed, but some horses will work hard on a low-energy cubed feed with plenty of good quality preserved forage and/or grass. Each horse should be considered individually and the compound chosen appropriately.

Concentrated compounds have become popular in recent years. These feeds are often called 'balancers' and consist of a concentrated version of a regular compound, which is fed in much smaller quantities of around 500 g per day to a 500 kg horse (in contrast to 2–4 kg of a regular compound). Balancers appear to have high nutrient levels, including protein, but only because these nutrients are expressed on a percentage, or gram/milligram per kilo basis. However, the nutrients per daily rate (e.g. 500 g) is what matters. For example:

Balancer: 26% protein and 11 MJ DE/kg   Medium energy cubes: 11% protein and 10 MJ DE

Feed 500 g = 130 g protein and 5.5 MJ DE   Feed 3 kg = 330 g protein and 30 MJ DE

These balancers can be fed just with forage, in which case they act as a broad-spectrum micronutrient supplement with extra good-quality protein. Because of their relatively low starch level, they can usually be added safely to a forage and compound feed diet to 'top up' nutrients and add some extra calories. They will never add a substantial amount of calories (energy) because less than 1 kilo is usually fed. However, this should still be done with care, to ensure that micronutrients are not overloaded.

Specific cereal balancers are also available, and these are an ideal way to ensure a cereal-based diet is balanced. One manufacturer has developed a ready-mixed oat and oat-balancer compound, using old-fashioned varieties of oats. The result is an ideal, balanced way to feed oats.

Ingredients of compound feeds

Compound feeds are manufactured using a wide range of the feed ingredients listed throughout this chapter. Good-quality protein is provided from oilseeds or oilseed meals, peas and/or beans. Soya bean meal and sunflower meal are commonly used, and linseed meal is used also. Some feeds contain whole processed beans or seeds (such as soya beans and linseed) and these provide high levels of oil as well as the protein. Peas and beans must be cooked (steam-flaked or micronized) before adding, to get rid of undesirable substances. Flaked peas are

Forages ('long')

Alfalfa hay	Good source of fibre, protein and calcium.
Grass hay (including single species, e.g. timothy, ryegrass or mixed, e.g. meadow)	Good source of fibre and the most versatile feed. Can vary in nutrient content, especially in protein and energy.
Haylage, including single grass species or mixed, as hay	Can vary widely in nutrient content. Best type for horses is high dry matter (>65%) and high fibre.
Cereal hay	Fibre-rich and equivalent to hay, but can vary in nutrient content.
Cereal straw	Fibre-rich and relatively low-energy; ideal for weight loss while fulfilling appetite (but ensure good dentition).
Silage	Often too low in dry matter and too high in protein and energy for most horses.

Forages (processed)

Dehyrated alfalfa chop (may have molasses added to bind dust from shattered leaves)	Good source of fibre, protein and calcium and more nutritious than alfalfa hay. Ideal to increase forage quality if only grass hay is available. Can be used to replace concentrate (on a weight, not volume basis).
Dehydrated grass chop	Good source of fibre, protein and much more nutritious than grass hay. Can be used as a partial hay replacer or a concentrate feed replacer (on a weight not volume basis).
Pelleted alfalfa or grass	As above; dehydrated forage is chopped and pelleted; ideal to soak for old horses with poor dentition.
Nutritionally improved straw pellets	Used as high-fibre compound feed ingredient; useful for obese animals.
Blends of chopped straw and dehydrated forages (grass or alfalfa)	Designed as hay replacers and useful for horses with RAO (but expensive). Commonly fed with compound feed; helps greedy horses by slowing intake rate of cubes.
Molassed straw chops	Often about 40% molasses; can be useful to mask supplements, but little other use.
Chopped hay or straw	Useful chaff product if dust extracted; may be a little unpalatable.

Straights

Cereal grains, e.g. wheat, barley, maize (corn), oats, and naked (hull-less) oats	Rich in starch and phosphorus (P) and low in calcium (Ca) (unbalanced Ca:P ratio) and lysine. Traditionally used to increase energy intake of working horses; more suitable alternatives are available nowadays. Oats are the safest; maize the highest energy. Maize is often added to compound feeds for colour. All have high GI; oats the highest.
Cereal grain by-products, e.g. wheatfeed, wheatbran, rice bran, oatfeed	More useful than whole grains because of higher fibre and lower starch levels, but still unbalanced Ca:P ratio. Common ingredients in compound feeds. Rice bran is a useful source of oil and energy.

Straights (cont.)

Oilseed by-products, e.g. soya bean meal, sunflower meal, linseed meal	Useful providers of good-quality protein (soya is the best); common ingredients in compound feeds.
Whole oilseeds, e.g. soya beans, linseeds	Available cooked, therefore ready to feed. Excellent sources of good-quality protein and energy. Linseed is also rich in alpha linolenic acid (essential omega-3 fatty acid).
Legume seeds, e.g. peas and beans	Traditionally used to provide protein; more suitable alternatives are now available (e.g. soya). Peas often used in compounds for colour.
Soya hulls	Source of high digestible fibre and ideal ingredient to supply energy without starch.

Compound feeds (fortified with micronutrients)

Cubes (nuts/pellets)	Generally more suitable formulation since no need to look good to horse owner. Huge range available; most useful are high-fibre, low-starch varieties available from low to medium energy.
Coarse mixes (sweetfeeds); may contain chopped forage, herbs and dried vegetables in addition to pellets and processed cereals	Formulated to be pleasing to look at, so often contain unnecessary ingredients such as flaked peas, maize and dried carrots. Most relatively high in starch and not necessary for most horses.
Chaff blends (processed forages with micronutrient pellets added)	Often sold as low-calorie feeds; some are complete feed, i.e. can be fed as sole diet with no added forage. Often very expensive.
Balancer-type products	Concentrated pelleted compound normally fed in small quantities (<600 g per day). Useful to supply micronutrients and good-quality protein without too much energy or starch.

Roots, succulents and others

Sugar beet (molassed and unmolassed)	Useful feed high in digestible fibre and balanced mineral profile. Underused because of feeding by volume after soaking, rather than weighing before soaking. Quick-soak (10 minutes) micronized versions are available.
Vegetables, e.g. turnips, carrots, mangols, fodder beet	Useful additions to a winter ration of dry feed (i.e. hay and concentrates). May help boost the appetite.
Fruit, e.g. apples and pears	As for vegetables.
Molasses	About 60% sucrose and highly palatable so useful to mask supplements. Contrary to popular belief, horses digest sugar well; however a high GI, so excess intake associated with higher risk of health problems.

Table 6.5 Notes on horse feeds available in the UK.

usually added to coarse mixes for their green colour rather than their nutritional value. Milk or whey powder is sometimes added to provide protein, which is of good quality: adult horses can digest lactose, the carbohydrate found in milk.

Energy was traditionally provided by cereal grains, as well as the oilseeds. Barley, wheat and maize should always be cooked, and oats can be fed whole provided the horse has good teeth. Oats should be processed in a veteran feed. Maize is the highest-energy cereal and, because of its very high starch and energy content, is of little use in most compounds. It is usually added to coarse mixes in small quantities for its yellow colour. Nowadays, highly digestible fibre from sources such as soya hulls, sugar beet and wheatfeed and vegetable oils are also used. For lower-energy compounds, less digestible fibre sources including oat husks and hairs (oatfeed), processed straw and grass pellets are used.

Cubed feeds tend to be higher in fibre and lower in starch than mixes, simply because they do not need to contain cereals to give the 'muesli' look of a coarse mix. However, some cubes may contain high levels of barley and are therefore relatively high in starch. Individual feed labels should be read for ingredients and for both starch and fibre levels.

In coarse mixes, vitamins and minerals are often added to a concentrate pellet that also contains good-quality protein. Some vitamins are coated in animal fat or gelatin during their manufacture, so care should be taken if a wholly vegetarian diet is preferred. Macrominerals including sodium, calcium, phosphorus and magnesium may also be mixed into the feed. Minerals are also available as compounds, for example magnesium oxide, also called calcined magnesite (50% magnesium), sodium chloride (39% sodium) and calcium carbonate (40% calcium). Despite the fact that some are not absorbed efficiently, quarried macrominerals are natural sources of essential nutrients, and are generally safe to feed. Many minerals are also available in soluble forms, but these supply less of the mineral per gram of compound. The macromineral potassium is often left out of compound feeds because forages are rich in potassium and most equine diets already supply excess even before a compound feed is added.

Other compound ingredients include a whole range of substances, many of which are available as separate supplements. Herbs are often included for their aromatic properties, which may help feed intake (and certainly appeals to the horse owner), but they are not usually added at therapeutic levels. Garlic and mint are probably the most commonly used. Aromatic herbs including mint, oregano and rosemary may be included for their volatile oil content, which give a good, long-lasting aroma. Other ingredients may include probiotics, cod liver oil and nutraceuticals (see page 104) such as glucosamine.

Compounds are usually mixed with a liquid to bind dust and help with pelleting; traditionally molasses was used, which also improved palatability. Molassed coarse mixes tend to be rather dark and sticky and are going out of favour. Nowadays, molasses and vegetable oil mixtures and clear, sweet cereal syrups are often used. Additives to help preserve the feed (e.g. mould inhibitors and antioxidants) may also be included, although only authorized additives are permitted and these must be declared on the statutory statement label.

Traditionally, compound feeds were concentrates, designed to add extra energy and protein to a forage diet. Nowadays, a huge variety of compounds are available, and specific characteristics are sometimes used to describe them. The following is a guide:

- High oil: 5% +

- High fibre: 10% +

- High protein: 12% +

- Low starch: > 10%

- Low energy: > 9 MJ DE/kg.

Supplements

Supplement is a term generally used to mean a feed that is given as an addition to the basic daily ration, in relatively small quantities of grams rather than kilograms. The legal term for a supplement is a 'complementary feeding stuff', which needs to be fed with other feeds to form the entire daily ration. (Compound feeds are also classified as complementary feeding stuffs as most compounds are meant to be fed with forage, not as a complete feed.)

Hundreds, if not thousands, of different supplements are available for horses, and the choice on shop shelves can be overwhelming. Although rules and regulations about packaging and marketing claims exist, many manufacturers are skilled at bending these, and horse owners can be left feeling guilty that they may not be doing the best for their horse if they are not feeding the latest supplement. However, not all horses need supplements all the time and many are not 'missing out' without them. Supplements should be given only when necessary, and the explanations in this section will help readers decide what supplements are useful, and when.

If something sounds too good to be true, then it probably is. Horse feed and supplement manufacturers generally do not have large research budgets like pharmaceutical companies, simply because they do not turn over such large sums of money. Therefore supplements are often formulated on *theories* of nutritional need or nutraceutical functions, rather than proven evidence. Some supplements are very expensive and there may be alternative ways of supplying the same nutrients. This is not to say that all supplements are a waste of money, because many are absolutely essential for a balanced diet in some horses, and many non-nutrient products (e.g. herbal and neutraceutical – see later this chapter) are very effective. Also, it is a myth that supplements containing 'base' material on which the relevant nutrients are mixed are of poor quality or somehow less useful than 'pure' ingredients. A base may be included to make the supplement more palatable, or to round the daily amount up to a whole scoopful, or to dilute out an ingredient that may cause harm if overfed in error.

A selection of supplements in a shop.

Labelling and nutrient declarations

As explained earlier, supplements are classified as complementary feeding stuffs and the rules about their labels are the same as for horse feed. When considering a supplement, the ingredients should be scrutinized, and the manufacturer contacted if inadequate information appears on the tub or literature.

One area in which confusion can occur is with the analytical declarations on supplements (the protein, oil, fibre and ash amounts). These constituents are given as percentages so, in order to make useful sense of them, the actual grams of each should be calculated from the daily amount that is fed. For example, if a supplement is 20% protein and is fed at a rate of 50 g per day, the actual amount of protein the horse receives daily is 10 g. Compare this to a 10% protein feed of which 2 kg is given per day – a total supply of 200 g per day.

Confusion can also occur when comparing supplements from different suppliers, because some declare nutrients per kilo of product, and some per daily amount or scoop full. The actual daily amount given to the individual horse must be calculated for each product in order to make a fair comparison.

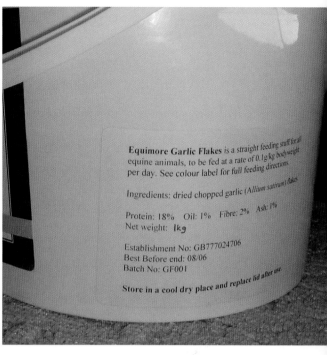

Equimore Garlic Flakes is a straight feeding stuff for all equine animals, to be fed at a rate of 0.1g/kg bodyweight per day. See colour label for full feeding directions.

Ingredients: dried chopped garlic (*Allium sativum*) flakes

Protein: 18%   Oil: 1%   Fibre: 2%   Ash: 1%
Net weight: 1kg

Establishment No: GB777024706
Best Before end: 08/06
Batch No: GF001

Store in a cool dry place and replace lid after use

Statutory statement on a tub.

Vitamin and mineral supplements (broad spectrum)

Broad-spectrum vitamin and mineral supplements are the most useful type because, even with the micronutrient-fortified compound feeds that are available, many horses do not receive all the micronutrients they require. These products contain balanced proportions of all the micronutrients (see Chapter 4), with the exception of salt; therefore they are generally safe to add to most diets. Since many nutrients interact with others, adding single nutrients where they are not actually needed can be unhealthy and in some cases could cause a deficiency of another nutrient. If the full nutrient profile of the forage is not known, broad-spectrum supplements can be added to balance the diet, which is likely to be short of a micronutrient or two. Horses fed forage who do not require compound feed are likely to be deficient in salt and some micronutrients (see Chapter 8) and they will eventually suffer from deficiencies if not supplemented.

Since micronutrients are added to compounds to balance those that may be missing from forage, if the full recommended amount of compound feed is given along with forage, in theory the horse's entire nutritional requirements will be met. However, if the compound feed given is formulated for a different class of horse then it is wise to add a broad-spectrum vitamin and mineral supplement. Examples of this might be a horse over 25 years old, or a hard-working horse, who actually hold their condition on forage and the full recommended amount of a low-energy compound feed. (It would, of course, be even better to give a feed formulated specifically for that class of horse.) Furthermore, if less than the full recommended amount of compound feed is given with forage, the horse's micronutrient requirements may not be met, and again, a broad-spectrum vitamin and mineral supplement should be fed. The feed sack label should be investigated to find the recommended amount, which may differ between brands. Compound feeds are formulated in such a way that nutrients are included in a set amount of feed. For example, if Brand X coarse mix is recommended to be fed at 4 kg per day to a 500 kg horse, and a horse requires only 2 kg along with forage to maintain his condition, then he will be receiving only half of the micronutrients he requires. In this case a broad-spectrum supplement will top up the levels of micronutrients and thus avoid deficiencies.

Of course, compound feeds can only be formulated to fit with average forage, and an absolutely ideal concentrate feed or supplement could only be formulated from information gained from forage analysis. Specific broad-spectrum supplements exist, and these can be very useful. For example, there are products designed to be fed to horses at pasture, to older horses, to hard-working performance horses, and products to be fed with specific forages such as haylage.

Feed blocks of hardened molassed mineral and/or vitamin mixtures are often given to horses at pasture. These products are designed to be licked, but because horses do not have a sense of balanced intake, under- or over-supplementation is easy. Therefore, the intake of such blocks must be monitored carefully.

Even broad-spectrum supplements may be short of sodium and other macrominerals. In fact most horse feeds, including compound feeds, are short of salt (sodium chloride). Salt can be antagonistic to other nutrients in a feed or supplement, and the individual horse's requirements depend on exercise levels, and thus may vary dramatically from day to day. Therefore, salt is best added to the diet separately.

The macromineral content of broad-spectrum supplements is variable, because these nutrients are needed in quantities of grams per day, and the chemical compounds that supply them are often only 50% or less of the actual mineral; therefore it may be difficult to fit enough macrominerals into a small scoop or two of supplement. In addition, with the exception of sodium (salt) as mentioned, macromineral levels in many forages are adequate for most horses.

Some forages may be short of calcium or magnesium, but these will generally not contain adequate energy or protein to maintain condition when fed alone, so horses on such forages would normally be receiving other feed.

Salt and electrolyte supplements

All horses require extra salt (sodium chloride) in their diets because, as explained earlier, most horse feeds including forages do not supply enough sodium.

Chapter 8 describes suitable amounts to add. Any salt is suitable and it can be bought from the supermarket. Salt licks are available, but are often not ideal because there is no control over how much is eaten. As is the case with mineral blocks, not all horses will help themselves to the correct amount of salt from a lick – some will overdose themselves and some will not take in sufficient. Salt licks are safe to use if the horse's intake is monitored, although working horses (who do not overdose themselves from licks) should have extra salt added to their feed even if they are being offered the lick. It would constitute over-eating a salt lick if a 2 kg salt lick lasted less than 2 weeks for a horse in hard work, or a month for a horse in light work.

In addition to needing extra common salt (see Chapters 8 and 10), working horses may also need electrolyte mixtures. Electrolytes are salts that occur in the body in an ionized form, which means they have an electrical charge. These electrolytes control fluid balance within and around all body cells. Macronutrients that act as electrolytes also have other roles in the body (see Chapter 4). The most important electrolytes are sodium, chloride and potassium; less important are calcium and magnesium. Electrolyte supplements have two uses:

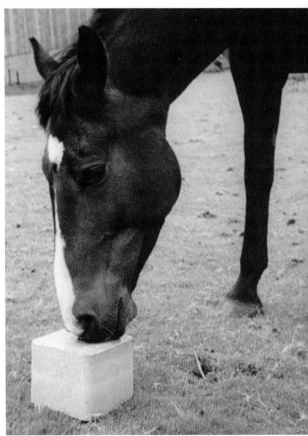

Horse licking a salt block.

1. To assist water uptake in a dehydrated horse, when they are mixed with water to make an isotonic 'oral rehydration solution' (ORS). Isotonic means at a similar concentration to body fluids.

2. To replace electrolyte minerals lost in sweat or during diarrhoea, when they are added to the feed or given via a syringe.

It is not possible to replace the large amounts of electrolytes lost from substantial sweating in an isotonic solution and therefore they must be added to the feed. A product that makes it clear how to use electrolytes should be chosen. A cheaper alternative to a commercial electrolyte, which can be used for an isotonic solution or added to feed, is a 50:50 mixture of salt (sodium chloride) and lite salt (a blend of sodium chloride and potassium chloride). Magneisum and calcium are not strictly necessary in an electrolyte product because the amounts of magnesium and calcium lost in sweat and relatively small and will be replaced in a well-balanced diet before losses lead to problems. More information about electrolytes, and how and when to supplement them, is given in Chapter 10.

Specific nutrient supplements

A number of specific nutrients are available for supplementation, some singly and some as combinations. Probably the most widely used and most useful combination is vitamin E and selenium. These two nutrients can be added to most diets safely, in appropriate amounts, without causing imbalances in other nutrients. Vitamin E and selenium are powerful antioxidant nutrients (see Chapter 4) and many horse feeds do not supply enough to working or recuperating horses. Single minerals such as magnesium and iron should be added to the diet with care, and ideally a nutritionist consulted to assess the entire diet, since excesses of single minerals can cause deficiencies of others. As discussed in Chapter 4, iron deficiency in the horse is rare, and iron toxicity is more likely. Anaemia (reduced red blood cell count) is usually caused by infection or inflammation, which should be diagnosed and treated by the vet. Treating most cases of anaemia with iron supplements is ineffective, and could imbalance the diet. In excess, iron can cause liver damage.

Supplements for specific problems

A huge variety of supplements targeted for specific problems are available, including those for calming, for good quality hooves, for a shiny coat, for hormone problems, and any other problem a horse owner has ever mentioned. These supplements usually contain specific nutrients and herbs, or a blend of both and/or any other feed material or additive that is available. Such specific supplements should be added to the diet with care and only after the basic diet has been balanced. The market for such supplements is lucrative, because horse owners are keen to solve their horses' problems and will pay relatively large sums of money if they believe a supplement will cure a problem. Some of these supplements will be unnecessary after the horse's basic diet is balanced and management problems sorted out. For example, a horse with RAO (previously called COPD) may no longer have symptoms if kept outdoors permanently with adequate shelter and rugs, fed haylage and no hay, and given a well-balanced diet rich in antioxidants.

Nevertheless, some of these supplements do appear useful, but because of limited scientific evidence to support their use, there is little an owner can do to be sure of results apart from trial and error. Learning more about nutrients, herbs and other ingredients, then studying the product information and calling the manufacturer's helpline for more information of the specific ingredients of a product is wise.

It would take a rather large book to describe and assess all the available supplements, so a short description of various types of 'problem-solving' supplements is given in Table 6.6. Note that these are simply examples, and some products may contain ingredients other than those mentioned.

Type/function of supplement	Typical ingredients	Notes
Calmatives	Tryptophan; B-complex vitamins; herbs; magnesium	Plenty of anecdotal, but no scientific evidence exists; there is no evidence that tryptophan calms horses. The herb valerian is on the list of prohibited substances for competition. Perhaps their use has an effect on the owner or rider's attitude to their horse, which in turn will affect the horse's behaviour. Less intensive management, good training and handling are more important than supplementation.
Hoof problems	Biotin, methionine; calcium, zinc, copper; essential fatty acids	There is some evidence that biotin helps some horse, and at least 15–20 mg daily should be fed long term. Foot balance is more important than nutrients.
Skin problems	Essential fatty acids (EFAs); herbs; zinc	Little proven evidence in horses, except for the use of linseed (rich in EFAs) for horses with skin conditions. The theory is strong and there is evidence of efficacy in other species. Ensuring a barrier to midges and flies is more important than supplementation for horses suffering from sweet itch.
Respiratory problems	Antioxidants, inc. vitamin C; herbs	Plenty of anecdotal evidence, and some scientific evidence of antioxidants to boost lung function in horses with RAO. Management and ensuring a dust and mould spore-free environment is much more important than supplementation for horses with allergic airway disease.
Hormone problems	Herbs inc. *vitex agnus castus*	Little evidence of efficacy in horses.
Blood boosting	Minerals inc. iron, copper; B-complex vitamins	Some contain iron levels that are too high, and broad-spectrum supplements are more useful. Diagnosis of the problem is imperative for under-performing horses or those with anaemia.
Laminitis	Various vitamins; minerals inc. magnesium; herbs antioxidants	No supplement can prevent or cure laminitis, but a broad-spectrum supplement with extra antioxidants will aid healing and recovery. Management is the best preventative measure.
Immune system function	Glutamine; antioxidants; herbs inc. *echinacea*; yeast	Little evidence for the use of these in horses, but the theory is strong and there is evidence of their usefulness in other species. Diagnosis and veterinary treatment of underlying problem is more important than supplementation in most cases.
Joint problems	Glucosamine, chondroitin; zinc, manganese; essential fatty acids; MSM; hyaluronic acid (HA), amino acids inc. glutamine; cod liver oil; cider apple vinegar	No strong evidence of efficacy in horses, but plenty of good scientific evidence in other species. No evidence for HA given orally. Plenty of anecdotal evidence exists. Many ingredients are sourced from mammals, fish or shellfish.

Table 6.6 'Problem-solving' supplements and what they are likely to contain.

Note that, by their very nature, these supplements contravene competition rules, because they are being fed for a physiological effect on the body, rather than to balance the diet. However, most of their ingredients are unlikely to be tested for at present, therefore many competitors continue to use them. In the future, competition authorities may begin to test for the metabolites of specific ingredients in the horse's body.

Nutraceuticals

Some of the supplements or their ingredients may be described as 'nutraceuticals', a term which combines 'nutrient' and 'pharmaceutical'. They are sold as complementary feedingstuffs, but are not nutrients. Instead they are intended to have a disease treatment or preventative effect or some other physiological effect on the body. A wide range is available, including:

- Proposed performance enhancers: creatine, carnitine, dimethylglycine, coenzyme Q10 and HMB; none of which are yet proven to be useful in horses.

- Joint supplements including glucosamine, chondroitin, methyl sulphonyl methane (MSM), for all of which there is plenty of anecdotal evidence, but little scientific evidence.

- Antacids, which are sold for horses prone to gastic ulceration, and for those who crib-bite.

In most cases, evidence for the use of nutraceuticals in horses is anecdotal, despite the claims made by manufacturers. Probably the most effective is glucosamine, for horses with joint disease. There is no evidence available to support the use of hyaluronic acid or hyaluronate as an oral supplement for joint problems, despite its success when used intra-articularly (injected into the joint). Some research has shown antacids to be effective in reducing cribbing in affected horses.

Despite the fact that nutraceuticals are sold as feeds, clearly their use is not nutritional. In the future many may become unavailable if EU law is enforced in the UK.

Plant antioxidants

In addition to certain nutrients that act as antioxidants in the body (see vitamin E in Chapter 4), certain plant components also have antioxidant actions. Bioflavonoids are colourful plant constituents that have a variety of healthy effects on the body, including potentiating the effect of vitamin C, and beneficial effects on blood vessels. Further research is necessary to prove their effectiveness in horses and they should not be considered a cure-all. Nevertheless, introducing colourful vegetable matter or supplements to stabled horses with no access to grass could be beneficial.

Probiotics and prebiotics

'Probiotic' means 'for life' and was formerly a term used for any substance that boosted the health of the microbes in the digestive tract (gut). Nowadays, probiotic is used to describe live microbes that either colonize the gut or boost the health of microbes already there, and the term 'prebiotic' is used to describe inactive substances, such as soluble fibre, that boost the health of gut microbes. Probiotics were developed originally to enhance the growth of farm animals by boosting the health of their digestive tracts, which in turn enhances weight gain and immune function. Both live bacteria, which colonize the gut, and live yeast, which do not, are classed as probiotics. Both must be able to withstand the acidic conditions of the stomach to have their beneficial effects, which are believed to occur in the small intestine (bacteria) and the hindgut (yeast).

Research has proved the usefulness of yeast for horses and much anecdotal evidence exists for live bacterial and prebiotic products for horses with various problems.

Live yeast products work by helping to remove excess sugar and starch from the hindgut, and causing lower levels of lactic acid, thereby helping to maintain a more healthy pH (acid-base balance). They also remove oxygen, helping to maintain the normal oxygen-free (anaerobic) environment within the gut, and boost the numbers of the fibre-digesting bacteria. Dead yeast cell walls also act as prebiotics, stimulating beneficial microbes and helping to excrete pathogenic bacteria.

As mentioned, prebiotics are feed components that cannot be digested by the horse's own gut enzymes and are therefore available to the microbes instead. Prebiotics include oligosaccharides such as fructooligosaccharides (FOS) and mannanoligosaccharides (MOS) and inulin, all of which are classed as soluble fibre. Research has shown that ingestion of prebiotics stimulates beneficial bacteria, particularly bifido bacteria. MOS binds to pathogenic bacteria, preventing them from attaching to the gut wall and 'flushing' them out of the gut. Yeast cell walls contain MOS.

Probiotic and prebiotic supplements may also contain digestive enzymes to help boost the horse's own supplies, and other substances that may help the gut, including mineral clays such as fuller's earth (bentonite), which absorb excess gas and water and minimize the drop in pH (acidification) present in the hindgut during starch overload.

Probiotics and prebiotics are useful for horses with digestive disturbance and those on high-starch, low-fibre diets. They are also useful for older horses, especially those with impaired dental function. Situations where these supplements are useful also include:

- Sudden change in diet.

- Administration of certain drugs, including antibiotics and dewormers.

- Stress from a new situation, travel, exercise or inappropriate housing and/or feeding.

- Competition stress.

- Dehydration.

- Inadequate dietary fibre.

- Overeating starch and fructans and laminitis caused by this.

- General unthriftiness or weight loss.

- Illness, especially with loss of appetite, digestive problems or infections.

Research has shown extra benefits for broodmares and growing horses fed live yeast. Lactating mares fed live yeast produced milk of better quality and had foals with improved growth rates compared to those not supplemented. Growing ponies fed live yeast had improved growth rates and daily weight gain in one study. Some research studies have shown increases in fibre, protein, calcium and phosphorus digestion in horse supplemented with live yeast, perhaps as a result of the effects on the gut environment.

There does not seem to be any advantage in feeding probiotics or prebiotics to healthy horses on high-fibre diets, although there is also no harm known to arise from doing so. It is perfectly normal for millions of microbes to be lost in the faeces every day, and the internal populations adjust to this loss.

Herbs and herbal blends

A huge number of herbal supplements are available for horses, including those used in blends for specific problems (as described above). Herbs can be effective and many modern medicines have been developed from substances in plants. However, in this context herbs are used as treatments and ideally a medical herbalist should be consulted for a horse with a specific problem. Most of the herbs used in products available off the shelf are relatively safe, but should always be fed strictly as recommended.

Herbs are sold as complementary feedingstuffs (feed supplements,) yet they are most often fed for their physiological effects rather than as a source of nutrients. Great care should be taken in feeding herbs to competing horses to ensure that no prohibited substances are fed inadvertently. (Competition rules state that no substance that affects any of the physiological systems should be fed to competing horses, and this rule should be taken literally – i.e. herbs should not be fed to competing horses. In reality, most of the metabolites of herbs – breakdown products in the body – are not yet tested for, the exception being valerian.)

Certain herbs are safe for general use and can form part of the ration; examples are mint and garlic. Garlic is a useful plant with a myriad of health benefits, and the bulbs are particularly good for horses with respiratory problems. However, garlic should not be overfed because, in high quantities of over 200 g per day, it can cause anaemia via abnormalities in red blood cells.

Garlic flakes.

Vegetable oils

Oil has over twice the calories per gram compared to grain; therefore it is a useful supplementary feed for horses with high energy requirements, such as hard-working and underweight horses. Although the natural diet of the horse is low in oil (about 3–4%), horses cope well with relatively large amounts of oil in their diets. Amounts of up to 0.6 ml per kilogram of bodyweight (300 ml for a 500 kg horse) can be fed safely, provided it is introduced gradually. 300 ml of oil weighs about 270 g (1 ml oil weighs about 0.9 g). Any vegetable oil is suitable, and some studies suggest that corn (maize) oil is the most palatable. Other oils that are fed to horses include soya, sunflower, linseed and blends. Vegetable oil from the supermarket is acceptable for horses.

Vegetable oils are almost pure oil, therefore they do not supply protein or carbohydrate to the horse. However, in addition to supplying plenty of calories, they are rich in essential fatty acids, which can improve the horse's skin and coat. Linseed oil is the richest plant source of the omega-3 series fatty acid, linolenic acid, particularly beneficial for the skin and coat. Oils are generally refined chemically, but mechanically extracted 'cold-pressed' oils are available, although they tend to be more expensive.

Vegetable oil is particularly useful for horses with rhabdomyolysis (see Chapter 15), performance horses with poor appetites (see Chapter 10) and horses who need to gain weight (see Chapter 8).

Fish oils

Fish liver oils such as cod liver oil are rich sources of the very long chain omega-3 series fatty acids EPA (eicosapentaenoic acid) and DHA (docosahexaenoic acid), which are transformed from α linolenic acid in the body. Although not classed as essential, they are thought to have more profound anti-inflammatory effects than α linolenic acid, from which they would be made in the body. These are useful to support joint function, and there is plenty of anecdotal evidence for their use in horses. Fish oil products supply extra vitamins A and D, therefore they should be incorporated into the ration with care.

Some owners choose to feed purely vegetarian diets to their horses and they should avoid fish oils.

Treats

Horse treats should be considered supplements, although they are usually fed in such small quantities that they do not unbalance the diet. A large variety is available, and most contain sweeteners such as sugar and/or molasses.

A variety of horsy treats.

chapter 7

Pasture

PASTURE PROVIDES AN ideal environment for horses in addition to a natural source of food. It gives horses the freedom to move about and express normal behaviour. Most horses obtain at least a portion of their daily diet from pasture herbage, yet often pasture is considered simply as turnout. However, if the aim is to maintain a productive pasture it may even be possible to reduce your feed costs! Ideally, all horses should live at pasture at all times, but in practice this may be difficult.

Types of pasture, grass species and productivity

Before they were domesticated, horses would graze and browse a variety of grass, herbs, tree leaves and other plants, obtaining a mixed diet and never being forced to graze on harmful weeds or confined to pasture heavily infected with parasites. Nowadays, domesticated horses are generally fenced in and have less choice about which plants they eat. From an agricultural viewpoint, grazing pasture is developed and maintained to produce as much grass as possible of a high nutritional quality. Short-term leys of single grass species are often re-sown every few years before re-ploughing and new species of grass have been developed that are more nutritious than old-fashioned types. However, this type of pasture is not ideal for horses. During spring and summer it may over-supply calories, protein and non-structural carbohydrates, and in spring, it under-supplies fibre. Furthermore, the suitability of pasture for a particular horse depends on intake rate as well as the actual herbage. Horses who tend to eat very large amounts of herbage quickly are at risk of gaining too much fat or developing laminitis.

Well-maintained permanent pasture or natural grassland is believed to be the best for horses, with a good turf and a good mix of grass and herb species, but managed to maintain productivity and avoid invasion of undesirable weeds and

A horse in open pasture.

poisonous plants. Such mixed species pasture would be considered 'rough' by an intensive cattle farmer, but most horses – perhaps with the exception of hard-working performance horses and lactating Thoroughbred broodmares – have nutrient requirements lower than those of production animals such as cattle.

Useful grass species that are palatable to horses include a mix of ryegrass, crested dogtail, creeping red fescue, rough and/or smooth-stalked meadowgrass and a small amount of white clover. Herbs, including dandelion, ribwort plantain, burnet and sainfoin are thought to be liked by horses. Even if these are planted with care, some may not persist over time, and pasture should be assessed on an ongoing basis to check that suitable plants are persisting. A varied diet probably provides a more balanced supply of micronutrients than just grass.

Ploughing and reseeding pasture is a last resort because it creates disturbance that takes years to settle down again, and there are much less drastic ways of improving pasture for horses. Having a good turf for horses is useful because it helps resist poaching, retains water in dry weather and aids fertility. Simply spreading seed on existing pasture is a useful way of improving it, especially in areas that have been overgrazed or poached, and it will also help avoid weed growth.

The area of grazing land required per horse depends on many factors, including whether or not the horse will be out permanently, what type of soil is present, how the pasture is managed and the pasture productivity. A general guide is one acre per horse plus one acre of improved grassland. However, low-quality permanent pasture may support just one horse per four acres.

Rosehips (*left*) and hawthorn (*right*).

Grass growth

In the UK, grass has a growing cycle that most horse owners are aware of. Rapid growth in the spring, when soil temperatures reach about 5 °C, produces protein-rich grass with relatively high levels of non-structural carbohydrates (sugars and fructans) and low levels of structural carbohydrates (fibre). The actual levels depend on the species of grass, but during spring all types of grass are risky for horses susceptible to excess weight gain and laminitis. Actual growth rates depend on environmental conditions, and grass needs adequate supplies of light, rain and soil nutrients in order to grow. Grass will stop growing when the soil temperature drops below 5 °C.

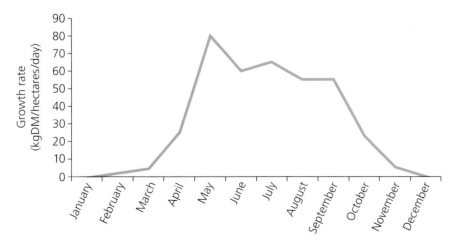

Figure 7.1 Typical grass growth throughout the seasons.

Pasture as feed

Pasture is an ideal feed for horses, but it does vary in nutrient composition throughout the year. Nutrient value depends on stage of growth, species of grass and fertilization, and on day to day environmental conditions (rainfall, temperature and sun). Spring grass tends to be relatively low in fibre and high in water-soluble carbohydrates (WSC) including sugar and fructans. WSC in growing ryegrass may be as high as 30% of the dry matter, and protein about 16% (of the dry matter). Growing spring grass is high in water, therefore has a low dry matter of about 20%. As grass matures it becomes higher in fibre because of the increased proportion of structural material, and therefore lower in WSC and protein.

Horses are selective grazers and prefer new growth, and leaves rather than stems. If grass becomes short, they will begin to browse and eat tree leaves, hedges and shrubs. Forcing horses to overgraze grass may cause the plants to become so eaten down that they cannot recover. Alternatively, if excess grass is available on a pasture, some may mature and produce seed, which results in a reduction of the nutrient value of the grass and, over time, changes the grass mixture of the pasture.

Supplying the correct amount of pasture grass can be a challenge, and most horses at pasture will be able to eat ad lib. During spring and summer, however, such a situation may over-supply nutrients to ponies, good doers and horses at maintenance (not working), causing weight gain. In such cases grass intake may need to be restricted, and an ideal method for this is strip grazing. Although mature grass is a more ideal feed for horses and ponies with low nutrient requirements, unfortunately the quantity of herbage available may make it a less desirable choice. Despite the fact that new grass growth is more nutritious, it is easier to limit the intake of a horse on a small area of well-grazed pasture that is strip-grazed.

It is useful to have an idea of how much grass a horse eats at pasture, but this is variable and depends on a number of factors including grass availability, sward length and rate of intake. A general guide is that horses will eat around 1 kg dry matter per hour in an average pasture.

Grass feeding values for horses

Estimating energy values of pasture grass for horses is difficult, but most plants contain between 8 and 10 MJ of digestible energy per kilo of dry matter. Managed temporary grassland of single species such as ryegrass will tend to be higher in energy. The protein quality of grass is good, because it contains good levels of essential amino acids. As grass matures, total protein level and digestibility will drop. Lipid content is relatively low at around 4–6% of dry matter, and the omega-3 linolenic acid is the main fatty acid. Vitamin content of growing pasture is good – grass is rich in vitamin E, betacarotenes, the precursors of vitamin A and the B-vitamin folic acid. More mature grass is higher in vitamin D than younger grass because of the presence of dead leaves, which contain vitamin D_2.

Mineral content of grass is highly variable and difficult to predict. Normal ranges are, however, available and these are shown in Table 7.1. Horses grazing on all but the most wet, acid-soil pasture in the UK are unlikely to be short of calcium, phosphorus, potassium or magnesium. However, sodium and micro-minerals (trace elements) may be in short supply, depending on the area. Some UK pasture is short of copper and/or selenium, iodine and zinc. Iron, manganese and cobalt shortages are unlikely, with most herbage containing plenty of these minerals for horses.

Nutrient	Low	Normal range	High
Calcium (g)	<2	2.5–5	>6
Phosphorus (g)	<2	1.5–4.5	>4
Magnesium (g)	<1	1–2.5	>2.5
Potassium (g)	<12	15–30	>35
Sulphur (g)	<2	2–3.5	>4
Zinc (mg)	<10	15–50	>75
Iron (mg)	<45	50–150	>200
Manganese (mg)	<30	30–200	>250
Iodine (mg)	–	0.1–0.4	–
Selenium (mg)	<0.02	0.03–0.2	>0.2
Cobalt (mg)	<0.05	0.06–0.3	>0.3

Table 7.1 Normal ranges of mineral content of pasture grass in the UK (per kg dry matter).

Adapted from P. McDonald et al (2002) *Animal Nutrition*, 6th ed., Pearson Prentice Hall.

Most grassland will fulfil most horse's nutritional requirements – with the exception of minerals – provided they can eat enough. Exceptions are hard-working horses such as eventers and racehorses. Broad-spectrum or bespoke supplements should be fed to pasture-kept horses who do not require additional feed, to ensure their mineral requirements are met.

Pasture maintenance

Looking after your pasture will provide your horse with an ongoing supply of nutritious feed, and reduce the parasite burden your horse picks up. Regular removal of droppings, resting the grass, ensuring the sward isn't eaten too short, using other species to graze the grass, topping, removal of weeds and managing poached ground are all strategies to maintain a productive pasture.

Removal of droppings

Removing droppings from your horse's pasture regularly will help to control parasite infection and help to maintain overall pasture production. The life cycles of the horse's most important internal parasites involves them hatching from eggs into larvae in the droppings. The larvae move out of the droppings into the surrounding pasture, where the horse picks them up, thus starting the life cycle again (see Chapter 8).

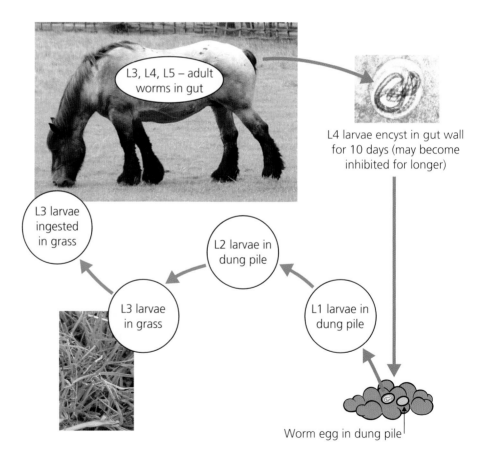

Figure 7.2 Diagram of small redworm life cycle and pasture infection.

The only method that controls parasites is to break their life cycle. Removing droppings before the larvae move out into the pasture prevents re-infection. Killing parasites inside the horse with drugs also breaks the life cycle, until the horse is re-infected by the pasture.

More and more horse owners are having their horse's droppings analysed for worm eggs, since this reflects the worm burden. Such faecal analysis can be carried out by your vet, or a laboratory, and is a very useful indicator of redworm infection. Such tests do not, however, reflect tapeworm infection. See Chapter 8 for more information about parasite control in horses.

Horses avoid grazing close to their droppings (it is the faeces, rather than urine, that they avoid), and this leads eventually to a patchy appearance in the pasture, described as 'roughs' and 'lawns'. The areas covered in droppings will grow lush and long and the nutrients from the faeces will encourage the growth of weeds such as nettles. The rough areas will eventually spread because mares and geldings tend to face into these areas to defecate, thereby extending them. Regular removal of droppings and/or grazing the pasture in rotation with cattle and sheep – who will graze the roughs refused by horses – helps avoid pasture wastage via these areas.

Grazing other species such as cattle and sheep on horse pasture is particularly helpful, especially if the pasture is a large area and droppings are not removed regularly. This is because, while sheep and cattle are not affected by the parasites that affect horses, they do ingest the larvae; therefore helping to 'clean' the pasture. If such controls are not available, 'rough' areas of longer grass around droppings should be cut (topped) – but, if droppings *are* removed regularly, roughs will not appear.

Grazing sheep on horse pasture has practical advantages.

A weedy field with rough areas.

Harrowing droppings to spread them is another technique to help avoid the development of roughs and lawns, but must be done with care if the pasture is not to be spread with worm larvae. Harrowing should only be done on warm, sunny days so that any worm larvae are dessicated and killed, and horses should be moved off pasture that has been harrowed, which should then be rested.

Optimal grazing

Optimum pasture productivity depends on the herbage being treated as a crop. Grasses are generally hardy, vigorous plants that withstand regular cutting and actually grow bushier with regular topping. Allowing horses to 'harvest' the grass by grazing, but moving them before it has been grazed too long to re-grow is the key. Ideally, grass should be grazed to no lower than a height of 5 cm before horses are moved and the grass allowed to recover. If grass plants are overgrazed, re-growth will suffer and the plant may eventually die. In addition, weed seeds are more likely to be able to take hold. 'Horse-sick' pasture tends to develop from overgrazing, which has led to under-productivity and even the death of much of the grass, and allowed weeds the opportunity to grow and flourish.

Since horses are very selective grazers, who will pick out preferred grass species, they can consequently be very wasteful grazers, and overgrazing of their preferred areas is a common problem. Splitting pasture into sections, even small areas, and moving horses periodically to new areas will help grass to maintain productivity. Aim to move the horses when the grass is grazed down to a length of 5 cm, and allow the grass to re-grow to about 10 cm before re-grazing. If the grass grows longer than this, ideally have it topped before allowing your horses to graze it.

Leaving grass to mature and produce seeds results in a less productive pasture, with grass of a lower feed value. However, allowing grass to go to seed may, over several years, alter the species in the pasture to a less ideal mixture.

Pasture that is used for horses who must have their grass restricted is difficult to maintain, and in some cases the pasture may have to be sacrificed for the health of the horse. The best option might be to allow the area to be trampled and overeaten, and the horse then given supplementary forage whilst turned out on such an area. Alternatively, strip grazing, mentioned earlier, is an ideal way to control grass intake without sacrificing the grass. Temporary electric fencing can be used to section-off areas, and then moved each day, or twice daily if possible, to allow access to new grass.

above left A horse grazing in very mature pasture.

above right Using electric fencing to provide strip grazing.

Weed control

Weeds are plants growing where they are not wanted and although some plants considered to be weeds are undesirable in horse pasture others, including flowers such as dandelions and yarrow, are desirable. If pasture, is grazed very short, or badly poached, a variety of undesirable weeds, including thistles, nettles, docks and ragwort may invade bare areas of soil.

The best method of suppressing weed proliferation is encouraging a dense, healthy sward of grass. Weeds should be dealt with before they seed, and ragwort must be removed as soon as it is identified because it is highly poisonous to horses (see below). Some weeds, including thistles and nettles, may be controlled by cutting regularly throughout the season, as soon as the plant grows up enough to do so. Cutting is not a useful method of controlling some species, including docks and ragwort, because the plants will simply regrow vigorously. In small areas, weeds can be pulled – which is a more permanent method than cutting. Herbicides should be used with care – they will kill desirable plants as well as undesirable ones. Also, care should be taken not to spray within several metres of any watercourses, and horses must be moved off the pasture until all traces of the sprayed plants are gone. Expert advice should be taken on herbicide use.

Despite its usefulness for its nitrogen-fixing properties, clover is sometimes considered a weed by horse owners. White clover is highly palatable for horses (unlike the red variety, which is not) and if too much is available the pasture may provide a diet too high in protein and water-soluble carbohydrate for most horses. Unfortunately, a number of practices associated with grazing horses will tend to encourage the growth of white clover. These include the removal of droppings, heavy grazing associated with high stocking rates, light grazing over winter and no rest periods. Specialist advice on controlling white clover should be taken.

Poisonous plants

Ragwort (*Senecio jacobea*) is classed as an injurious weed under the Injurious Weeds Act 1959, which means that land owners or occupiers must control it via legal means if they are asked to do so. The Ragwort Control Act 2003 makes this more likely, because of more stringent and specific rules. There is also a voluntary Code of Practice to Prevent the Spread of Ragwort (2004), which recommends that horse pasture and hay fields, plus neighbouring land, should be kept ragwort-free. Ragwort is highly poisonous to horses, and can cause death even from ingestion of tiny amounts over many years. It contains alkaloids that damage the liver. Growing ragwort is not usually eaten by horses, but if it dies, e.g. is trodden or cut into hay, it becomes palatable. In its first year of life, ragwort is in a rosette stage, flat on the ground, and although it may be difficult to spot, it should ideally be dug out or sprayed at this stage. The following year the plant will grow tall, flower and then deposit thousands of seeds. These plants should be dug out in spring before flowering and seeding. Care must be taken to remove all root fragments because otherwise these will regenerate and produce new plants. Cutting second year plants as an emergency method to stop the production and spread of seeds is acceptable, but further action should be taken to remove the plant because cutting only encourages growth.

Sheep will graze the rosette stages of ragwort plants, and some people use this as a method of control. However, sheep are also affected by its poison and – although much larger amounts need to be ingested for the plant to be fatal to this species – this practice should not be encouraged.

Some other poisonous plants found in the UK, that horses should not be allowed access to, are listed below. For a full list, a specialist book should be consulted.

Bracken, acorns, yew, laburnum, mistletoe, knotgrass, monkshood, hemlock, hellebore, henbane, iris, daffodil, narcissus, St John's wort, deadly nightshade, larkspur, foxglove, hemp, columbine, corncockle, horsetail, bluebell, honeysuckle, poppy, buttercup.

(top) Ragwort plants at the rosette first year growth stage and *(below)* the flowering second year growth stage. Both are highly poisonous to horses.

above left Horses at risk, grazing in a field with ragwort.

Fertilization and other treatments

Soil analysis should be carried out to investigate the needs of the pasture. Pasture soil should be maintained at a pH of about 6.5–6.8, to ensure mineral uptake by the grass. Some pastures will benefit from the alkaline effects of lime, but expert advice should be sought before it is applied, and horses must be removed from the pasture until all the lime is washed into the soil. Calcified seaweed is a useful additive for horse pasture, because it supplies minerals and has an anti-acidic effect similar to lime. Horses do not have to be removed from pasture after the application of seaweed.

Fertilization of pasture should be carried out with care and with expert help. Simply adding nitrogen to grass pasture is not ideal, because this may cause an unwanted flush of grass, will encourage the growth of some species at the cost of others in a species-rich permanent pasture and will encourage the growth of docks, thistles and nettles if the grass is overgrazed and bare areas are present. Nitrogen fertilizers will also affect the mineral content of the herbage. However, the application of nitrogen does help to reduce excess white clover in horse pastures. Ensuring that some nitrogen-fixing leguminous plants are present is useful and these include clovers and vetches, but the total amount should be limited. Farmyard manure is believed to be more beneficial than chemical fertilizers because it provides a slower release of nutrients, and adds to the organic matter of the soil – however, after is it applied, pasture should be rested for 4–6 weeks.

A severely poached field.

Minimizing poaching

Horses tend to poach pasture partly with their hooves, which are often shod, and partly through their social activities, which include congregating in specific places and rolling in areas that have already become a little poached. In addition, if horses are brought out of the pasture to stables and fed, they learn to anticipate this and will congregate around gateways. Gateways and entrances to shelters may need to be filled with hardcore or ground protection plastic grates if they are to survive the winter without becoming too muddy.

Allowing sheep to graze horse pasture will help alleviate the effects of poaching as well as keeping the grass clean and the roughs eaten down. The hooves of sheep tend to level out areas poached by horses, and these can then be reseeded the following spring. Poached areas need to be sown with grass seed to avoid the proliferation of weeds.

Shelter, fencing and access to water

Horses at pasture should have access to shelter at all times; during summer to get away from flies and in winter to give some protection from rain and wind. Horses can survive outside at very low temperatures, but wetting does increase heat loss, especially if a wind is present. Natural or man-made shelters are suitable, and each should have adequate ground treatment to avoid excess poaching.

Fencing should be suitable for horses, i.e. safe with no protruding nails, loose wire or sharp edges. Barbed wire should be avoided because it can cause horrific injury to horses. Many people still prefer traditional post and rail wooden fencing, although well-maintained electric fencing (which can be set up with wooden posts and two or three lines of wide tape) is probably safer. A line of

Providing horses with access to shelter in bad weather is very important, even if they still choose to stand outside.

Drinking from a trough.

electric tape can be run along the top of wooden fencing to stop horses chewing. Fencing rails or tight wire are safer than stock wire fencing made up of grids, which horses may get their hooves stuck through. The benefit of electric fencing is that horses learn to avoid it; therefore even injuries from broken wooden fencing are avoided.

Watering containers in pasture should be mobile or have hard standing around them, to avoid excessive poaching. Troughs should be cleaned out regularly and pipes should be buried or insulated to avoid freezing during winter.

chapter 8

Practical feeding

KNOWLEDGE ABOUT HOW the horse processes and uses nutrients, and the range of feeds available, gives an understanding that helps owners to formulate a practical ration, or daily feed regime. Before a ration is formulated, there are some basic horse-care strategies that need to be addressed. Maintaining digestive system health, including dental care and protection against parasites, is important to ensure efficient digestion and utilization of dietary nutrients. After these practical points have been attended to, an appropriate ration can be put together or formulated. There are both simple and more complicated ways of doing this, the latter of which include calculations, but are more accurate and assess all nutrients. All methods require knowledge of the bodyweight and bodily condition of the horse. Finally, there are plenty of practical guidelines to ensure good feeding practice, including storage of feed, when to feed, how to feed, and how to deal with feeding-related problems.

Dental health

As explained in Chapter 2, horses have hypsodont teeth, which mean they continue to grow out of the gums throughout the horse's life. If the horse lives long enough, at some point each tooth will grow right out and be lost. As the teeth grow they are worn down by the horse's tough, fibrous diet and eventually, in the very old horse, their rough surfaces become smooth. This continual growth means that there is a high risk of uneven wear and sharp edges. Because of the side to side (lateral) as well up and down movement of the lower jaw, and the fact that the teeth on the lower jaw are closer together than those of the upper jaw, sharp edges tend to form on the outer edges of the upper jaw teeth and the inner edges of the lower jaw teeth. These edges need to be removed. In addition, some teeth can become more dominant than their opposite tooth, and these need to be rasped back.

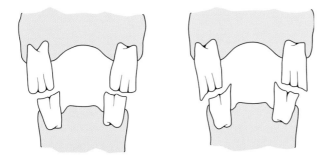

Figure 8.1 Transverse section of skull, showing hooks on teeth.

Horses should be checked by a qualified equine dental technician or vet at least every year and whenever problems are suspected. Older horses or those with problem teeth should be checked at six-monthly intervals. Qualified equine dentists in the UK are known as dental technicians and details can be found via the British Equine Veterinary Association (BEVA) and the Department for Farming and Rural Affairs (DEFRA).

Horses have evolved to eat a high-fibre diet, mostly from ground level. When a horse eats from head height, his teeth do not meet (occlude) at the same place as when he eats from the ground with his neck stretched down. Therefore a stabled horse fed a grain and hay diet from head height may suffer more dental problems than a grass-kept horse through inappropriate occlusion over many

An equine dentist at work.

Half-chewed food on the ground; the consequence of quidding.

years. If dental health is ignored and a horse develops a problem with his teeth, he may not be able to chew properly and therefore will not be able to utilize his feed fully. Nutrients may be wasted and, in the worst case, the horse will be at risk of choking.

Teeth should be checked regularly regardless of any signs of problems. However, signs that indicate a problem include quidding, where food is half-chewed then rejected (see photo); mouth discomfort (and possibly head unsteadiness) when bitting and during riding; long pieces of forage in the faeces; bad breath, and unexplained weight loss despite a suitable diet.

Horses who have not had regular dental care throughout their lives may develop problems with their teeth (such as a severe 'wave mouth' with chewing teeth of different lengths) that cannot be remedied by dental treatment. Specific feeding strategies for horses with dental problems, lost teeth or an inability to chew are given in Chapter 11.

Internal parasite control

Horses are susceptible to a range of internal parasites, which tend to be called worms, despite the fact that some are not actually worms. Many horses carry a certain level of worms without illness, but in some cases worms can kill. Most internal parasites of horses cause unthriftiness or even illness, either through damage to the gut wall, 'stealing' nutrients, or migration through the body and organs. They can cause colic, poor growth, weight loss, diarrhoea and in some cases, death. Therefore, all horses should have a programme of worm control. Individual horses have different control needs, depending on how they are kept; therefore the vet should be consulted to help with the worm control programme.

Description and life cycle of major parasites in horses

Intestinal parasites were mentioned in the previous chapter about pasture management, because the most effective control regime of internal parasites includes maintaining a clean pasture with as low a population of parasites as possible. However, some horse parasites are not picked up from pasture, having a slightly different life cycle.

Important intestinal parasites of horses are small redworms (small strongyles), large redworms (large strongyles), tapeworms, bots, and in foals, roundworms (ascarids). Many other intestinal parasites exist, but these will be controlled if the important parasites are controlled.

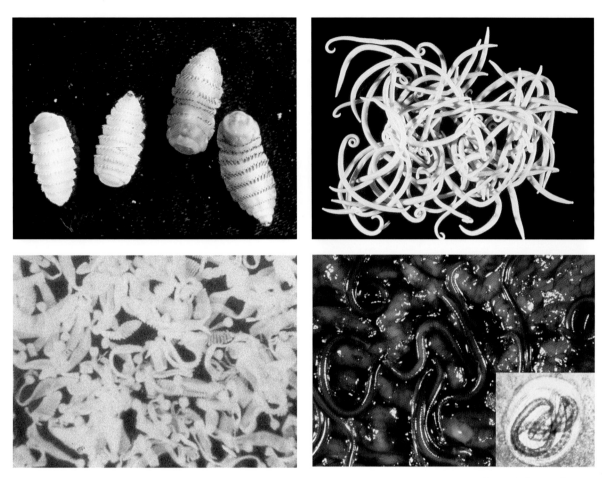

The main types of internal equine parasites.

top left Bots.
top right Roundworms.
bottom left Tapeworms.
bottom right Redworms, (*insert*) an encysted small redworm.

Small redworms

Small redworms (small strongyles or cyathostomins) are 'plug' feeders, attaching themselves to the gut wall and feeding on the blood vessels. They can cause debilitating disease and can be present in very large numbers. Small redworms have a short life cycle of just 6 weeks, so regular deworming is necessary. However, the newer drugs have a longer effect than just one life cycle, with moxidectin suppressing the appearance of small redworm eggs in the dropping for 13 weeks after dosing. Eggs in the horse's droppings hatch to infective larvae within 5–7 days, and these infective larvae are picked up by the horse during grazing. The ingested larvae burrow into the wall of the large intestine, and form tiny cysts. After 10 days of the encysted stage, the maturing larvae hatch out and become adults. Sometimes during winter their emergence is inhibited, resulting in large numbers of larvae emerging from the gut wall en mass in the spring, causing colic, diarrhoea, weight loss and even death. The condition is sometimes called 'larval cyathostominosis'.

All types of deworming drugs (almost universally referred to as 'wormers') kill susceptible small redworms, but unfortunately some worms have built up a resistance to the benzimidazole drugs (including fenbendazole, mebendazole and oxibendazole). If resistance is suspected, the vet can help to monitor the effectiveness of these drugs with the use of faecal worm egg counts carried out before and after deworming with a benzimidazole drug. The encysted stages of small redworms are more difficult to kill, and are controlled by either a single dose of moxidectin or a 5-day course of fenbendazole (although the latter may not be effective against resistant worms).

Large redworms

Large redworms (large strongyles) are particularly dangerous because, rather than burrowing into the gut wall, they travel through and out into the horse's body, damaging arteries and organs. The most common species, *Strongylus vulgaris*, migrate to the arteries supplying the intestine, which can lead to spasmodic colic, and can also cause fatal aneurysms, which may kill the horse instantly. The larvae spend 2–4 months in the arteries, causing inflammation and physical restriction of blood flow. After this time they migrate back to the gut to become egg-laying adults. Large strongyles have a 6-month life cycle, so just twice yearly deworming will help to control them. The ivermectin and moxidectin drugs kill adult and migrating stages of large redworms.

Tapeworms

Tapeworms do not feed directly from the horse, but hook onto the gut wall and absorb nutrients from the contents of the intestine. Tapeworms tend to accumulate at the junction of the small intestine and the caecum of the horse (the ileocaecal junction), where they may cause blockages. The risk of colic in this area is increased when tapeworms are present, and they can cause both impaction colic and spasmodic colic. Reproducing tapeworms shed sections of tail containing eggs, which are expelled in the horse's droppings. The eggs are eaten by tiny mites called oribatid mites, which tend to be most active on grassland during the summer months. The mites are also present in hay and straw. The tapeworm develops in the mite for around 2–4 months, and then becomes infective to the horse when the mite is eaten. After about 4–6 weeks, adult tapeworms will be developed in the horse's gut. Adult tapeworms can be controlled by a single dose of praziquantel or a double dose of pyrantel. Horses should be dosed twice yearly, in around April and October.

Bots

Bots are the larvae of bot flies that live in the horse's stomach over winter. Adult bot flies are killed by the frost, so dosing with a drug active against bots (e.g.

ivermectin or moxidectin) after the first frost will clear the horse's stomach from bots and help to reduce the bot fly population for the following year. Yellowish-white bot fly eggs are laid on the horse's coat (often on the legs) and should be removed by scraping carefully with a sharp knife, helping to reduce infection. The eggs hatch and irritate the horse, causing licking, which introduces the larvae into the horse's mouth. From there they burrow into the back of the tongue, then eventually emerge and migrate to the stomach. The following spring the larvae loosen their hold and pass out in the droppings, burrow into the soil and finish their life cycle by emerging as flies, ready to produce another population.

Roundworms

Roundworms are a common cause of colic in foals, where they can physically block the intestine. There is some resistance built up to roundworms as a foal grows. Roundworm eggs are passed in the droppings, and develop into infective larvae within the egg. The eggs are sticky and tend to cling to the mare, the foal's muzzle and all around stables and pasture. If these eggs are eaten, the larvae hatch out and penetrate the gut wall, migrating through various organs to the lungs. The worms then work their way up the airways, are coughed up and swallowed, ready to develop into egg-laying adults in the small intestine. The eggs of the roundworm are tough and can remain viable in the environment for 10 years. All the deworming drugs kill roundworms, and treatment should begin when foals are 1 month of age.

Controlling internal parasites in horses

Surveys have shown that although many horse owners use some sort of worm control for their horses, they often do so in a haphazard way. More efficient pro-grammes would help their horses to have lower worm burdens. The key to con-trolling intestinal parasites in horses is to break their life cycles. Methods of breaking the life cycle include preventing them from being eaten by the horse by clearing faeces from the pasture, or killing reproducing adult worms in the gut with the use of 'worming' drugs more scientifically known as 'anthelmintics'. The most effective way to control worms is to prevent them being eaten by horses, and regularly removing droppings from pasture is the best way to do this. Redworm larvae move out of faeces and become infective within 5–7 days depending on conditions, so droppings should be removed every 4–5 days. Droppings should ideally be moved outside the pasture and composted to create enough heat to kill any eggs or larvae within it. Parasitic worms that affect horses do not affect other grazing species and, as mentioned in Chapter 7, allowing sheep or cattle onto pasture grazed by horses helps to 'clean' it, removing worm eggs and larvae. Stabled horses can also be infected and stable hygiene is vital.

Ideally the aim of treatment with drugs is to prevent worm infections rather than treat them. These drugs kill the adult egg-producing worms (or the larvae, in the case of bots) and some also kill developing stages. They should be used at specific intervals throughout the year to help minimize contamination of the horse's pasture with worm eggs and larvae. Unfortunately, no single drug on the market controls all the intestinal parasites of horses – this is why strategic deworming programmes must be followed. Table 8.1 helps outline the main parasites and how they can be controlled with drugs.

Despite the fact that many different brand names of 'wormer' are available, these consist of three main groups: benzimidazoles (including fenbendazole, mebendazole and oxibendazole), macrocyclic lactones (ivermectin and moxidectin) and tetrahydropyrimidines (pyrantel), plus a relatively new drug for horses, praziquantel. Praziquantel is only effective against tapeworms. It is important to find out which drug each branded product contains, in order to ensure a strategic treatment programme that controls all the different parasites.

Parasite	Latin name	Life cycle and notes	Time to control	Drug to control
Small redworms (Strongyles)	Over 40 species of *Strongylus*	Rapid 6-week life cycle. Encyst in gut wall for 10 days, or longer over winter (inhibited); may cause cyathostominosis if mass emergence in spring.	6–13 week intervals (according to drug) at all times when grazing, including winter.	Any, but benzimidazole resistance may occur. 5-day course of fenbendazole or moxidectin required to kill inhibited (and developing encysted) stages.
Large redworms (Strongyles)	*Strongylus vulgaris, edentatus* and *equinus*	6-month life cycle; migrate through arteries, feeding on the walls. Can cause fatal damage.	Minimum 6-monthly intervals.	Ivermectin, moxidectin or 5-day course of fenbendazole.
Tapeworms	*Anoplocephala perfoliata, magna* and *mamillana*	6-month life cycle with oribatid mite as intermediate host.	Spring and autumn, 6 months apart.	Praziqantel or double dose of pyrantel.
Bots	*Gastrophilus intestinalis*	Larve of bot fly, over-winter in horse's stomach.	Winter, after first frost (adult flies killed).	Ivermectin/moxidectin
Roundworms (ascarids)	*Parascaris equorum*	Large adults, young worms migrate through organs including lungs.	From 1 month old, monthly until 6 months, then 6–8 weekly.	Any, but check wormer for 'age from' use.

Table 8.1 The main horse parasites and their control with anthelmintic drugs.

Different types of drug have different dosing intervals and these must be followed in order for the programme to be effective.

All horses on the same pasture should be treated at the same time, and foals should be treated from the age of 4 weeks. It is often recommended that the same drug should be used for one year, then a change made to a different drug for the next year. This cycle is meant to help prevent the development of worms that are resistant to the drugs, as has happened in some areas with the benzimidazole drugs. In theory this gives a 3-year cycle because there are only three different types of wormer; but benzimidazole drugs should not be used for a whole year unless it is confirmed that there is no resistance to them. The vet should be consulted about running faecal egg counts to investigate whether or not benzimidazole drugs are effective on individual horses.

Horses should never be under-dosed for their bodyweight and if in doubt, dose for 10 or 20 kg more bodyweight. The deworming programme should be carried out throughout the year, even for horses allowed only a few hours at pasture during the day. Worms are not just a summer problem because the eggs and larvae can survive frosty conditions. A strategic plan is given in Table 8.2, see page 130.

below left Some anthelmintic drugs in syringes.

below Administering an anthelmintic.

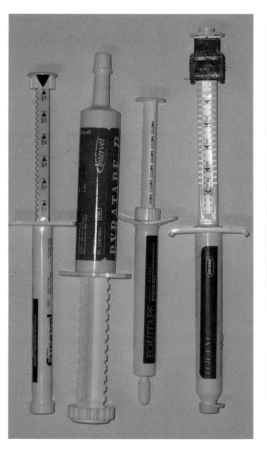

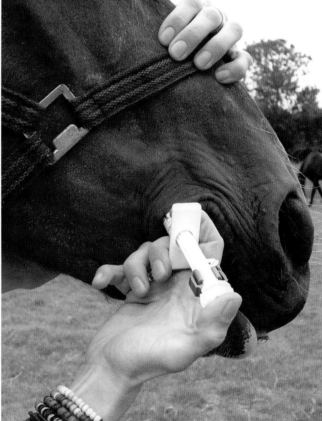

	Small redworm	Large redworm	Tapeworm	Bots	Sample Annual Programme 1	Sample Annual Programme 2
January	May become inhibited				Moxidectin	5-day Fenbendazole (i.e Panacur Guard)
February						
March			2 x Pyrantel or Praziquantel		2 x Pyrantel or Praziquantel	2 x Pyrantel or Praziquantel
April	Every 6–13 weeks (depending on drug) throughout entire year	Ivermectin or Moxidectin or 5-day Fenbendazole **not less** than every 6 months			Ivermectin every 8 weeks or Moxidectin every 13 weeks	Pyrantel every 6 weeks
May						
June						
July						
August						
September	Rotate drug annually		2 x Pyrantel or Praziquantel		2 x Pyrantel or Praziquantel	2 x Pyrantel or Praziquantel
October						
November	May become inhibited			Ivermectin or Moxidectin after first frost	Ivermectin or Moxidectin after first frost	Ivermectin or Moxidectin after first frost
December						

Table 8.2 A strategic worm control plan.

Faecal egg counts can be carried out by the vet or a laboratory (usually advertised in equestrian magazines) to help ensure that the deworming programme is effective. Counts can also be used to help plan the programme, which may be more economical for large yards with many horses, or where owners wish to minimize the use of drugs with their horses and/or on their land. In such cases, a faecal egg count is carried out and, with veterinary advice, the horses treated only when their counts are over a specified number of eggs per gram. All horses must be treated at the same time with the same drug. Veterinary advice is essential with such a programme, because the count only reflects egg-laying adult parasites, not developing, migrating or encysted stages, or tapeworms. Tapeworm infection cannot be diagnosed effectively with faecal egg counts and requires a blood sample. However, new techniques that involve molecular biology are currently being developed and they should provide a sensitive method of diagnosis for the future.

When a new horse with no known deworming history arrives at a yard, this horse should be isolated and treated strategically before being incorporated with others. First, a double dose of pyrantel should be given to control tapeworms, and this will also kill small redworms. Two days later, a dose of moxidectin should be given to control bots, large redworms and inhibited encysted small redworms. The horse should then go onto the same programme as the other horses on the yard.

Herbal anthelmintics are available, but are not subject to the same rigorous tests of effectiveness that the pharmaceutical drugs are; therefore they should be used with care and faecal egg counts must be carried out to assess their effectiveness in individual horses. Worms can kill horses and their control must be taken very seriously.

Practical diet formulation

Formulating a diet means putting together a feed ration to meet the horse's nutritional requirements. Nutritionists use complex computer programmes to help formulate rations, but horse owners can carry out similar calculations at home with a calculator. The steps in planning what to feed or assessing the current diet are:

1. Determine the horse's bodyweight and condition.

2. Decide whether the horse is in appropriate condition or needs to either lose or gain weight.

3. Investigate the horse's nutritional requirements, which depend on his level of work, stage of life and reproductive status.

4. Choose suitable forage and feed and calculate the amounts required to meet requirements for nutrients.

5. Add vitamin and mineral supplements if necessary.

6. Add other health-promoting supplements if necessary.

For those who do not wish to get into such detail, the alternative is to simply choose a forage and a compound feed and feed appropriate ratios, adding a broad-spectrum supplement if less than the recommended amount of compound is enough for the horse to maintain condition. In this way, steps 3 and 4 are missed out. Such a simple approach works better if branded compound feeds are used as the concentrate, making the choice of feed easier for horses in work, growing horses and pregnant or lactating mares.

Whatever method is used to calculate what to feed, the horse must be assessed on an ongoing basis and the diet adjusted as appropriate, because each individual has slightly different requirements, and most requirements are based on an 'average' horse. Ponies and other good doers tend to need less energy intake to maintain weight, and some hot-blooded horses may require more than typical amounts.

Establishing bodyweight and condition

Before selecting or appraising a horse's diet, an assessment should be made of the horse. A subjective assessment 'by eye' is helpful because it can tell a great deal about the general health of the horse – although this technique is more useful to people with lots of experience with horses. A disadvantage of this 'overall look' approach is that it can be difficult to notice changes when the horse is observed every day. Objective assessment is a more reliable method, and will supply information that is useful in diet selection.

In order to formulate a suitable ration, two basic criteria need to be assessed. First, the horse's bodyweight needs to be determined, to help estimate the horse's normal intake of feed, and thus calculate his nutrient requirements. Second, his actual condition or body-fat covering needs to be appraised, to determine whether or not this condition is suitable for the individual horse or whether it needs to be increased or reduced. This appraisal can be made by using the technique known as condition scoring; a relatively objective and standardized method of estimating body fat covering (see below). To ensure consistency, all methods of weight estimation and condition scoring should be carried out by the same person in the same way at the same time of day, and the horse should be stood square on a level surface.

Determining bodyweight

The most accurate method of determining bodyweight is with calibrated scales. Scales can be fitted in a yard and some large competition yards find them invaluable for monitoring their horses' bodyweights. Research has shown that performance horses function better within a specific weight range. Mobile scales for horses are available, but are expensive at around £2,000–3,000 (UK cost in 2006). Some horses are reluctant to stand quietly on them and need to be trained to do so. Public weighbridge scales can also be used, but may not be accurate for weights under a tonne (1,000 kg), and the vehicle or vehicle and trailer may need to be weighed with and without the horse in order to arrive at an accurate figure. Whenever the horse is weighed for comparative purposes, this should be done at the same time relative to feeding and exercise because weight fluctuations will occur depending on when the horse urinates and defecates and on his hydration status.

The horse's bodyweight can be estimated from his height, but this is an inaccurate method. Weightapes can also be used to estimate weight; these are inexpensive and easy to obtain. They are not always accurate, especially for horses with odd conformation, those who are very underweight or overweight, and pregnant mares. They are, however, fairly useful for horses in average condition, with average conformation. (Tapes that are specific for either ponies or horses are available, and these tend to be more accurate for their appropriate types.)

Weightapes are useful for monitoring weight changes, provided they are used in a consistent manner. The tape should be placed around the horse's body in a specific way (see photo) with the tape lying underneath the horse's abdomen

Mobile horse scales.

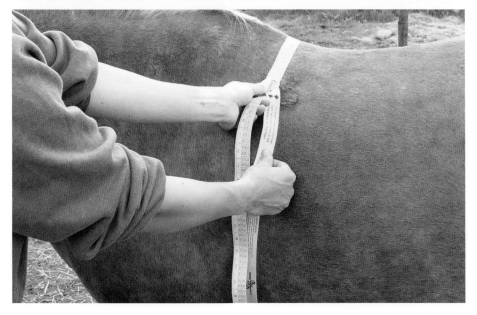

Using a weightape.

where the girth would lie (just behind the elbow), and sloping back to behind the withers. Where the tape meets should thus not be the top of a vertical line, but of one sloping like a backslash (/). The reading should be taken after the horse has breathed out.

A more accurate method of bodyweight estimation, rather than just using girth measurement, is to couple this with a length measurement and apply a formula to both. To do this, the horse should be standing square on a level surface. This technique involves first obtaining a girth measurement, with the tape applied as above – although a simple tape measure can be used in this case. Then, the body length is measured from the point of shoulder to the point of buttock (tuber ischii) as in the photo. The measurements in centimetres are then put into the calculation below:

$$\text{Bodyweight (kg)} = \frac{(\text{heart girth} \times \text{heart girth}) \times \text{length}}{11877}$$

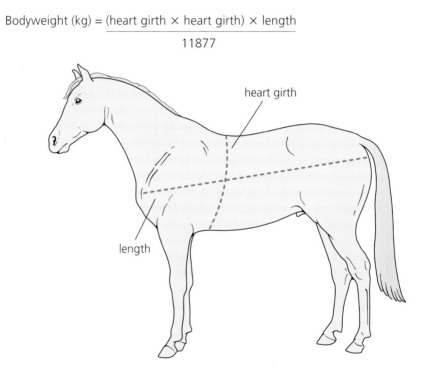

Figure 8.2 Measuring a horse's heart girth and length.

Knowing a horse's bodyweight is not only useful in terms of ration formulation but also for administering correct drug doses, monitoring health, maintaining optimal performance in athletic horses and assessing growth in young horses.

Condition scoring[1]

Although bodyweight measurements help to estimate total feed intake and allow the horse's overall weight to be monitored, they do not describe anything about body fat covering. Body condition scoring is a method of assessing body fat covering, i.e. how fat or thin a horse is. Body fat tends to be laid down in specific areas and these are examined during the condition scoring process. Assessing body fat can help to evaluate energy (calorie) intake and if necessary adjust the feeding regime to be more appropriate to the particular animal. Condition scoring can also help determine whether an athletic horse has an appropriate body fat covering for the specific discipline. Both excess and too little body fat are unhealthy, limiting the horse's ability to perform optimally and being linked to increased risk of disease and even a reduced life expectancy. Condition scoring is a useful method that can be used by anyone. There are several different systems, and recently research workers have adjusted original systems to make them more suitable for specific breeds, e.g. Warmbloods.

The most straightforward system was published by Australian researchers Carroll and Huntington in 1988, who adapted a system published 8 years previously by a British lady, Anne Leighton Hardman. The adapted system involves a visual and tactile assessment of fat covering of the neck, back and ribs, and pelvis, giving them a score from 0 to 5, including half-scores. If the pelvis score differs by 1 or more points from the back and ribs or neck score, it is adjusted by half a point towards these other scores. If both the latter scores are an equal amount over and under the pelvis score, it remains unaltered. The final pelvis score is the horse's condition score (see Table 8.3, page 136).

The following are tips to help with condition scoring:

- Stand back and take a good look at the overall shape of the horse.

- Then move close and feel the relevant areas. Note how easy it is to feel the bones, including the shoulder and the ribs, under the skin and fat.

- Note that the abdomen (belly) is not used because its shape is affected by factors other than body fat, such as gut fill.

A more complex system using a scale of 1 to 9 and examining six rather than just three areas of the body was published by Henneke and colleagues in 1983, and has since been adjusted and updated. This system is more specific, though more complicated to use. It helps to avoid incorrect scores in very old horses who may have a prominent spine and pelvis as a result of muscle loss, but adequate body fat covering elsewhere. The fat covering along the neck, withers, behind the shoulder, ribs, tail head and along the top-line is individually assessed and scores are averaged to obtain an overall condition score. This system was developed using Quarter Horses and is therefore suitable for lighter types including Thoroughbreds, but not ponies, draught crosses or Warmbloods. In 2004, German researchers Kienzle and Schramme published an adapted 1 to 9 point system to suit Warmbloods, noting that these horses had more prominent hip bones than Quarter Horses at the same condition score, and that a crease down the back of a Warmblood did not indicate that he was overweight. They also published a slightly different formula to estimate the bodyweight of German Warmblood horses.

Fat does not turn into muscle, and as a horse gets fitter he generally uses body fat for energy, and develops muscle separately. If a horse is overweight, or the aim is to get him fitter, he will need to achieve a lower condition score. If, on the other hand, he is too thin, he will need to gain a higher condition score over time. Although condition scoring of pregnant mares is not accurate, the technique is still useful as a guide to ensure they are not overfed. Their swelling abdomens are not taken into account; this helps to avoid confusion between fat deposition and foal development.

Condition Score	Pelvis	Back and ribs	Neck
0 Very Poor	Angular, skin tight, very sunken rump with no fatty tissue detectable. Deep cavity under tail and either side of croup.	Skin tight over ribs, which can be seen easily. Backbone (vertebral spinous processes) sharp, prominent and easily seen.	Marked 'upside down' ewe neck, narrow and slack at base.
1 Poor	Rump sunken but skin supple. Prominent pelvis and croup with no fatty tissue detectable. Deep cavity under tail with visible 'poverty lines'.	Ribs easily visible. Skin sunken on either side of backbone. Spinous processed well defined.	Ewe neck, narrow and slack at base.
2 Moderate	Rump flat either side of backbone. Croup well defined but some fatty tissue evident; slight cavity under tail.	Ribs just visible. Backbone covered and spinous processes not visible but easily felt.	Narrow but firm.
3 Good	Covered by fat and rounded, but no gutter. Pelvis easily felt and skin smooth and supple.	Ribs just covered but easily felt. No gutter along back. Spinous processes covered but can be felt.	Firm but no crest (except for stallions).
4 Fat	Gutter to root of tail. Pelvis covered by soft fat and felt only on firm pressure.	Ribs well covered and only felt on firm pressure. Gutter along backbone.	Wide and firm with some crest.
5 Very fat (obese)	Deep gutter to root of tail. Pelvis buried in fat and cannot be felt. Skin stretched.	Ribs buried and cannot be felt. Back broad and flat with deep gutter along backbone.	Very wide and firm with folds of fat. Marked crest.

Table 8.3 Body condition scoring for horses (0–5 scale).

(Adapted from Carroll & Huntington, 1988).

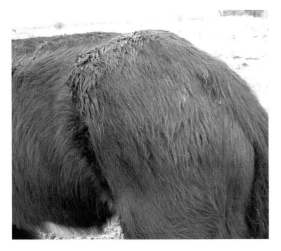 

The ideal condition score for any horse will depend on his job and his breeding. However, all horses should have a body fat covering suited to their role, and most horses should score about 3; good (0–5 system). Fit, well-muscled competition horses will tend to be closer to 2; moderate. Show horses tend to be at least 4; fat, and ideally should be kept in leaner condition. Overweight horses, like people, have a much increased risk of a variety of diseases, including laminitis; therefore all horses should ideally be kept below score 4. Horses above score 4 should have their feeding and exercise regimes changed immediately and expert advice sought on how to do this.

above left A thin horse who would have a condition score of 1.

above A fat pony who would have a condition score of 5.

Discipline	Suitable range of body condition scores (0–5)
Hacking and light work	2–3.5
Showing	3–3.5
Dressage	2–3
Horse trials	2
Endurance	2
Showjumping	2–3
Polo	2
Western sports	2–3
Driving sports	2–3
Racing	2

Table 8.4 Suitable body condition scores for horses in different disciplines.

Formulating the ration

Once the horse's bodyweight and body fat covering (condition score) have been assessed, a ration can be formulated which involves feeding forages, an appropriate amount of compound food and such broad-spectrum vitamin and mineral supplements as are necessary to balance the feed. Alternatively, the more mathematically minded can investigate actual requirements of individual nutrients and use this information to select suitable feeds, including compounds and straights.

The simple method

The simplest method is based on an estimation of daily intake and a forage to concentrate ratio, as laid out in Table 8.7. Horses' daily intakes normally vary from 1.5 to 3% of bodyweight and, typically, horses at maintenance or in light work are fed 2% of their bodyweight (See Table 8.5). (You will recall that 'maintenance requirements' are a description of the needs of a horse who is not in work). This figure can be increased for horses who need to gain weight.

Class of horse	Percentage bodyweight (dry matter)
Maintenance to light work	2%
Moderate to intense work	2–2.5%
Pregnant mare, months 9-11	2%
Lactating mare	2.5%
Obese horses on weight loss regime	1.5–2%

Table 8.5 Typical daily feed intakes (appetite).

The issue of dry matter (DM) can be confusing. It is a common error to assume that hay and concentrate are 100% dry matter; they are actually about 88% dry matter (12% water). There are two ways of deaing with this using the simple method. If the horse is stabled and fed hay and compound feed or grain, which are all approximately the same DM of 88%, the intake can be calculated on a fresh weight (as fed) basis, and the horse fed at 2.3% of bodyweight rather than 2%.

For example:
A 500 kg horse has a DM intake of 2% of his bodyweight = 10 kg
10 kg DM can be obtained from 10/(88/100) kg of 88% DM feed such as hay and cubes
= 11.36 kg hay and cubes

The second and more accurate way to deal with DM is to convert all feeds and forages to dry matter before including them in the diet (see Table 8.6 or refer to the feed label).

For example:
1kg of hay or cubes as fed = 0.704 kg DM (1 × 88/100, since both are 88% DM)
1kg haylage = 0.65 kg DM (1 × 65/100, assuming a haylage with 65% DM)
1kg spring grass = 0.2 kg DM (1 × 20/100, since spring grass is about 20% DM)

Hay	85–90%
Haylage	60–75%
Young spring grass	20%
Mature grass (late summer/winter)	28%
Compounds (mixes and cubes)	85–90%
Cereal grains	86–88%
Soaked sugar beet pulp	20%*
Fresh carrots	20%

*depends on how much water is used to soak

Table 8.6 Dry matter of typical horse feeds.

	Forage %	Concentrate %
Maintenance	80–100	0–20
Light work	80	20
Light work (ponies/good doers)	80–100	0–20
Moderate work	60	40
Moderate work (ponies/good doers)	70	30
Intense work	50	50
Stallion in breeding season	70	30
Pregnant mares		
Months 1–8	as for maintenance	
Months 9–11	60–70	30–40
Lactating mares		
Months 1–3	50	50
Months 3–6	60	40
Growing youngster		
Weanling	50	50
Yearling	50–60	40–50
2 year old +	as for maintenance	

Table 8.7 Recommended forage to concentrate ratios (based on Thoroughbreds and their crosses unless stated).

The ratios in Table 8.7 are strictly to be used as a guide, and many types of horses will not require such high amounts of concentrate feed as suggested. In addition, because of the wide range of feeds available, it is not always necessary to use these ratios. More information on meeting nutritional requirements without feeding moderate to high levels of concentrate feed is given after this section. Also, for horses who need to gain or lose weight, see the relevant section later in this chapter.

Example 1

500 kg Thoroughbred × Connemara in light work, in ideal body condition (hay as the forage):

Expected feed intake = 2% of 500 kg = 10 kg
Appropriate forage:concentrate ratio = 80:20
$$= 8 \text{ kg forage and 2 kg concentrate}$$
$$\text{(DM levels)}$$

Adjust to actual levels of feed as fed = (8/0.88) = 9 kg forage and (2/0.88) = 2.3 kg concentrate

With average hay, a low-energy compound feed would be suitable for this horse. Note that if the feed is recommended to be fed at 3–4 kg, the above diet would need to be supplemented with a broad-spectrum vitamin and mineral supplement.

Example 2

450 kg Thoroughbred eventer in moderate work, in ideal body condition and eats up well (hay as the forage):

Expected feed intake =2.5% of 450 kg = 11.25 kg
Appropriate forage:concentrate ratio   = 60:40
$$= 6.75 \text{ kg forage and 4.5 kg}$$
$$\text{concentrate (DM levels)}$$

Adjust to actual levels of feed as fed = (6.75/0.88) = 7.7 kg forage and (4.5/0.88) = 5 kg concentrate

With average hay, a moderate- to high-energy compound feed would be suitable for this horse, and should be split into three meals per day. Alternatively, a higher energy forage such as haylage could be fed, and then a low- to moderate-energy compound would be suitable.
E.g. Same horse (haylage with 65% DM as the forage)

Adjust to actual levels of feed as fed = (6.75/0.65) = 10.4 kg forage and 5 kg concentrate (as above)

Example 3

570 kg Warmblood mare in the final trimester, in ideal body condition (hay as the forage):

Expected feed intake = 2% of 570 kg = 11.4 kg
Appropriate forage:concentrate ratio = 70:30
$$= 8 \text{ kg forage and 2 kg concentrate}$$
$$\text{(DM levels)}$$

Adjust to actual levels of feed as fed = (8/0.88) = 9 kg forage and (2/0.88) = 2.3 kg concentrate

With average hay, a low-energy compound feed would be suitable for this horse. Note that, if the feed is recommended to be fed at 3–4 kg, the above diet would need to be supplemented with a broad-spectrum vitamin and mineral supplement.

Choosing the compound feed

As described in Chapter 6, a wide variety of concentrate compound feeds are available and it is not necessary to feed any horse, no matter how hard-working, high levels of dietary starch nowadays. Most horses would benefit from higher levels of fibre and oil rather than high-starch compound feeds. In fact, the latest research shows that growing horses should be fed diets high in fibre and oil and that dietary starch should be kept to a minimum. Check starch levels of stud and youngstock feeds before choosing them, and try to source feeds with starch contents under 20%. The more concentrate is fed to the horse, the more important it is to select feeds with low starch contents.

The simple method of ration formulation was probably first developed for horses stabled full time with hay as the only forage, and using traditional compound feeds. Nowadays, many horses are turned out to pasture for at least part of the day, even during winter, and more nutritious forages are available, making the forage:concentrate ratios less useful. In addition, other types of compound feed are available, including concentrated 'feed balancers', designed to be fed in small quantities. Therefore, this simple method is a very loose guide to feeding, and is most useful where average hay is fed with traditional compound feeds.

Current best practice using the simple method

In reality, most horses should be fed forage ad lib, allowing them a more natural and healthy eating pattern, therefore the forage:concentrate ratios should be used loosely. The exceptions are: an obese horse, a horse whose 'normal' appetite is greater than 2.75–3% of his bodyweight per day (e.g. more than 15 kg per day for a 500 kg horse), or a greedy performance horse just before competing or hunting. These horses would tend to gain weight on ad lib forage, therefore their forage intake should be limited to 2% of their bodyweight, and forage with a relatively low nutrient content selected. (For further information, see Feeding for Weight Loss, this chapter.)

Ad lib feeding allows the horse to eat as much forage as he chooses, and extra feed would be added if and when necessary to maintain condition, rather than adhering to a set forage: concentrate ratio and limiting forage. The forage should be chosen according to the horse's circumstances.

For horses with increased nutrient requirements, including those in moderate or intense work, growing horses, pregnant mares in their final trimester and lactating mares, a more nutritious forage such as haylage may be necessary. Alternatively, a high-energy forage such as quick-dried grass or alfalfa can replace up to a third of the usual forage. Careful choice of forage may result in no concentrate feed being necessary, although some vitamin and/or mineral supplementation will probably be necessary. Very hard-working horses, lactating mares and young hot-blood horses (e.g. Arab, Thoroughbred) are always likely to require some concentrate feed.

> **Note:** diets can be formulated from no prior knowledge of the horse, but because of the large variation in individual energy requirements, in practice this is less accurate than utilizing information about the horse's current ration.

When starting to make up feeds in practice, it is useful to know the weight of a scoop of each type of feed used, so that changes can be made more accurately. Once the weight of one scoop is known, the scales can be put away. For a quick guide, the typical weight of feeds in a typical plastic horse feed scoop (2.5 litre volume) is given in Table 8.8. Note that the scoop is filled level, not heaped.

A plastic bowl scoop with a capacity of 2.5 litres.

Feed	2.5 litre level scoop
Cubes/nuts	1.7 kg
Coarse mix (basic)	1.4 kg
Hay-replacement chaff	300 g
Molassed chaff	300 g
Quick-dried grass	178 g
Quick-dried molassed alfalfa	400 g
Molassed sugar beet pulp nuts	1.6 kg
Oats	1.2 kg

Table 8.8 Typical weights of feeds in one level 2.5 litre plastic 'bowl' scoop.

Feeding for weight gain

If a horse is healthy but too thin, i.e. the condition score (fat covering) is too low, and he needs to gain weight, more calories are required in the diet. Horses gain weight by eating more energy per day than they require for their daily activities, so there is some left to put into store, as fat. Increasing dietary calorie (energy) supply can be achieved in a variety of ways, but the most effective method is to increase the energy content and overall amount of the forage first. Then, if necessary, the compound feed could be increased or changed to a higher-energy feed. Finally, extra calorific additions can be made to the diet, such as sugar beet pulp and vegetable oil.

Forage

Always offer forage ad lib to an underweight horse and, as mentioned above, change to a more nutritious forage, higher in energy. Changing the forage rather than the concentrate usually has more impact on dietary energy because most horses are fed more forage than concentrate feed.

So, for example, changing from:
9 kg fresh weight late-cut hay (7 MJ/kg DM) = 56 MJ energy
to:
9 kg fresh weight early-cut hay (9 MJ/kg DM) = 71 MJ energy
gives a total increase of 15 MJ energy per day.

Whereas changing from:
3 kg fresh weight pony nuts (9 MJ/kg DM) = 23.8 MJ energy
to:
3 kg fresh weight conditioning cubes (12 MJ/kg DM) = 31.7MJ energy
gives a total increase of just 7.9 MJ energy per day

(These calculations incorporate the 0.88 figure for dry matter.)

Earlier cut leafy hay is higher in energy than later cut stemmy hay. Most hay-lages tend to be higher in energy than hay, but there are exceptions. Therefore the energy content of the forage should be ascertained as accurately as possible. Another way of increasing the energy supplied by the forage portion of the diet is to replace some long forage (e.g. hay or haylage) with quick-dried chopped forage, such as grass or alfalfa. Both are available without added molasses (see Chapter 6) and this form is more suitable if they are to be fed in quantities of more than a kilo per day. Replacing 2 kg of a 7 MJ/kg DM hay with 2 kg of quick-dried grass (around 11 MJ/kg DM) will add about 7 MJ energy. Quick-dried forages are light and fluffy, or not as dense as most other feeds, so just 1 kg will fill a regular water bucket. The original forage should still be offered ad lib, with the quick-dried forage offered in a large trough or bucket alongside.

Concentrate feed

After the relevant changes have been made to the forage portion of the diet, the concentrate feed could either be changed to a higher-energy (conditioning) feed, or the current feed could be increased to the maximum recommended amount. When increasing the amount of concentrate feed, the rules for maximum starch intake must be adhered to. Starch intake must be restricted to a maximum of 2 g starch per kg of bodyweight per meal, which is 1 kg of starch per meal for a 500 kg horse. Feeding a maximum of 2 kg concentrate to a 500 kg horse per meal is a safe general guide. Ideally, the actual starch level of the feed of choice should be ascertained. If straight cereals are to be fed, refer to Chapter 6 for the starch contents of straights.

If large amounts of starchy feeds are given in an attempt to put weight on a horse, the result may be the opposite of what is desired. Large meals of starchy feed cause overflow of undigested starch into the hindgut, causing gut disturbance (see Chapter 4), which in turn disturbs normal digestion and absorption.

Compounds containing higher levels of fibre and lower levels of starch are safer to feed in larger quantities and these are a better choice for weight gain. Medium-energy, high-digestible fibre and oil compounds are ideal for weight gain, despite the fact they are often marketed as 'endurance horse' or 'slow-release energy' feeds. Sometimes, simply increasing the amount of concentrate feed is all that is necessary, and weight gain is possible from feeding 4 kg rather than 2 kg of low-energy pony nuts per day. It is the total amount of dietary energy that causes weight gain or loss, not specific types of concentrate feed. The feed bag label or the company helpline should be consulted for more information on maximum recommended amounts of individual compound feeds.

If chaff or chop is added to concentrate feed, a high-energy version should be used, for example quick-dried grass or alfalfa with or without added molasses and/or oil.

Extra calorific additions

Adding moderate- to high-energy feeds to the current diet will also help promote weight gain. Sugar beet pulp is a palatable, medium-energy feed that can be fed safely in much larger quantities than many horse owners feed it. It should be weighed before soaking, because after soaking about three-quarters to four-fifths of the weight is water (which has no calorie content). The energy level in sugar beet is similar to a medium-energy compound feed, yet it is very low in starch and high in digestible fibre. Sugar beet can be fed instead of, or with, the concentrate feed, and it can safely be fed at quantities similar to concentrates – i.e. up to half of the total diet. Total meal size (excluding chaff or chop) should not exceed 0.4 kg per 100 kg bodyweight (2 kg for a 500 kg horse), including the dry weight sugar beet pulp (before soaking). Simply changing to a more nutritious forage, increasing the concentrate feed and adding 1 or 2 kilos of sugar beet per day will in most cases cause appropriate weight gain.

If more calories are required than can be fed with all of the above recommendations, then vegetable oil can be added. Vegetable oil is the highest-energy horse feed available, and horses cope well with much higher levels than normally fed. Introduce oil gradually, increasing up to a maximum of about 60 ml per 100 kg bodyweight (around 300 ml per day for a 500 kg horse). Feeding 300 ml oil (about 270 g, since 1 ml oil weighs about 0.9 g) adds an extra 9.5 MJ of energy to the diet.

Feeding for weight loss

Horses with condition scores of 4 or over should lose weight, because such fatness is associated with a range of diseases including laminitis. Horses lose weight by eating less energy per day than they require for their daily activities, so they use energy from their fat stores.

Decreasing dietary calories (energy) is easy in theory, but can be difficult in practice. The biggest challenge is reducing dietary energy while, at the same time, fulfilling the horse's need to chew and the need for gut fill. The most effective regime includes very low-energy forage that keeps the horse chewing while also restricting energy intake.

Forage

The lowest-energy forage should be obtained for horses on a weight loss regime. Late-cut stemmy hay, or late-cut stemmy high-fibre haylage are lower in energy and better choices than early-cut leafy forages. Straw is a useful forage for weight loss, and it can be either fed alone, or mixed with hay or haylage to reduce the overall nutrient content of the forage. Straw is perfectly safe for horses if introduced gradually, fed with ad lib water and fed only to horses with good dental function. Many horse owners worry about feeding straw because they have heard of it causing impactions and colic, but these colic cases are usually a result a horse who has not adapted to eating straw being stabled suddenly on a straw bed and effectively being given ad lib straw. The horse then nibbles straw all night and impactions can result.

Most pasture grass is a medium- to high-energy feed that tends to be eaten quickly. Therefore, most fat horses should have their grass intake restricted, either by a strip-grazing regime or by being turned out on a pasture that has been grazed well down, and being given supplementary low-energy forage. Strip grazing can be carried out with electric fencing that is moved regularly to allow access to new grass. The amount of new space per day is adjusted according to the horse's condition.

A horse wearing a grazing muzzle.

Supplementary low-energy forage should always be offered where there is very little grass available, to avoid starving and the intake of large amounts of soil. Muzzles can be used to reduce the intake rate of grass, and they are successful for many horses. However, muzzles that allow *some* grass intake should be used to avoid unhealthy long periods of fasting. Supervision and special care is needed for horses wearing muzzles to avoid abrasions caused by rubbing, catching in fences and suchlike.

If the forage is downgraded to a less nutritious type, no extra concentrate is fed and pasture access is restricted and the horse still does not lose weight, then forage should be restricted to 1.5% of the bodyweight per day (7.5 kg DM forage for a 500 kg horse, or about 8.3 kg average fresh weight hay). This forage must be fed in several small batches over 24 hours to avoid long periods of fasting. Fasting for more than a few hours is very unhealthy for horses. Fat horses or ponies who are fasted have a high risk of a potentially fatal disease called hyperlipidaemia. This condition is more common in ponies and donkeys and is a real risk for very overweight animals who have their forage restricted too severely (see Chapter 13).

Any other additions?

No concentrate feed should be given because it is not necessary, regardless of what some feed bag labels state. Absolutely no cereals, starchy or sugary feeds should be given, because fat horses are often insulin-resistant and such feeds will worsen this problem. However, if other horses on the yard or in the pasture are being fed, low-energy feeds may be necessary to avoid fighting. Carrots or plain chopped straw chaff can be fed or, if cost is not an issue, hay replacer chaffs or specific 'good doer' or 'low calorie' compound chaffs can be used.

A source of micronutrients must be fed to horses on weight loss regimes because low-energy forage will be short of some essential nutrients. Either a broad-spectrum supplement with plenty of macrominerals included, or a bespoke product for horses on calorie-restricted diets (e.g. some balancer-type products) should be fed.

The fat horse should be exercised as much as possible. Exercise increases the daily energy requirement; therefore, on an energy-restricted diet, fat stores will be used up to meet the increased requirement. As with all exercise programmes, workload should be increased gradually to avoid injury. Exercise also boosts the action of insulin and helps to normalize the blood nutrient and hormone profiles of fat horses, which in theory makes them healthier and less at risk of laminitis.

More precise calculations for ration formulation, using nutrient requirements

For the purpose of this section, nutrient levels from the latest published nutrient requirements will be given. These levels are the minimum requirements. The publication is called *The Nutrient Requirements for Horses* and was produced in 1989 by the National Research Council in the USA. It is, in fact, now rather out of date, and a new edition was expected by 2005, but was not available by the time this book was written.

The 'nutrients' that will be worked with in this section are energy, protein and lysine (an indicator of protein quality), the requirements of which have not been reassessed dramatically since 1989 (unlike those of some other nutrients, including vitamin E). Typical dry matter intakes and the different classes of horse (working, growth and reproducing) have been outlined in the previous section.

Although formulating feed rations by these methods *should* provide optimal nutrient levels for any given horse, it remains the case that individuals show differences in factor such as metabolic rates, growth rates, temperament, etc. Therefore, the individual horse must always be monitored closely and, if necessary, observed factors such as condition, growth and performance should take precedence over theoretical requirements in determining adjustments to the ration.

Energy requirement equations

Energy requirements are described below as megajoules (MJ) of digestible energy (DE) per day. BW is bodyweight.

Maintenance

Horses from 200–600 kg   DE = (5.9 + 0.13 BW) MJ

Horses over 600 kg   DE = (7.61 + 0.1602 BW − 0.000063BW²)

For example:

Daily energy requirement of a 500 kg horse at maintenance:

5.9 + (0.13 × 500) = 70.9 MJ DE

Working horses

Predicting energy requirements for working horses is very difficult because of the huge variation in factors, including individual temperament, type of work, environmental conditions and suchlike. Ongoing research is investigating more accurate ways of measuring the energy requirements of exercise in horses but, for the purpose of this section, conversion factors will be given for light, moderate and intense work. A similar situation exists for reproducing and growing horses. Different breeds and how they are managed – e.g. stabled or turned out at all times in addition to their temperament – will affect individual energy requirements. Again, conversion factors that provide a guide are given.

Working horses generally

Light work	Maintenance DE × 1.25
Moderate work	Maintenance DE × 1.5
Intense work	Maintenance DE × 2

Breeding stallions

Maintenance DE × 1.25 (as for light work)

Pregnant mares

0–8 months	As for maintenance DE
9 months	Maintenance DE × 1.11
10 months	Maintenance DE × 1.13
11 months	Maintenance DE × 1.2

Lactating mares

200–299 kg BW

0–3 months	Maintenance DE + (0.04 BW × 3.318)
3 months to weaning	Maintenance DE + (0.03 BW × 3.318)

300–600 kg

0–3 months	Maintenance DE + (0.03 BW × 3.318)
3 months to weaning	Maintenance DE + (0.02 BW × 3.318)

Growing horses (4–24 months of age)

Maintenance DE + $((4.81 + 1.17x - 0.023x^2) \times ADG) \times 4.184$

Where x is the age in months and ADG is average daily gain in kg. For guidance, the average daily gain for horse who will weigh 500 kg when mature is: 0.65 kg at 6 months; 0.5 kg at 12 months; 0.35 kg at 18 months and 0.2 kg at 24 months. (For practical illustration, see Example 2 on page 150.)

Growing horses in training (up to 24 months of age)

Growing horse DE $\times$ 1.5

After 2 years, the growing horse's nutrient requirements are similar to an adult's (for more information see Chapter 9).

Weight gain and loss

For weight gain, the total DE for each class or life stage of horse should be multiplied by 1.1. For weight loss, the total DE for each class of life stage of horse should be multiplied by 0.9.

Protein and Lysine requirement equations

Crude protein requirement is calculated from the energy requirement for all classes apart from lactating mares, whose protein requirements depend on milk production rates. For ease, a percentage of total dietary protein is given for lactating mares. Lysine requirements are calculated from crude protein.

		Crude protein (g/day)	Lysine (g/day)
Maintenance & work		(40 × DE)/4.184	0.035 × crude protein (g)
Breeding stallions		As for maintenance	0.035 × crude protein (g)
Pregnant mares		(44 × DE)/4.184	0.035 × crude protein (g)
Growing horses:	weanlings	DE × 12	0.5g × MJ DE
	1 to 2 years	DE × 10.8	0.45g × MJ DE
		Crude protein, total diet	
Lactating mares	0–4 months	12–13%	0.035 × crude protein (g)
	4 months +	10–11%	0.035 × crude protein (g)

It can be seen that lysine should be 3.5% of the total protein for all classes apart from growing horses up to 2 years, who require more.

Dietary energy, protein and lysine requirement calculations

Example 1: Pregnant mare in final trimester, 450 kg bodyweight.

Digestible energy = $5.9 + (0.13 \times 450) \times 1.2 = 77.28$MJ

Crude protein = $(44 \times 77.28)/4.184 = 813$g
    which is equivalent to 9% protein in the total diet if the mare was eating 9 kg dry matter per day (2% of her bodyweight)

Lysine = $0.035 \times 813 = 28.45$ g.

Example 2: 7-month old Thoroughbred weanling colt with an average daily gain of 0.65 kg, a bodyweight of 230 kg and an expected adult bodyweight of 500 kg.

Digestible energy = $5.9 + (0.13 \times 230) + (4.81 + 1.17x - 0.023x^2) \times$ ADG$) \times 4.184$
        = $(35.8) + (7.72 \times 4.184)$
        = 68 MJ

Crude protein = $68 \times 12 = 817$ g
    which is equivalent to 14% protein in the total diet if the weanling was eating 5.75 kg dry matter (2.5% of his bodyweight per day)

Lysine = $0.5 \times$ DE = 34g
    which is equivalent to 0.04% of the total dietary protein.

Example 3: 575 kg fit Thoroughbred eventer in intense work.

Digestible energy = $5.9 + (0.13 \times 575) \times 2 = 161$ MJ

Crude protein = $(40 \times 161)/4.184 = 1539$ g
    which is equivalent to 10.7% protein in the total diet if the horse was eating 14.4 kg dry matter (2.5% of his bodyweight per day)

Lysine = $0.035 \times 1539 = 53.9$g.

Readers who wish to study these calculations in more detail can refer to the NRC 1989 publication cited, and other scientific equine nutrition textbooks. An outline of all the known nutrient requirements for a 500 kg horse at maintenance was given in Chapter 4. For further details on feeding performance horses, breeding stock and youngstock, old horses, and sick horses or those on box rest (i.e. confined), refer to the relevant chapters.

Practical feeding guidelines

Access to water

Ideally, horses should have access to clean, fresh water at all times; although they are well adapted to drinking just once a day, they will choose to drink more often when given free choice. Water intake varies widely according to feed, and intake by a horse grazing spring pasture (80% water content) is very low. An average horse on a dry diet in a moderate to cool environment will consume about 25–30 litres per 24 hours (about 5 litres per 100 kg bodyweight), but this is an estimate and individual intake varies. Automatic waterers and self-filling troughs are less labour-intensive than buckets, but make it difficult to monitor intake, unless meters are fitted. Water does not need to be withheld after feeding because it does not 'wash out' the stomach contents. Water buckets and troughs should be

Water should be fresh, and available from clean containers.

cleaned regularly, especially field troughs, which may easily be forgotten. Water buckets in stables should be emptied and filled with fresh water every day, rather than being simply topped up.

Storage and hygiene

Feeds should be stored in a cool, dry, rodent-proof place. Excess heat and sunlight can reduce the potency of the vitamins in fortified feeds. Mouldy feed should never be given because it could contain poisonous mycotoxins, which are produced by mould fungi. Horses are, by nature, fussy feeders, and will refuse feed that they have eaten close to a period of illness in the past. Feed containers should be kept clean and ideally washed out after every use. Accessories such as mixing spoons and scoops should also be kept clean. Grain and compound feeds should not be kept longer than their recommended use-by dates because they contain the eggs of mites, which will hatch in humid, warm weather. Neither the mites nor infested feed are poisonous to horses, but they do make feed unpalatable and have a strong, musty, sweet smell. A heavy infestation will look like sand sprinkled around the feed, and the mites, which are tiny, may be seen moving slowly. The mites will quickly infest other feeds in the feed room, and if they are suspected the feed must be removed and destroyed, and the whole feed room thoroughly cleaned. Keeping floors and walls clean and clear of spilled feed will help reduce the risk of cereal mite infestation.

A clean, tidy feed room will help with feed hygiene.

All hay, no matter how dust-free it appears, should be soaked or steamed for around half an hour before being fed. Even the cleanest-looking hay contains huge amounts of dust and mould spores, which can cause respiratory disease and recurrent airway obstruction (RAO, previously called COPD) in stabled and field-kept horses. Haylage is a better choice of forage for stabled horses. Grain, chaffs and dry compounds (those not mixed with molasses or oil) should be dampened with water before feeding – particularly grain, which can be very dusty.

Soaking hay – the water should be discarded afterwards.

Design and use of feed containers

Feed containers should ideally not have metal handles or any other attachments that could cause injury, and should be of such design that they can be cleaned easily. Containers made entirely from plastic, or rubber flexible buckets such as tub trugs (see photo) make excellent feed bowls. Ideally, all feed including forage should be placed at ground level, to encourage a normal eating posture and helping to ensure more normal wearing of teeth. However, large troughs for hay might be necessary at pasture, to limit wastage and avoid excess poaching. (At pasture, the area where horses are fed may need to be moved regularly to avoid poaching. Also, bear in mind that horses who tip their feed out on the ground may take in too much soil if bowls are placed on muddy

A safe feed bowl without metal handles.

areas.) Special hay mangers are available for the stable, which fit into the corner and allow a more natural eating posture. Haynets must be used with care. They are useful to minimize wastage and to extend eating time in horses fed very palatable haylage, but they do not allow a healthy posture and horses are at risk of getting their feet caught in them. At all times they must be tied to a breakable string. It has been known for horses (particularly shod horses) to get a foot caught in a haynet, struggle, and sustain such injuries that they have been euthanized.

Maximum amounts

All feeds with the exception of 'long' forage (e.g. grass hay) should be given in as many small meals per day as possible, and starch intake should be restricted to a maximum of 2 g starch per kg of bodyweight per meal, which is 1 kg of starch per meal for a 500 kg horse. Feeding a maximum of 2 kg concentrate to a 500 kg horse per meal is a safe general guide. It is not necessary to feed chaff with compounds, but adding it to pelleted feeds may help slow the rate of intake in greedy horses.

Make all changes gradually

Changes to the diet should be made gradually, to allow the gut microflora, digestive enzymes and nutrient transporters to adapt. Sudden changes may cause gastrointestinal disturbance and diarrhoea, and in some cases, colic. This rule applies to all feed and forage, and it is particularly important when introducing starchy feeds, vegetable oil and changing to new forage. Forages can vary widely in their nutrient content and, as mentioned earlier, impaction colic in a horse stabled suddenly on a straw bed is not uncommon. A pasture-kept horse who is going to be travelled should, if possible, be fed the forage he will be given in the box or trailer for a 7–10 days before travelling (see also Feeding and Transportation later this chapter).

When to feed

The old rule of not feeding within one hour before or after exercise is based on horses who worked hard and received large quantities of concentrate feed. Horses fed forage ad lib and no meals (e.g. those at pasture) can be exercised without feed being withdrawn, providing adequate warm-up periods are given. An hour should usually be allowed between a moderately large concentrate meal and exercise, to allow for digestion and the associated changes in circulation and fluid distribution. However, endurance horses can be trained to eat during their races, at the vet gates. Feeding small amounts of concentrate and free-choice forage (ideally grass) will do no harm and is likely to have benefits, including increasing fuel supply (from the concentrate) and an acid-buffering effect on the stomach. Horses performing in endurance events (including eventing) will benefit from having access to forage and plenty of water right up to the start of the competition, because the forage holds water within the gut, giving a useful reservoir of fluid during the extended period of exercise. Sprinting racehorses may benefit from having forage restricted to 1% of their bodyweight (no less) during the final 12 hours before their event, to reduce the extra weight of forage and fluid in their digestive tracts.

Feeding-related behavioural problems

Many horses, particularly in yards, anticipate feed time with great enthusiasm, and sometimes exhibit aggressive behaviour or noisy behaviour such as door banging. The first step in avoiding such unwanted behaviour is to ensure that horses are not hungry before meals are fed. Ideally all horses should have access to forage at all times, so they should not have fasted for long periods before being fed concentrate. Second, it should be noted that concentrate feed acts as a strong reward for behaviour, so a horse who exhibits any particular behaviour just before feeding is likely to repeat that behaviour in the future. The person feeding must therefore be aware of their timing, not giving a horse feed straight after he bangs the stable door, or exhibits aggressive behaviour such putting his ears back and threatening to bite. Horses will learn very quickly that they have to stand back in their stable if feed is not given until they carry out the required behaviour. The person involved must be committed to the retraining. It is a mistake to shout at horses banging stable doors, because the attention shouting gives them may, itself, act as reinforcement for that behaviour (i.e. the behaviour is more likely to be repeated).

When feeding groups of horses at pasture, the dominance hierarchy should be considered in order to minimize aggression at feed times. Placing feeds in a triangle or circular shape rather than a straight line has been shown to reduce aggression, possibly because all the horses can watch each other while maintaining their distance.

Feeding and transportation

Travelling tends to cause dehydration, because of the lack of free access to water, and sweating. Horses should be fully hydrated before a prolonged journey, particularly if travelling to a competition or event, because just 2% dehydration impairs performance. Fresh, clean water and forage should be freely available right up to the time of departure. On long journeys, water should be offered during every rest stop; preferably every 3–4 hours and at intervals of no more than every 6 hours.

During journeys of more than an hour or two, horses should always be offered forage to avoid periods of fasting and the resulting gut problems. Soaked hay or haylage are better than dry hay, to increase water intake. Offer horses travelling for more than an hour or two soaked sugar beet pulp and/or dampened dried grass or alfalfa, or soaked high-fibre cubes or grass nuts. Whatever is fed during a journey must have been incorporated into the daily diet prior to travelling, to accustom the horse's digestive system to that feed, so pre-planning is an important factor in travelling. For horses who travel regularly, soaked sugar beet pulp is an ideal daily feed, since holds many times its weight in water. For very long journeys, salt can be added to the soaked feed.

Never hang nets of hay or haylage outside the trailer or horsebox because these will pick up pollution and dirt from the road. Store extra nets in the trailer or box, or in bags in the towing vehicle.

Forage should be available on all but the shortest journeys.

Note

1 The section of this chapter on Condition Scoring makes reference to the following sources:

Leighton-Hardman, A. C. (1980) *Equine Nutrition*, Pelham Books, London, pp9–17.
Carroll, C. L. & Huntington, P. J. (1988), *Body condition scoring and weight estimation of horses*, Equine Veterinary Journal, 20, 41–45.
Henneke, D. R. et al (1983), *Relationship between condition score, physical measurements and body fat percentage in mares*, Equine Veterinary Journal, 15, 371–372.
Kienzle, E. & Schramme, S. (2004) *Body condition scoring and prediction of bodyweight in adult warmblood horses*, Pferdeheilkunde 20, 517–524.

chapter 9

Feeding for reproduction and growth

Correct nutrition is fundamental for healthy new life, and unbalanced diets in both the broodmare during pregnancy and the young, growing horse may cause irreversible damage later in the young horse's life. During growth, overfeeding is potentially more damaging than underfeeding. Much of our knowledge of nutrition for growth and development has come from studies of Thoroughbred horses; therefore it should be extrapolated with care to general riding horses and ponies. Stallions, and broodmares during the first 8 months of pregnancy, do not have higher nutrient requirements than adult horses at maintenance. In practice, however, all individuals should be fed according to their condition. During the final 3 months of pregnancy the mare's requirements rise as the foal develops, and during the first 3 months of lactation, the mare's requirements are at their highest. Refer to the Appendix for the nutrient requirements of breeding horses and youngstock.

Feeding broodmares

Prior to conception

Conception rates are best in mares on a rising plane of nutrition, whose body-weight has been increasing from lean to good in condition scoring terms (score 2 on the 0–5 scale) during the preceding period. The ideal situation is turnout on good grass, although this depends on the time of year the mare is being covered. Thoroughbred mares sent to stud early in the season (who may be under artificial light), should ideally be kept in lean to good condition then their feed increased for the final few weeks before they are covered. If they are already pregnant, their body fat covering should be monitored very carefully and they will

A group of mares and foals.

usually be on increased feed by late pregnancy (see below). Broodmares should not be overweight – the mare's condition score should be checked several months before she is covered, so that adjustments can be made to her diet to ensure she is in good, not fat condition.

The first 8 months of pregnancy

During the first 8 months of pregnancy, the mare's nutrient requirements are no different from those of a resting non-pregnant mare. The foetus does most of its growing during the last 3 months, and this is the period when the mare's nutrient requirements increase. If the mare is in work, she should be fed according to the level of exercise. The diet should be carefully balanced with adequate micronutrient supply, adding a broad-spectrum supplement if necessary.

The final 3 months of pregnancy

The mare's nutrient supply should be increased gradually, and special consideration should be given to micronutrients. The growing foetus not only requires adequate minerals for ongoing development, but must also lay down stores in the body for use during lactation, because the mare's milk does not supply adequate levels. During this time, the foetus begins to take up more and more space in the mare's abdomen, and some mares may have a reduction in appetite. The mare's condition should be monitored carefully, and she should remain in good, but not fat, condition. For good fertility after foaling, she should ideally be on a rising plane of nutrition once again. Such a regime is difficult if the mare has been allowed to gain too much fat in the early stages of pregnancy.

For a mare foaling in summer, good spring grass is the ideal feed in late pregnancy, but for a mare foaling in later winter or spring, the ration might need to be adjusted more radically. Mares may eat less than 2% of their bodyweight as their final month approaches, and the quality rather than quantity of feed may need to be increased. Ideally, the quality of the forage should be increased to reduce reliance on compound feed. Some grass hay could be replaced with alfalfa hay, haylage could be fed instead of hay, or a couple of kilos per day of chopped quick-dried grass or alfalfa could be fed in addition to ad lib forage. Most mares on forage of average quality will require compound feed, at a ratio of about 20% of the diet during months 9 and 10 and rising to 30% of the diet for the final month of pregnancy. However, these are guidelines and each individual mare should be fed according to her condition. For ponies, pony crosses, some Warmbloods and other good doers, a low-energy compound may be sufficient and a stud feed will not be necessary. In such cases, a broad-spectrum supplement should be added to increase micronutrient supply.

Research has shown that feeding mares supplementary vitamin E and selenium during their final 3 months of pregnancy has beneficial effects on the immunoglobin concentration of their colostrum, which resulted in better acquired immunity in their foals. Total diet levels should be about 2,000 mg (200 mg/kg diet) vitamin E and 3 mg (0.3 mg/kg diet) selenium for a 500 kg mare eating 10 kg dry matter. The mare should ideally be allowed access to the environment in which she is to foal for a couple of weeks prior to the expected foaling date to allow her to produce relevant antibodies that she can then pass on to her foal in colostrum.

During lactation

The mare's nutrient requirements are at their highest during lactation, when she might be producing as much as 20 kg of milk per day. Her energy requirements double during this time. Mares generally produce about 3–4% of their bodyweight per day in milk during the first 12 weeks of lactation, then about 2–3% during the next 12 weeks. During early lactation the mare will produce milk at the cost of her own body tissues, and weight loss during this time is common. Ideally, the mare and foal should be turned out on good grass, which gives the mare plenty of good-quality feed and gives the foal room to move around and develop normally. For mares with limited access to pasture, special care should be given to

A mare, with her foal suckling.

choosing good-quality forage, and a compound concentrate feed may need to be fed, at 30–40% of the total ration (depending on the forage quality). If straight cereals are fed, they must be supplemented with a source of good-quality protein (e.g. soya bean meal) and minerals (e.g. a broad-spectrum supplement with good calcium levels) to ensure good-quality milk.

The mare can be fed at 2.5% of her bodyweight. Clean, fresh water should be available at all times; a lack of water will suppress milk production. Ongoing assessment of the mare is important, and condition scoring every couple of weeks is useful and will help to avoid over-zealous feeding in an attempt to maximize milk production without the mare losing weight.

Feeding stallions

In theory, stallions at stud do not have higher nutrient requirements than non-breeding stallions or geldings. However, some stallions become restless during the breeding season, spending time pacing and less time eating, and their rations need to be adjusted accordingly. Concentrate feed should be added as necessary. Each stallion should be fed individually, aiming for a good but not fat condition (score 2 to 3 on the 0–5 scale) and ideally kept well exercised. Working stallions should be fed according to their exercise level.

As for all types of horses, special care should be given to ensure micronutrient supply is balanced, because poor sperm quality in stallions has been attributed to deficiencies in vitamins. Always ensure adequate intake of vitamins E and A, and if the stallion holds his condition on forage alone, feed a broad-spectrum supplement.

Feeding youngstock

Both nutrient supply and its timing and the overall amount of feed have huge effects on the growing youngster. The ideal situation is a smooth growth curve; slower, more gradual growth over a longer period is healthier than producing a fast-growing youngster who matures more quickly. We will investigate nutrient requirements first, followed by practical feeding and weaning strategies and how these affect growth and development.

The newborn foal

Newborn foals should be up and suckling within 2 hours of birth, and many will take their first drink within half an hour to an hour. Foals are born without their own immunity, and must obtain colostrum containing immunoglobulins from the mare within the first 12 hours after birth. These important immunoglobulins can only pass through the foal's intestinal wall for up to 24 hours after birth. If the

A newborn foal.

mare has lost her colostrum through leakage, or for some other reason the foal does not receive it, colostrum replacement is necessary, either from another mare or as a commercial product. Colostrum is rich in vitamin A; therefore this will also need to be replaced if necessary, either via the commercial colostrum product or injection by the vet.

(Subsequent to the initial immunity provided via the colostrums, the foal continues to acquire immunity via antibodies from the mare for the first 3 to 4 weeks of life.)

Suckling also encourages the passage of the meconium, which is present in the large intestine at birth. If the meconium is not passed, the foal will show signs of discomfort and straining, and veterinary assistance should be sought.

The first few months

Foals grow most rapidly during their first 3 months of life, and for the first few weeks usually rely primarily on their dam's milk for nutrition. Suckling foals will take in up to 3% of their bodyweight in milk (dry matter) at around 10 days, and this will drop to about 2% at about 40 days. Most foals start to nibble at their dam's feed and forage within 10–21 days of age. If there is a problem with the mare's milk supply and the foal is not growing normally, creep feed should be offered, starting with milk pellets, and changing gradually to a proprietary young foal feed, preferably one based on fibre rather than starch.

Researchers have found that foals who developed crib-biting had spent more time suckling as foals, and more time nuzzling their dams, which could indicate hunger and reduced milk supply. Such foals would also be at risk of gastric ulcers, and starchy concentrate feed is contra-indicated. Further research is necessary before solid conclusions can be drawn, but there is good evidence that concentrate feeds high in fibre and fat are healthier for growing youngsters than starchy feeds. This is explored further in the section on weaning.

For foals with normal growth rates, grass intake should be encouraged by keeping the mare and foal at pasture whenever possible, or good quality forage should be offered as an alternative for stabled or early foals.

The purpose of creep feed for pre-weaned foals is to help their digestive tracts adjust to such feed in preparation for weaning, thus ensuring that growth interruption is minimized. Weaning is a stressful time and both feeding and management regimes must be optimized to minimize stress. Forage adaptation is more important than concentrate because, during and after weaning, the foal will rely on plenty of forage for normal physical and mental development. Overfeeding concentrate feed either before or after weaning is unhealthy and increases the risk of developmental abnormalities. As a general guide, a maximum of 0.5 kg of concentrate per 100 kg bodyweight should be fed pre-weaning. A 240 kg 6-month-old foal who will have an adult bodyweight of around 500 kg would be fed a maximum of 1.2 kg concentrate feed pre-weaning. The type of concentrate feed should be selected according to the breed or type of foal, and the individual condition of that foal, which will depend on grass availability and the mare's milk production. It should not be assumed that all foals will require youngstock or stud feeds, and a low-energy maintenance concentrate may be more suitable for pony and pony cross foals, Warmbloods, other good doers and those in good condition.

Although condition scoring is not directly applicable to foals, similar techniques can be used to monitor their body fat covering. The normal average daily weight gain for Thoroughbreds is around 1–1.5 kg per day for the first 4 months, dropping thereafter to 0.7 kg at 6 months, 0.45 kg at 12 months and 0.35 kg at 18 months. Growth rates should not exceed these figures, and would be expected to be less in pony and draught-type breeds.

Weaning welfare

Research studies investigating the behaviour of foals around weaning time and during their first year of growth have enhanced the understanding of this stressful time, allowing the development of practical strategies that help reduce problems. Hopefully the days of box-weaning foals, giving them a little forage and buckets of weanling concentrate feed are over. High-fibre and low-starch diets are healthier for foals, especially during weaning, and the development of higher energy fibre-based feeds that support growth allow this guideline to be followed. Research has shown that foals given feed high in fibre and fat concentrates appeared less stressed, performed more grazing behaviour and were more inquisitive and calmer than those fed traditional concentrates high in starch and sugar. High-starch diets increases the risk of weanlings developing abnormal behaviour such as crib-biting. In fact, one research study showed that following weaning, foals fed starchy concentrates were four times more likely to develop crib-biting than those fed forage-based diets. Yet another reason for avoiding diets high in starch and sugar for growing youngsters is the high glycaemic index of such diets, which will be explained further later in this chapter (Avoiding Developmental Abnormalities).

Despite the fact that age at weaning does not appear to affect mature height or weight, ideally foals should be weaned at a minimum age of 6 months, by which time they will be eating independently and have a reduced milk intake. Foals should be offered the feed they will be given post-weaning at least several weeks before being taken away from their dams, so that their digestive systems are adapted to the diet. Sufficient nutrient supply to replace any dam's milk still being ingested should be given, but ideally in a feed based on fibre and fat, rather than a starchy concentrate. Forage should be of the highest quality, to reduce the need for concentrate feed, and grass hay can be 'upgraded' by offering quick-dried alfalfa or grass alongside. Foals not previously adapted to their post-weaning diet have a slowed growth rate that may be followed by a compensatory growth spurt, which exposes them to the risk of developmental abnormalities such as orthopaedic disease.

Weaning should be carried out gradually rather than abruptly, because this reduces stress. Stress is unhealthy in the foal and will also cause reduced appetite, which could in turn cause a slowed growth rate and the associated problems mentioned above. The ideal situation is to start with a group of mares and foals, from which single mares can be removed one at a time. If this is not possible, foals must be given company when separated from their mare. Weaned foals should have access to pasture (ideally all the time) and other horses or foals to socialize with. Pasture supplies the best feed for growing weanlings, and even late-born foals who are weaned during winter should be allowed access to pasture for as long as possible, with supplementary forage.

The aim for growing youngstock should always be to attain a steady increase in bodyweight and height. Compensatory growth spurts should be avoided by avoiding periods of underfeeding (especially around weaning) but rapid growth rates must also be avoided by adjusting the ration accordingly. After weaning, foals should never be allowed to get too fat; a lean condition is preferable to fat. Ideally, every fortnight the youngster should be weighed (from which average daily weight gain can be calculated) and have his height measured and condition (body fat covering) assessed.

From 6 months to 2 years

The most important factor in feeding youngstock is to monitor the individual and adjust the ration accordingly. Forage, ideally fresh growing grass, should always make up most of the ration. Pasture is the ideal environment for a growing youngster, providing good food and natural exercise, so youngsters are best kept outside, with good shelter and free access to water, ideally on a large pasture with hills. However, care should be taken to adjust the diet according to grass intake, because spring grass is very nutritious and can, in a matter of weeks, result in a very different diet from that in late winter. Concentrate feed should be reduced as pasture grows in the spring, and/or as the youngster is turned out for longer periods.

If, for any reason, forage cannot meet nutrient requirements then concentrate feed should be added with care, starting with small amounts and adjusting on an ongoing basis. Feed recommendations on bags of compounds are often too high, and should be referred to with care. The protein and energy requirements of youngstock are often overestimated, probably because of the traditional need to push the growth of Thoroughbreds as fast as possible for sales. Other breeds reared on pasture with little extra feed do not suffer the many problems that young, growing Thoroughbreds do, including joint and bone abnormalities or developmental orthopaedic disease (DOD) – see next section this chapter. Moderate underfeeding of young horses does not affect mature height or length, but just lengthens the time it takes for the horse to reach mature stature.

A general guideline is to feed weanlings 450 g of concentrate for every month of age until the age of 9 months, then decrease this by half and continue until the horse is 2 years old. An 8-month-old foal would receive 3.6 kg feed, and a 14-month-old yearling would receive 3.1 kg feed. This level of feed is too much for ponies, cross-breeds and youngsters with access to good grass, and would be applicable only for fast-growing breeds during winter with poor to moderate grass hay. Ponies, cross-breeds and other good doers could be fed good-quality forage and a good broad-spectrum growing horse supplement. For youngsters who require concentrate, compounds are the best choice because of their balanced nutrient profile. The correct balance of micronutrients and a source of good-quality protein (essential amino acids) are essentials for healthy growth and development.

As a general guide, young horses (Thoroughbreds and their crosses) achieve 60% of their mature weight and 90% of their mature height by 12 months of age.

A yearling at grass.

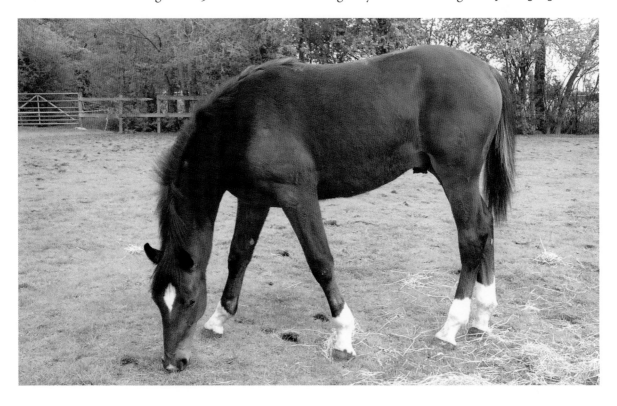

Expected weight as a percentage of adult weight at 6, 12 and 18 months (adult weight kg in brackets)

	6 months	12 months	18 months
Thoroughbred (500)	46	67	80
Arab (450)	46	66	80
Quarter Horse (450)	44	66	80
Pony (180)	55	75	84
Draught horse (600)	34	52	69

Expected height as a percentage of adult height at 6, 12 and 18 months (adult height in brackets)

	6 months	12 months	18 months
Thoroughbreds (16 hh)	83	90	95
Quarter horses (15 hh)	84	91	95
Part-bred Arabs (15.2 hh)	83	92	95

Table 9.1 Normal growth patterns for young horses.

After 2 years, the growing horse's nutrient requirements are similar to a mature adult, and feed should be appropriate to the type of horse and workload.

Avoiding developmental abnormalities

The term developmental orthopaedic disease (DOD) was coined in the 1980s to describe all the skeletal and joint problems seen in growing horses. DODs include osteochondritis dissecans (OCD), physitis (inflammation of the growth plates), subchondral bone cysts, angular limb deformities, flexural limb deformities and juvenile osteoarthritis. Normally, long bones lengthen at growth plates on either end as the young horse grows, and both the centre and the ends of the bones gradually ossify from cartilage into dense bone. There is also another growth plate at the end of each long bone, where cartilage gradually ossifies but leaves a layer of cartilage that becomes the articular (joint) cartilage. In the various forms of DOD, these normal processes are in some way disturbed.

Some types of DOD, such as angular limb deformities and physitis, often correct themselves but others, including OCD and subchondral bone cysts, often do not. In OCD and subchondral bone cysts there is a failure of the normal ossification of the ends of the long bones, in a process called osteochondrosis (OC). This abnormal development can cause lesions in the articular cartilage, and flaps may chip off. Many of these cases require surgery, the outcome of which is usually successful. OC is not simply caused by excess dietary energy, nutrients and rapid growth, but these, as well as nutrient imbalances, do seem to play important roles and should be avoided. There is a genetic predisposition to this condition, but further research is necessary before any screening programme or suchlike can be put into place. Certain breeds, including Warmbloods and Thoroughbreds are at higher risk.

While exercise does not appear to be linked to OC, clinical signs may be seen after exercise, probably resulting from displacement of a fragment of cartilage. Nevertheless, controlled exercise has a protective effect on the bones and joints of growing horses. High-protein diets do not seem to be linked to OC, yet such diets are usually high in energy and this could be the reason why protein was once believed to be the culprit. Various mineral imbalances have been implicated in cases of OC, including high phosphorus, low copper, and high zinc to copper ratios (greater than 5 zinc: 1 copper). Mineral intake should certainly be balanced, with a calcium to phosphorus ratio of at least 2:1, 20 mg copper per kilo diet (dry matter), and no more than 5 times that amount of zinc (preferably 40–60 mg/kg). More recently, diets with a high glycaemic index(i.e. those high in starch and sugar) have been linked to a higher risk of DOD. This effect is likely to occur through large fluctuations in blood glucose and insulin causing changes in bone maturation processes. A concentrate feed based on fibre and fat (with adequate good-quality protein) would therefore be a healthier choice than a feed based on starch and sugar.

With regard to cases of angular and flexural limb deformities and physitis many, as mentioned, are essentially self-correcting, although supportive treatment including hoof trimming and plastic shoeing (and sometimes joint surgery) may be required. In all cases, care should be taken that the foal is receiving a balanced diet and is not being overfed.

Feeding the orphaned foal

Caring for an orphaned foal involves a huge amount of work and should not be taken on lightly. In addition to meeting demanding nutritional needs, the foal's normal development depends on a mother-figure to help him learn about appropriate behaviour. An equal helping of love and leadership is very important, because a well-loved foal who is allowed to rule his handlers becomes a very dangerous adult horse.

If no foster mother can be found, the orphan can be hand-reared. Initially, provision of colostrum is the first priority, followed by a suitable milk replacer.

Commercial milk replacers are available, and should be fed following instructions for the first few days. After that time, the milk powder should be gradually diluted and a final milk substitute of around 10% dry matter, with fat of around 1% and protein of around 2% is appropriate. Most powders need to be diluted in 9 parts water to obtain 10% dry matter. Foals will take in between 2 and 3% of their body-weight in milk per day, and should be fed every few hours for the first couple of weeks. Most foals can be trained to take their milk from a bucket, helped by allowing them to suckle a finger dipped into the milk, then lowering their head into the bucket, which is best placed at the foal's shoulder level. Fresh faeces from an adult horse who has been treated for parasites should be made available to the orphan, from which he can nibble to help develop healthy gut microflora. Foals will naturally eat faeces for this purpose. Concentrate feed and leafy forage can be introduced within the first couple of weeks to encourage the foal to eat solid feed. Milk pellets can be mixed with youngstock feed to supplement liquid milk replacer.

Orphaned foals can be weaned off milk replacer when their solid food intake is at least 1 kg of creep feed (including concentrate and milk pellets) and 1 kg forage, based on a cross-bred or Thoroughbred horse expected to make around 400–500 kg mature weight.

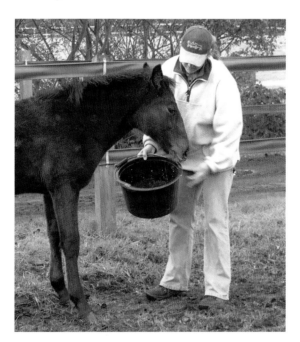

Feeding an orphaned foal from a bucket.

chapter 10

Feeding for physical performance

IN CONTRAST TO OTHER large herbivores such as cattle, horses are usually kept for their athletic ability rather than to produce meat or milk. Despite this, working horses have traditionally been fed in the same way as production animals, with emphasis on dietary protein and high levels of concentrate feed. Such diets are unsuitable for horses and miss out important factors such as dietary energy and electrolyte minerals.

Feed provides the nutrients that are used as fuel for physical exercise. Nutrient supply during training is at least as important as supply during competition. In fact, it is likely that more can be done to improve an individual's performance with nutrition during training than during the actual competition. Exercise of any type requires similar nutrients and horses used for different disciplines may not require significantly different diets. However, certain strategies may help to produce optimal performance.

Can performance be improved by adding a specific feed? Despite the fact that many commercial feed companies would like to think so, there is little evidence to support such a claim. It is more likely that correct nutrition can help a horse to reach his genetic potential. In trying to manipulate the diet to maximize performance, care should be taken to avoid competing horses having prohibited substances in their blood during competition.

Energy supply

Energy is the most important dietary factor for exercise. Energy fuels exercise, and when a horse starts to work (exercise), energy production in the body must increase dramatically from resting levels. Energy is not a nutrient as such, but is extracted by the body from other nutrients, primarily carbohydrates, oils and fats. Protein is used for energy to a much lesser extent, although some amino acids are used as a source of energy by some body cells.

Racehorses at the finish: feed provides the nutrients that are used as fuel.

Energy can be extracted by horses from all types of carbohydrate, including fibre. Very often, horses are initially fed any low-energy bagged feed along with forage then, once in work, their feed is changed to a moderate- or high-energy version. In reality, there is no such clear distinction. Horse move around all day, and this requires energy. In fact energy is required even when the horse is asleep! The difference is the rate of energy supply that is required. Once a horse starts to use his muscles more intensively, e.g. when he starts to trot and canter, the energy requirement – and thus supply – will increase many times over. Moderate- to high-energy bagged (compound) feeds are marketed for working horses because many will require the higher energy they supply. However, many other working horses will thrive on low-energy compound feeds, particularly if they are fed high-quality forage.

How energy is extracted from feed

Feed is broken down to its constituent parts during digestion and absorption. As explained in previous chapters, carbohydrates are broken down into small, single-sugar units or volatile fatty acids; fats are broken down into fatty acids; protein is broken down into amino acids. These small units can be used in the body's metabolic 'mill' for energy production. Horse feeds are generally described as having a certain amount of digestible energy per kilo, e.g. 8 or 10 MJ. When the feed is digested by the horse, its constituents supply this amount of energy. Different types of nutrients provide different amounts of energy, and this is the reason why high-fat feeds tend to be higher in energy than equivalent starchy grain feeds. A gram of the carbohydrate, starch, yields about 4 kcal (17 kJ) energy, and a gram of vegetable oil (fat) yields about 9 kcal (38 kJ) energy. Therefore 1 cupful of oil is higher in energy for the horse than 1 cupful of grain.

Energy storage in the body

If there was no way of storing energy in the body, the horse would need to eat food all the time, even during exercise. However, the body stores both carbohydrate and fat, which can be used when the horse begins to exercise. As explained in Chapter 4, protein is not normally used for energy, and plays other roles in the body. However, protein will be used for energy in the form of amino acids extracted from muscle and organs if a horse is starved, or if exercise is so strenuous or prolonged that the body has run out of all other energy stores.

Carbohydrate is stored as muscle and liver glycogen, and some free blood sugar (glucose). About 95% of glycogen is stored in the muscles. Glycogen is a large molecule made up of units of glucose, just like starch (the storage carbohydrate of plants). There is a limit to how much glycogen the horse's body can store – there is not an infinite supply. Glycogen stores in the average Thoroughbred horse are about 4,500 g, which is equivalent to about 75 MJ. The liver glycogen stores play an important role in maintaining blood glucose within very narrow limits, which is important for normal body function. Glycogen is used during exercise, and the rate at which it can be broken down and used for exercise depends on the concentration in the muscles. High concentrations can be broken down more quickly, which would benefit horses competing in sprinting disciplines or short jumping events.

Fat is stored in the body in much larger quantities than carbohydrate. Most of the body's fat is stored in adipose tissue under the skin and around the internal organs, with a small amount within the muscles. An average Thoroughbred horse has about 25 kg of fat stored in his body, equivalent to about 640 MJ. Excess fat stores are unhelpful for performance horses, because they add extra weight, which increases energy expenditure, and because they inhibit heat loss.

	Mass (kg)	Energy (MJ)
Glycogen	4.5	75
Fat	25	640

Table 10.1 'Fuel' stored in an average 500 kg horse.

The currency of energy

The energy extracted from dietary nutrients is ultimately converted to a substance called ATP (adenosine triphosphate). For energy to be used by the body, the ATP has to be split, releasing energy; a process that is going on all the time. One of the three phosphate molecules ATP contains is split off, and it becomes ADP (adenosine diphosphate). The released energy can be used for muscle contraction, but there is some wastage and about three-quarters is lost as heat. The body then converts this ADP back into ATP using the energy from food, via a complex metabolic 'mill'. There is only a small supply of ATP in the horse's body at any one time and, once the horse starts exercising, the ADP must be restored to ATP if the horse is to carry on exercising.

A racehorse galloping.

How energy is produced

There are three main energy pathways that 'fuel' the body; each uses a different biochemical pathway and produces ATP at different rates:

1. The ATP-phosphocreatine (PC) pathway.

2. Anaerobic (or lactic acid) pathway.

3. Aerobic pathway.

The ATP-PC pathway

How the body selects which pathway to use depends on the intensity of exercise and the supply of oxygen from breathing. It is important to note that the horse rarely uses just one pathway exclusively – in most circumstances a combination of pathways is used.

The ATP-PC pathway is a 'back up' because it can only fuel up to 5 or 6 seconds of maximal activity. It uses a compound called phosphocreatine (PC) that is stored in the muscles to regenerate ATP from ADP. It can produce energy instantly but stores of PC run out very quickly and after the 6 seconds the body will rely on other fuels to regenerate ATP so that it can continue exercising. The ATP-PC pathway would be used for a horse escaping a predator, or jumping one large fence.

The anaerobic pathway

Anaerobic means 'without air' or oxygen, and the anaerobic pathway can meet rapid, large requirements for energy. Using oxygen for energy supply from nutrients is much more efficient but not rapid enough to meet the energy needs from high-intensity exercise, such as a short sprint or an explosive jumping effort. The anaerobic pathway can use only muscle glycogen as fuel; this is broken down via a process called glycolysis. Glycolysis produces a substance called pyruvate, which is then processed to release energy (regenerate ATP) with the resultant by-product lactic acid. This rapid energy pathway cannot carry on producing energy because lactic acid builds up and interferes with continued muscle contraction, and because it uses glycogen at a very rapid rate. Lactic acid used to be thought of simply as a bad waste product but in fact high rates of production reflect a horse capable of high-intensity exercise. Furthermore, it is not really a waste product, because it is re-circulated and can either be used for ATP regeneration (along with oxygen in the aerobic system) or converted back to glucose in the liver, where it can be stored as glycogen. Lactic acid does not persist in the muscles for longer than about 15 minutes, and the muscle soreness or stiffness or other problems that occur after exercise and the following day are not caused by the presence of lactic acid, which is long gone by that time.

The aerobic pathway

Horses cannot continue a maximal effort using just the anaerobic pathway for more than a couple of minutes, so for any exercise with a duration longer than that, aerobic pathways must also come into play. Even our 'powerhouse' equine athletes such as Thoroughbred racehorses or showjumpers cannot use just anaerobic pathways of energy supply, because their efforts often need to last for longer than a couple of minutes.

Aerobic means 'with air' or oxygen and the aerobic pathways of energy can use both carbohydrates and fat for energy supply. Energy supply is relatively slow, but this system can supply much greater amounts of ATP than the others, so it can support exercise of long duration. The processing of carbohydrate (glucose) starts in the same way as it would for the anaerobic pathway (with glycolysis), but then oxygen is involved and the pyruvate produced from glycolysis enters an aerobic metabolic pathway called the TCA (tricarboxylic acid) or Krebs cycle. Fatty acids enter this aerobic metabolic pathway one step on from pyruvate. Fatty acids can only be processed for energy release with the use of oxygen.

Energy production and fuel sources

Whether carbohydrate or fat is used for energy production depends on the intensity of the exercise and on how much fuel is left in store. Even thin horses have large reserves of energy as fat, and if exercise is of a relatively low intensity, it could carry on for days before fuel runs out. However, while fat is a useful supplier of energy for exercise (supplying more energy per gram than carbohydrates), its drawback is how slowly the energy can be supplied – alone, it cannot support anything but the very low-intensity exercise of walking and slow trotting. Thus, as the horse begins to exercise, both fat and carbohydrates will be used, but once he begins a slightly fast trot or canter he starts to use mainly carbohydrates and, as he increases his speed further, he will be unable to use fat as an energy source. After exercise of long duration at moderate to high intensity, the horse's muscle glycogen stores will decrease dramatically and he will depend for energy increasingly on blood glucose and, once again, on fat. At this stage, the speed of exercise will inevitably drop. Horses, like other athletes, cannot continue to exercise if muscle glycogen and blood glucose run out – before this time fatigue would set in as a result of a weakening of the central nervous system, which depends on adequate blood glucose to function.

Which fuel the horse uses depends then, on his fitness levels and the composition of his diet as well as the intensity and duration of exercise. As mentioned, fat is a useful supplier of energy in terms of energy per gram, but the energy derived from it is supplied slowly. Nevertheless, performance horses used to eating diets with a higher than average fat content do adapt to using fat more efficiently, thus sparing their supplies of muscle glycogen to some extent.

There is, in fact, much confusion about feeding fat to horses, and what constitutes a high-fat diet. A regular diet for horses contains about 4% fat, whereas a regular human diet contains about 30% fat. Human nutritionists find it odd that a high-fat diet for horses would be 10% fat! Scientific research into high-fat equine diets have been inconclusive in proving that fat boosts performance in horses, and many of the trials were flawed. What we do know is that high-starch diets are not particularly healthy, and so replacing some of this starch with fat

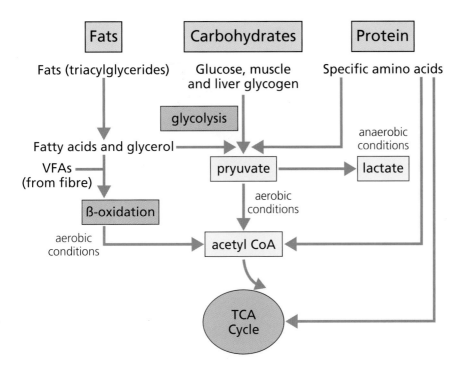

Figure 10.1 Simple diagram of the energy metabolic mill.

probably has benefit for horses. However, performance horses must have adequate supplies of muscle glycogen for optimal performance, and overfeeding fat should be avoided until further research is done. A maximum of 20% fat (as a percentage of total energy supplies) should be fed.

It should be noted that when a horse uses carbohydrate or fat as an energy source, he is not using these nutrients as they are fed, or even absorbed. Only glucose compounds and single fatty acids can be used in the energy pathways. This confusion leads to the myth that fibre feeds cannot support exercise. As explained in Chapter 4, fibre is fermented in the horse's hindgut, producing volatile fatty acids (VFAs) that the horse can absorb. Of the three VFAs that are produced in large quantities, two – acetic and butyric acid – can enter the horse's energy-producing 'metabolic mill' in the same way as fatty acids from dietary oil. The third VFA, propionic acid, can be converted into glucose in the horse's liver, and subsequently used to make glycogen in the liver or muscles. In addition, many fibrous feeds also contain some non-structural carbohydrates such as sugar (grasses) and starch (alfalfa). Although propionic acid levels increase in grain-fed horses, some is still produced in fibre-fed horses. Horses fed no grain at all still seem to be able to synthesize muscle glycogen and store adequate levels of carbohydrate in their muscles. However, research that determines the optimum level of

Eventing is a sport that requires sustained energy production.

non-structural carbohydrates in the performance horse's diet is yet to be carried out. Until more is known about how to optimize muscle glycogen stores, it is wise to feed some non-structural carbohydrates (e.g. starch and sugar) to performance horses. However, the high levels fed in days gone by, which had adverse effects on health, are now unnecessary because of other good sources of energy, including highly digestible fibre and oil.

What happens when energy supplies run out

When energy supplies run out and ATP can no longer be regenerated at a rate to fulfil requirements, exercise can no longer be sustained at the current level and fatigue will set in. Just when supplies run out will depend on the intensity and duration of exercise. A horse galloping at maximum speed using the ATP-PC and then anaerobic systems will, after a minute or two, feel fatigue and will have to slow down and start using the aerobic system. Fatigue in this case is not usually a consequence of the energy supply running out – it occurs because, at such high-intensity exercise, the muscles are flooded with lactic acid, creating an environment that disturbs muscle contraction.

During aerobic exercise of long duration, muscle glycogen stores can be depleted, and the horse will begin to rely on blood glucose from liver glycogen. Then, at some point, exercise intensity will slow as the body also uses fat as a fuel. Eventually, fatigue will be felt as a consequence of low blood sugar (hypoglycaemia) and other factors including a shift in brain chemicals. An exercising horse will almost never run out of fat stores and fatigue will set in as a consequence of these other factors before this happens.

Human athletes use a technique called muscle glycogen loading which involves eating diets very high in non-structural (starch and sugar) carbohydrate before a competition, sometimes with a fast or fatiguing exercise bout beforehand. In humans, this supercompensation of muscle glycogen stores can aid performance. Horses, however, already have superior muscle glycogen stores per gram of muscle as compared to human athletes, and it is not proven that glycogen loading works for them. More importantly, horses should not be fed large amounts of non-structural carbohydrates, because this can cause digestive disturbance, colic and tying up (rhabdomyolysis), therefore muscle glycogen loading should not be attempted in horses.

The replenishment of muscle glycogen stores in horses is dealt with later in this chapter – see Starch and Sugar.

Nutritional requirements for performance horses

So far, most of this chapter had been taken up with investigating energy supply, because this is the crucial nutritional factor for performance horses. It does not matter, for example, how high in protein the diet is; if energy supply if not met then a horse cannot perform optimally. However, requirements for other nutrients do increase for horses in regular exercise, and tables of nutrient requirements can be found in the Appendix.

Water and the electrolyte macrominerals

Along with energy, water is the other most important dietary factor for exercising horses. Water requirements are significantly increased in performance horses. The body cannot function without adequate water, and dehydration will have a detrimental effect on performance. A loss of just 2% of bodily water – equivalent to about 10 kg in a 500 kg horse – will affect performance via inadequate thermoregulatory (heat control) and circulatory function. As explained in previous chapters, water intake will depend on a variety of factors including moisture content of feed, temperature, workload and availability of water. Water is lost in breath, faeces, urine and sweat. (Refer back to Chapter 4 for more information about water requirements and functions in the body.)

Working horses can lose large amounts of water in their sweat, with sweat-loss rates of up to 15 litres per hour. Horses, like all other mammals, are efficient at maintaining body temperature in a process called thermoregulation – in fact, the horse can sweat at higher rates than humans and any other animals. If a horse could not sweat efficiently during exercise, his internal temperature would quickly rise to dangerous levels. Energy production in the muscles is relatively inefficient and three-quarters of the energy produced for muscle contraction is lost as heat. Sweating helps to dissipate the heat produced by the working muscles through evaporation of the water from the sweat. Sweating is more efficient in hot, dry climates and is less effective in humid environments, where the air is already saturated with water.

Sweat consists of water, a protein called latherin which helps spread the sweat, and electrolyte minerals, and it is more concentrated than body fluids, i.e. it is hypertonic. (Human sweat, by contrast, is hypotonic, or less concentrated – less salty – than human body fluids.) Horses can, therefore, lose large amounts of electrolytes (body salts) during exercise. The electrolytes lost in large quantities are sodium, potassium and chloride. Much smaller amounts of magnesium and calcium, and traces of iron, zinc, copper and other minerals are also lost in sweat.

Constituent	g per litre of sweat
Sodium	3–3.7
Chloride	5.9–6.2
Potassium	1.2–2
Calcium	0.08–0.24
Magnesium	0.024–0.2
Protein	2 (after first hour of sweating)

Table 10.2 Constituents of equine sweat, plus concentrations.

From: L. D. Lewis (1995) *Equine Clinical Nutrition: Feeding & Care*, Williams & Wilkins.

Dehydration during exercise causes impaired sweating; therefore inhibits the ability to lose heat. Dehydration reduces performance, causing early fatigue, and increases the risk of airway inflammation and colic. (Refer to Chapter 4 for signs of how to recognize dehydration.)

Exercising horses have increased requirements for water and electrolyte minerals, both of which are in direct relation to the extent of sweating during exercise. Both water and electrolytes will be replenished over several days of free access to water and the normal diet. However, replenishment of these nutrients more quickly is healthier and also important for subsequent performance in a horse competing over many hours or days. The most efficient rehydration takes place if the water the horse drinks contains a similar balance of salts to that of the body, therefore water containing electrolytes is more efficient at rehydrating horses than water alone. A half and half mixture of plain salt (sodium chloride) and lite salt (a mixture of sodium chloride and potassium chloride) can be added to water at a rate of 90 g per 10 litres to make an ideal oral rehydration solution. Such a solution will be at a similar concentration to the horse's body fluids, or 'isotonic'. (Note that it is the amount of water the salts are mixed into that makes the mixture isotonic, not the proportion of salts in a commercial electrolyte product.) Unfortunately, dehydrated horses will often not feel thirsty because their body dilution of sodium is normal as a consequence of their losing lots of both water and sodium in sweat. (Body sodium concentration affects the thirst mechanism – when sodium concentration increases, the thirst response is 'switched on'.) Sometimes giving some feed with a little salt in it will encourage a horse to drink. Plain water will not rehydrate a dehydrated horse so effectively as an isotonic solution because plain water will dilute the body fluids, 'switching off' the thirst response. In addition, this dilution will stimulate water loss via urination to normalize body sodium concentration.

Oral rehydration solutions, while replacing lost body water efficiently, will not supply enough electrolyte minerals to replace lost body salts for an intensively worked horse. The minerals lost in smaller quantities are usually replaced by the normal diet, but the amounts of sodium, potassium and chloride lost cannot usually be replaced by the normal diet, especially in horses who work at least every other day. These must be replaced by feeding either a commercial electrolyte mixture, or a homemade electrolyte mixture of half lite salt and half normal salt. If a commercial electrolyte is fed, it must supply enough minerals – a very hard-working horse may require 150 g per day of extra salts, over and above normal requirements. These electrolytes should be given in the feed, along with free access to water.

Rehydration is essential for performance horses who have been sweating heavily.

Make sure that fresh water is available to performance horses at all times. Allow horses who compete in endurance exercise (including long-distance rides and eventing) access to water right up until they begin the competition. These horses should also be given access to grass forage, which acts as a reservoir of water in the gut, helping to reduce the risk of dehydration.

Protein

Despite popular belief, although the protein should be high-quality, working horses do not require much increased levels of protein in their diets. As explained earlier, protein is not used to a great extent for energy production and therefore feeding higher levels of protein will not increase energy supply or have any performance-enhancing effect. Furthermore, dietary protein will not build muscle; only a carefully planned exercise (conditioning) regime will do this. In fact, excess protein could have detrimental effects, including excess water intake and loss, increased nitrogen excretion (which increases energy cost) and increased ammonia levels in the stable, which is a challenge to the respiratory system.

Daily protein intakes for athletic horses need be no more than 2.5 g crude protein (assuming about 80% digestibility) per kg BW, which is about 12.5% in the total diet for a racehorse eating 10 kg DM. Remember to take into account the protein content of the forage as well as any concentrate feed.

Antioxidant Nutrients

Several nutrients (e.g. selenium, vitamins E and C and carotenoids including betacarotenes) act as antioxidants or are involved in antioxidant processes (e.g. zinc, iron, copper and manganese). Exercise is associated with increased oxygen consumption and the horse has a phenomenal ability to take up oxygen and use it in the energy-producing pathways. Along with this use of oxygen comes the production of 'reactive oxygen species' or free radicals, which are a normal part of oxygen use in the body. These free radicals produce oxidative stress, and the body copes by quenching them with antioxidant nutrients. Further research is necessary to investigate whether higher dietary levels of antioxidant nutrients than those currently recommended may help to combat exercise-associated oxidative stress. Until then it seems prudent to supply higher levels of antioxidant nutrients to working horses, taking into account maximum tolerable levels.

Micronutrients

Many micronutrients are involved in energy supply and are therefore important to working horses. Unfortunately, research to date has been limited, and much more work needs to be done before we can be sure about optimum supplies of vitamins and minerals for working horses. Published nutrient requirements for horses are based on adequate levels to avoid deficiencies; therefore it is possible that optimal micronutrient levels for hard-working horses are much higher. Feeding more than published recommended nutrient levels is, in most cases, safe. However, there are several micronutrients that should not be over-supplemented; these include iron, selenium, vitamin A and vitamin D. In addition, single minerals should be supplemented with care. (Quantities have been discussed in Chapter 4.)

Calcium and phosphorus requirements rise a little with exercise, and again the ratio of the two is important. Exercising horses should be fed about 0.4% calcium, equivalent to 40 g per day for a horse eating 10 kg dry matter, and 0.25% (25 g) phosphorus. In contrast to sodium, potassium and chloride, little calcium is lost in sweat.

The macromineral magnesium is an activator of many enzymes involved in muscular contraction and work, and low levels have been associated with a loss of appetite; therefore optimal performance will depend on adequate magnesium. Little information about the requirements of hard-working horses exists, therefore a little more than published requirements should be fed to working horses – around 0.15–2% of the diet per day, or 15–20 g for a 500 kg horse eating 10 kg dry matter per day.

Balanced levels of trace minerals are essential for any horse's diet, but some are particularly important for athletic performance. Unfortunately it is not known whether exercise *increases* the requirement for these nutrients, but it is prudent to increase levels a little, bearing in mind maximum tolerable amounts.

Zinc is a component of over 200 enzymes, and is involved in cell growth, the production of red blood cells (the cells that carry oxygen to the muscles, where it is used to help produce energy to power muscle contraction), and immunity. Zinc is also involved in carbohydrate metabolism, where it is incorporated into insulin. Exercising horses should be fed at least 60 mg zinc per kg of diet dry matter. More can be given, but the zinc to copper ratio should not be greater than 5:1.

Iron plays a key role in oxygen carriage by the red blood cells and is involved in enzymes associated with energy metabolism. It has commonly been supplemented to performance horses, despite there being no proof that it helps boost performance. Over-supplementation is not recommended because, if fed in large quantities, iron is toxic, acts as pro-oxidant and inhibits the absorption of other minerals, including zinc and copper. Also, because it is so essential, iron is recycled efficiently by the body. Forage contains good levels of iron and healthy performance horses fed adequate forage should not suffer iron deficiencies. Exercising horses should be fed a total of 40–50 mg iron per kg dietary dry matter.

Contrary to popular opinion, iron deficiency in the horse rarely causes anaemia. Anaemic horses should have their problem diagnosed and the cause treated appropriately before dietary measures are taken. If substantial blood loss has occurred, then extra iron and copper should be fed to support red blood cell production, but iron itself should not be used as a treatment for anaemia. The most important factor is to get the cause of the anaemia diagnosed first, and that problem treated.

Copper and selenium are involved with enzymes and proteins that act as antioxidants. Copper is a scavenger of free radicals, plays a key role in energy metabolism and is needed for the production of haemoglobin, the red blood cells' oxygen transporter. Copper supplementation has also been shown to have a protective effect against DOD in Thoroughbred youngsters, and optimal levels in the young performance horse are probably higher than published recommendations. Feed 20 mg per kg dry matter to working horses and a little more (25 mg/kg dietary dry matter) for growing horses in work. Selenium has been the focus of research into its antioxidant properties in the horse, and recommended dietary levels for performance horses have been increased in recent years. A total daily dietary intake of 3 mg selenium for a 500 kg horse in intense work is recommended (around 0.24–0.3 mg/kg dietary dry matter), and this is still much lower than the 20 mg level, which is toxic to horses.

Exercise is not thought to increase the requirement for iodine, cobalt or manganese but, again, these may be increased slightly provided that maximum tolerable levels are considered.

Sub-optimal levels of dietary vitamins may result in decreased athletic performance, and research in human athletes has shown that supplementation improved performance in people with pre-existing vitamin deficiencies. As explained in Chapter 4, many of the B-complex vitamins are involved in energy production in the body, where they have essential roles in the pathways that regenerate ATP from the breakdown of fat and carbohydrates. Despite the fact that mature healthy horses generally receive adequate supplies of B-complex vitamins via microbial fermentation in their hindguts, performance horses may be short of these essential nutrients. This is because performance horses are often fed limited forage, therefore their hindgut microbial function may be inadequate and it is likely that deficiencies of B-complex vitamins could occur without supplementation. In addition, the metabolism of propionate (one of the volatile fatty acids produced from microbial fermentation) to glucose requires vitamin B_{12}; therefore performance horses fed high-concentrate diets probably require higher levels of this vitamin, because they produce relatively high amounts of propionate.

B-complex vitamins are relatively safe and do not cause toxicity if overfed, therefore it is prudent to supplement the performance horse's diet, particularly if the diet is low in forage and/or high in unfortified concentrate feed. Exercising horses should be fed at least 5 mg/kg dry matter (50 mg for 10 kg intake) vitamin B_1 (thiamine), and 2 mg/kg (20 mg for 10 kg intake) vitamin B_2 (riboflavin).

Vitamins C and E are important antioxidant nutrients, which means they stabilize body cells from damage, and are important for immunity. Exercise increases the oxidative load so, in theory, it would increase the requirement for antioxidant nutrients. Although horses can synthesize their own supplies of vitamin C, it is not known whether or not hard-working performance horses can synthesize enough. Recent research showed that supplementary vitamin C – the most important antioxidant in lung-lining fluid – boosted levels within the lungs of horses. Therefore horses stabled for most of their time (including most performance horses), who are exposed to high levels of respiratory allergens and irritants, could benefit from supplementary vitamin C. Ascorbyl palmitate seems to be better absorbed by horses than plain ascorbic acid, and at least 10 g per day needs to be fed.

Vitamin E is the most important antioxidant for stabilizing cell membranes, including muscle cell membranes. It is an important antioxidant for exercising horses, and recent research has shown that requirements, especially of performance horses, are probably much higher than previously thought. In addition, the vitamin E intake of horses drops dramatically once they have less access to green forage, so particular attention should be given to the vitamin E intakes of stabled performance horses. Aim for a total dietary level of 2,000 mg for a horse in light to moderately hard work, and 3,000–4,000 mg for a hard-working horse (based on daily intake of a 500 kg horse).

Horses tend to take in much of their vitamin A via betacarotenes, which they then convert into vitamin A in their bodies. Carotenoids including betacarotenes are important antioxidants and plays crucial roles in immune function. Performance horses probably require increased levels of vitamin A, but care should be taken not to over-supplement because vitamin A is toxic at high intakes. Fresh forage is a rich source of betacarotenes, and horses who have little or no access to pasture should be supplemented with vitamin A. Maximum levels in the diet should be 16,000 iu per kilo of diet (dry matter), equivalent to 160,000 iu for a 500 kg horse eating 10 kg dry matter. Maximum levels of vitamin D for performance horses should be 2,200 iu per kilo of dry matter, or 22,000 iu per 10 kg.

The belief that 'more is better' is definitely not true in the cases of both vitamins A and D. Both are toxic at high levels and care should be taken when adding supplements containing vitamins A and D to a diet high in fortified concentrate feed. Note that cod liver oil contains high levels of vitamins A and D. For signs of chronic toxicity of these vitamins, refer to Chapter 4.

Practical diets for performance horses

Exactly the same guidelines for feeding horses in general should be applied to the working horse, whether a privately owned, low-level competition horse or an elite racehorse or eventer. Common belief implies that elite performance horses require different management and feeding regimes from others, but these intensive regimes tend to cause a myriad of health problems including an increased risk of colic, respiratory disease, stomach ulceration, laminitis, tying up and oral stereotypies. These are just the problems that can be seen, but there is the potential danger that the low-forage, meal-based feeding regimes and confinement in stables to which so many performance horses are subjected may also cause other problems, including sub-optimal bone quality, behavioural disturbances and sup-optimal performance. If the horses' basic needs are kept in mind, many problems can be avoided and performance can be maximized.

Forage and fibre

Horses need concentrate feed only when forage cannot supply the nutrients they require, so for performance horses with high nutrient requirements it makes sense to source the most nutritious forage available, and feed as much as they will eat. As explained in Chapter 8, only very greedy horses, or those whose body-weight might affect performance (e.g racehorses and eventers) should have their forage restricted, and this never to less than 1% of their bodyweight per day (i.e. 5 kg dry matter forage for a 500 kg horse). Researchers in Kentucky have shown that racehorse performance is not detrimentally affected by this level of forage, fed right up to the day of a race.

The most suitable preserved forage for performance horses is haylage (see Chapter 6), because it is of superior hygienic quality and tends to be more nutritious than other forages, thus less concentrate feed is required. (If hay is fed, absolutely all, even the cleanest looking, should be soaked for at least 10 minutes before being fed to performance horses – for more information about why, see Chapter 13.)

Despite the advantages of feeding performance horses as much good quality forage as is practical, the fact remains that, in most cases, meeting the extra nutrient requirements of exercise necessitates the use of extra feed, because most horses cannot eat enough forage to obtain all the nutrients they require – hard work almost doubles energy requirements. However, gone are the days of having to feed grain and/or grain-based concentrate feeds to hard-working horses. Nowadays 'superfibres' are available that are used in compound feeds, making them equal to grain in energy supply, but with much higher fibre and lower starch levels. Such feeds can be given instead of grain and grain-based compound feeds

The most suitable preserved forage for performance horses is haylage.

without causing the problems of loss of appetite and increased risk of gastric ulcers, colic, tying up and laminitis. Many of these highly digestible fibre feeds are also high in oil, the most energy-dense feed there is.

	Traditional competition mix (typical values) (4 kg)	New 'superfibre' cubed feed (4 kg)
Crude protein (g)	480	480
Crude fibre (g)	320	760
Oil (g)	140	200
Starch (g)	1,200	400

Table 10.3 Constituents of two different types of compound feeds for performance horses.

Starch and sugar

Some dietary starch and sugar is probably beneficial for most performance horses (with the exception of those who tie up/suffer from rhabdomyolysis) to ensure maximal muscle glycogen stores, a factor that is necessary for optimal performance. Further research is necessary to help understand the link between the composition of diet and muscle glycogen storage, and manipulating the diet does not appear to affect muscle glycogen but, until more is known, it is prudent to feed some dietary starch and sugar. Exercise boosts the action of insulin, and feeds with a relatively high glycaemic index such as sugar and starch are safer for horses in work than for sedentary animals. However, as explained in Chapter 8, starchy feeds should be fed in maximum quantities of 2 g starch per kg of bodyweight per meal, equivalent to 1 kg starch per meal for a 500 kg horse. Higher levels than this risk gut disturbance and are a waste of money because digestion is inefficient.

Following exertion, horses replenish their muscle glycogen stores more slowly than humans, and it may take up to 2 days before levels are replenished after a particularly strenuous or very prolonged bout of exercise. Therefore, hard, fast galloping sessions should not be attempted more than 2 or 3 times a week, or on consecutive days, because muscle glycogen may not have replenished in between. This factor should be considered for optimal performance in sprinting and showjumping events, in which horses should not be worked very hard and fast for the 2 days leading up to the event, in order that optimal muscle glycogen stores are present.

Fat supplementation

Much research has been carried out on fat-rich diets for exercising horses, with conflicting results. Some studies showed performance benefits in horses fed fat-supplemented diets because of a sparing of muscle glycogen as a result of enhanced use of fatty acids for energy. However, other studies have shown no effects and there is no clear performance-enhancing effect in competition. Despite this, high-fat diets do have the following benefits for exercising horses:

- Lower heat load, particularly useful for endurance and eventers.
- Higher energy density (more calories per gram and per cupful), useful for fussy eaters.
- Results in lower reactivity and calmer disposition when replacing a high-starch diet.

Fat should be fed for several months prior to competition to allow the horse's body to adjust to digesting, absorbing and using it efficiently. Horses can, in theory, be fed up to 20% of their dietary energy as vegetable oil, which is equivalent to about 570 g per day for a 500 kg horse in moderate work. However, such high levels can imbalance the diet because oil is relatively nutrient-poor, and in practice, adding up to 0.6 ml per kg bodyweight (300 ml for a 500 kg horse) is well accepted by most horses, providing it is introduced gradually.

Feeding for specific disciplines

There is no reason to follow a specific feeding regime for a specific discipline. It is the type of exercise rather than the discipline itself that matters. Where physical training or conditioning is concerned, then the work needs to be discipline-specific – at least in the final period of training – but where the diet is concerned, this is not the case. Rations for working horses should be selected on the basis of how long the horse exercises and at what intensity, during both training and competition. Ensuring that nutrient requirements, especially energy needs, are fulfilled is the best nutritional method of enhancing performance in any discipline.

Unfortunately much more research is needed before we understand how to influence a horse's energy supply from feed. It is possible that different proportions of fibre, starch and oil might be appropriate depending on the intensity and duration of exercise, but currently this question has not been answered.

Certain disciplines do, of course make general requirements of the horse, and therefore of his energy output. Speed performers, including racehorses and showjumpers, will probably benefit from some dietary starch and sugar, but in all cases the levels must be kept within recommended maximums. Dressage horses must perform with control, and will benefit from a higher fibre, lower starch diet, supplemented with oil if extra energy is required. Eventers or any other horses competing over more than one day will benefit from meals of their normal diet being fed both after competition and then again later in the evening, particularly with respect to starch intake. Plenty of forage should be offered to these horses, and the final concentrate meal given at least 4 hours before competition starts the next day. Since prolonged exercise is associated with greater water and electrolyte loss, eventers and endurance horses tend to have heightened needs of these nutrients.

Endurance horses can be fed during competition; therefore more can be done to influence their performance from a dietary point of view. Periods of fasting of over 4 hours increase the risk of gastric ulcers, which are a big concern for endurance horses. Therefore, small feeds should be offered at every opportunity throughout the competition. Both high glycaemic index feeds (starchy or sugary) meals and forage (grass is ideal) should be offered. The unhelpful effects of a concentrate meal before exercise are overridden during exercise, and feeding relatively small amounts of starch or sugar during prolonged exercise will provide further supplies of fuel, and may enhance performance. Nutrients from forage and fat take much longer (many hours) to become available to the horse, and are not useful for fuel supply during exercise of up to 4 or 5 hours. Despite this, forage should be offered to help maintain stomach and gut health.

All equine athletes should be maintained in lean body condition for optimal performance. Leanness is particularly important for endurance horses and race-

It is the type of exercise, rather than the actual discipline, that dictates nutritional requirements.

Endurance rides make special demands of the horse, and vigorous veterinary checks are carried out.

horses because extra body fat is extra 'dead' weight, and inhibits heat loss. However, being over-thin may be unhelpful to endurance horses, and one study of horses in a 100 mile race showed that very thin horses were more likely to be eliminated as a consequence of metabolic problems. A body condition score of 2–3 on the 0–5 scale would be appropriate for an endurance horse or racehorse.

When Arab racing first became popular in the UK, many people who took part were enthusiastic amateur owners of Arabs. Some of these people tended to train and feed their horses inappropriately, and these horses therefore looked very 'whippety'. Most of the races were won, not by these horses, but by others prepared by handlers with a professional background in racing; the obvious difference being that the winning horses, whilst fit and well-muscled, carried a good deal more condition than the 'whippets'.

Salt paste warning!

Recent research investigating endurance horses has shown that horses given salt pastes (mixtures of salt and water syringed into their mouths) during prolonged exercise of moderate intensity are at high risk of gastric (stomach) ulceration. Therefore salt pastes should not be fed alone. Rehydration should be encouraged using oral rehydration solutions of the correct concentration, and the horse trained to accept the treated water before competition. Salts may be given in feeds throughout competition, in controlled amounts. Salt pastes may also cause other problems; if a horse does not drink enough after their administration, body fluids will be very imbalanced and exercise performance will be inhibited.

Effects of exercise on appetite

Loss of appetite is a common problem in hard-working horses, which makes meeting nutrient requirements a challenge. Why it occurs is not fully understood, but the following factors may play a role:

1. Vitamin B_1 (thiamine) deficiency.

2. Gastric (stomach) erosion and ulcers.

3. High blood propionate levels.

Thiamine (vitamin B_1) deficiency is a well-known cause of appetite suppression in farm animals. Performance horses could well suffer from such a deficiency arising from a shortage of forage, which results in a lack of microbial production of the vitamin in the hindgut. Thiamine, along with all the other B-complex vitamins, is safe to supplement and all performance horses should receive extra B vitamins. However, while supplementing thiamine alone to help boost appetite can be done, the basic diet – including forage and vitamin supply – should be examined and altered if necessary.

Up to 90% of racehorses in training suffer from erosion and ulceration of the gastric lining, which is attributed to the long periods of fasting along with a high-concentrate, starchy diet and low forage intake, and the physical splashing of gastric acid occurring during exercise. Gastric ulcers may be present without obvious symptoms and may cause loss of appetite without it being apparent that there is a health problem. Following the guidelines for more healthy feeding regimes explained in Chapters 8 and 13 will help avoid gastric erosion and ulceration. If ulcers are suspected, a vet should be contacted without delay.

Levels of specific blood nutrients are known to be a regulator of appetite in animals. Propionate, one of the volatile fatty acids produced from hindgut microbial fermentation in horses, is produced and absorbed in higher amounts in a horse fed high levels of concentrate feed. High blood propionate levels suppress appetite. Reducing the starch content of the diet reduces the proportion of propionate produced in the hindgut and could, in theory, help boost the appetite. Vitamin B_{12} supplementation has been shown to increase appetite in some horses fed a high-grain ration, and its role in the metabolism of propioniate could be the mechanism. Ideally, the cause of the problem (i.e. too much starch), should be dealt with, rather than just dealing with the symptom by feeding extra vitamin B_{12}.

Practical timing of feeding performance horses

A commonly asked question is when and what to feed before exercise and particularly before competition. Feeding grain-based concentrates within 4 hours before exercise inhibits the availability of free fatty acid and increases glucose uptake by the muscles, both of which are undesirable, especially for prolonged exercise. Endurance horses and eventers should have their concentrate meals fed at least 4 hours before competition and long training sessions. After that time they can be offered forage such as hay, haylage or grass. Endurance horses should be encouraged to eat forage right up to the start of their competition, because this acts as a reservoir for fluid in their guts, and will help slow the onset of dehydration. Horses undergoing endurance exercise should not be fasted before exercise, and withholding their normal feed for 10-12 hours before competition will reduce performance.

On the other hand, racehorses and sprint performers where speed matters should not be allowed ad lib access to forage for the 12 hours prior to competition. Intake should be restricted to 1% of their bodyweight for this period, ideally in several small meals to avoid long periods of fasting. Above this level, the extra weight of forage plus the water it holds could, in theory, affect performance. These horses should also have their final concentrate meal at least 4 hours before competition, again to ensure that the body starts to mobilize fuel for use, rather than being actively storing it away. It may be beneficial for racehorses and other high-intensity performers to have a meal of non-structural carbohydrates such as grain 4 or 5 hours prior to competition, to 'top up' body stores. (Note that this strategy is different from a glycogen-loading regime.)

Does feeding after exercise boost muscle fuel stores and affect subsequent performance? Horses replenish their muscle glycogen stores more slowly than humans, and feeding high levels of soluble carbohydrates post-exercise has not been shown to speed the replenishment. As mentioned earlier, horses can take up to 2 days to fully replenish their muscle glycogen stores after hard, fast or prolonged exercise, therefore such work should not be undertaken just prior to a competition during which maximal muscle glycogen stores are needed. There is no evidence that specific feeding regimes post-exercise maximize muscle glycogen stores in horses as they do in human athletes.

Avoiding prohibited substances

Performance horses compete under rules, the aims of which are to make competing safe and to avoid individuals gaining unfair advantages (or disadvantages, in some cases). Competition rules include a list of prohibited substances that must not be present in the horse's body during or after competition. Many horse feeds contain a variety of constituents and it is possible for a horse to be inadvertently fed something that is prohibited. Care should be taken to ensure this does not happen.

The rules of the British Equestrian Federation (BEF) state:

The following are prohibited substances:

Substances capable at any time of acting on one or more of the following mammalian body systems:

the nervous system

the cardiovascular system

the respiratory system

the digestive system other than certain specified substances

for the oral treatment of gastric ulceration

the urinary system

the reproductive system

the musculoskeletal system

the skin

the blood system

the immune system, other than those in licensed vaccines against infectious agents

the endocrine system

Antipyretics, analgesics and anti-inflammatory substances, cytotoxic substances, endocrine secretions and their synthetic counterparts and masking agents.

The Horseracing Regulatory Authority makes a very similar statement. The crux of the matter is that it is not just the actual substance that is ingested by or administered to the horse, but also why that substance has been given. For example, most herbs are not fed for their nutritional content, but for their active constituents, which have physiological effects on the horse's body in a similar way to a drug. If an owner or trainer feeds a herbal product that has an effect such as calming, then whether or not the herb's constituents can or do get tested for, this is breaking the rules. The BEF makes this very clear in their rulebook, and even state that: 'The use of any herbal or natural product to affect the performance of a horse or pony in a calming (tranquillising) manner or an energising (stimulant) manner is expressly forbidden by the FEI regulations.'

The BEF and the FEI (the International Equestrian Federation) are becoming more aware of the use of herbal products, which previously they had not tested for. It is likely that they will start testing for more and more herbal constituents in the future. The BEF make a point of stating that the FEI does not approve any herbal or natural product as not breaking its rules, therefore product packaging claims should be considered with care.

The BEF make an extra note that the FEI often detects caffeine and theobromine in samples. Caffeine and theobromine are possible contaminants of horse feed, because they are natural constituents of cocoa and coffee beans, which may contaminate grain ingredients during the process of feed manufacture. The BEF recommends that competitors check with their horse feed manufacturers to ensure that the feed is routinely tested for the presence of prohibited substances, and that competitors keep a small sample of each batch of their feed.

Many horse feed companies offer a guarantee on their feeds, but these guarantees are usually against caffeine and theobromine – the most common feed contaminants, and not against all prohibited substances. Chaff products generally do not carry guarantees because they are less likely to be contaminated and the mixing processes make it more difficult to take samples.

All competitors are urged to refer to the British Equestrian Federation website (see Useful Contacts) for the competition rulebook relevant to their discipline.

chapter 11

Feeding in old age

MORE HORSES ARE LIVING well into their twenties, and even into their thirties, probably because of improved veterinary care and deworming. Horses do not become old at a specific age, despite the claims made by commercial feed companies. A horse is 'old' when he shows several signs of ageing, which may include a dipping of the back, general joint stiffness or arthritis, and loss of efficient dental function. Horses should not be fed differently just because they have reached a certain age, and the *signs* of ageing, rather than actual age, should be used when considering an older horse's ration. Furthermore, it should be understood that older horses do not have different nutrient requirements *per se*, but the fact that they have lived for so many years means that they are more likely to have dysfunctional (or lost) teeth, gut worm damage, and possibly damage to the liver and other organs. It is these factors that may result in altered nutritional requirements. Also, old age in horses often brings with it different management, for example a horse may be retired and not clipped, and therefore may require less feed.

Nutritional requirements of the older horse

Old horses should have their basic diets assessed in the same way as any adult horse, i.e. nutritional requirements are based on whether or not they are working or reproducing (some mares continue to produce foals into their twenties), and energy intake is based on whether the horse is maintaining, losing or gaining weight. Researchers have suggested that older horses are less able to digest protein, fibre and phosphorus but this probably reflects worm-induced digestive dysfunction and poor dental function rather than old age itself. In cases of reduced digestive and absorptive abilities, it is prudent to ensure a high intake of vitamins and minerals for an old horse, perhaps providing an old horse at rest (maintenance) with the levels normally given to a younger horse in moderate

Old horses out at pasture.

work. However, healthy old horses with good physical condition should be fed a similar ration to any mature horse.

Although as yet unproven in horses, old age in other mammals is associated with a decline in immune function and an increased susceptibility to disease. Adequate dietary antioxidants should be fed to help maintain immune function, which may also help the age-associated increase in oxidative stress (free radical damage) in the body. There is as yet no evidence that synthetic antioxidant supplementation can help with this oxidative stress, and old horses should have access to fresh grass at every opportunity, and a source of vitamin E and provitamin A (carotenes) throughout the winter. Feeding quick-dried grass or alfalfa chaff and plenty of sliced carrots is one practical way of doing this. It has been recommended that extra vitamin C be fed to old horses showing signs of ageing, especially those with reduced liver function. Worm-induced damage or reduced hindgut function resulting from inadequate intake of fibre could impair the old horse's internal supply of B vitamins from microbial fermentation; therefore extra B vitamins should be supplemented.

Ensure a source of good quality protein, especially for very old horses, who are likely to have reduced absorptive ability. During winter when grazing is sparse, supplement hay with a compound feed or alfalfa chaff to increase the intake of essential amino acids. Alfalfa is a useful feed for old horses, but should not be fed in quantities greater than a couple of kilos per day for an average 500 kg horse.

It is important to feed older horses according to their own individual issues or problems, rather than simply feeding a veteran compound feed and whatever forage is available. Most importantly, their fibre requirements should be met even before their calorie needs are considered. Feeding more calories but not fulfilling fibre needs for an old, underweight horse will not result in weight gain, but instead could cause gut disturbance, diarrhoea, and further weight loss.

Dental function

The biggest challenge with feeding older horses is coping with the decline in dental function. Dental inadequacies can cause weight loss, choke and impactions. Quidding, when the horse drops balls of partially chewed food from his mouth, is one major sign of inefficient dental function; another is long pieces of forage (greater than a few centimetres) visible in the droppings. The horse may also drop feed from a bucket meal. The teeth may need to be rasped with a motorized rasp, which may have less of a loosening action than a hand-held rasp. Excessive rasping should be avoided, especially on loose teeth.

Unfortunately, while it should be considered essential, regular dental attention does not guarantee that an old horse's teeth remain functional, because the grinding surfaces may simply be worn so smooth that their grinding ability is reduced. Also, the hypsodont nature of horses' teeth (see Chapter 2) means that the teeth will eventually grow right out of the gum and fall out. There is no specific age at which this happens, but during and after a horse reaches 20 he should have his teeth checked more frequently. Loose teeth can cause a horse discomfort and/or pain, and a dental technician or vet may choose to remove the tooth, after which the horse might be able to resume chewing. Gaps can arise between teeth that are growing out, which can accumulate food material, in turn causing dental decay and gum inflammation. Wedged food should be cleaned out of the incisors (front teeth) on a regular basis, and the dental technician or vet will deal with food wedged between molars during their visits which, for older horses, should be at intervals of no more than 6 months.

For old horses with only slight dental insufficiency, choose soft meadow hay or haylage. Monitor them carefully to ensure they can cope with the forage, by looking out for quidding and the length of forage in the droppings. Give them access to good pasture as much as possible.

Old horses who struggle with forage must have their fibre requirements fulfilled from alternative feedstuffs. In early stages, the horse may cope with chewing short-chopped forage, such as hay replacer chaffs or quick-dried grass. These can be soaked in water for half an hour to soften, making them easier to chew. Molassed chaff should not be fed as a forage replacer because it contains straw, which is too tough for old horses with dental problems to chew, and contains too much sugar to be fed in large quantities. In later stages, when the horse cannot eat large quantities of chopped forage and eventually cannot eat any such forage, ground fibre (in pellets or cubes) and sugar beet pulp can be fed instead. Grass nuts and high-fibre cubes can be soaked to a mash to enable them to be eaten by a horse with even just a few functional teeth. Such feeds should have a crude fibre content of at least 18%. Forage replacement feeds should be given in several meals per day, ideally four or five but at least three, once the horse can no longer graze. A selection of different forage replacement feeds should be offered to encourage the horse to eat enough. Carrots and/or apples sliced very thinly can also help to tempt the horse. *Ensure horses who cannot cope with forage do not have access to it because they may try to eat it and choke.*

Ensure that enough is fed – a 15.2 hh horse weighing 500 kg should be fed 8–10 kg of feed per day, and if that horse cannot eat forage, he will need 8–10 kg of cubes/nuts and sugar beet (weigh before soaking) per day.

The gut of a horse with reduced chewing ability will have to cope with larger pieces of food material, which will have an impact on digestibility, passage rate and other factors. Larger pieces of forage travel through the hindgut faster, therefore there is less time for water to be reabsorbed in the colon, and this might make the droppings sloppy.

Maintaining healthy weight and coping with weight loss

Keeping older horses in regular exercise is recommended, provided it is appropriate to their individual capabilities. As in humans, strength in older horses declines and muscle mass is reduced, and more careful training regimes are required for older horses to keep fit. Old horses who are retired and have sedentary lifestyles will have reduced need for calorie intake, and excessive weight gain must be avoided in such horses to reduce the strain on the joints.

As is the case with all horses, old horses should be assessed individually and fed as appropriate. Old horses should not always be fed veteran or old horse compound feeds that contain higher energy than maintenance compounds, because they may not require them. Many healthy old horses would put on weight if fed recommended amounts of typical veteran compound feeds and this, as mentioned, would put extra strain on their musculoskeletal systems and is not to be advised. One feed manufacturer has developed two types of veteran feed; one high in calories for old horses who lose weight easily, and one with a calorie content similar to a maintenance feed for old horses who maintain weight easily. If such a useful choice of feeds cannot be sourced, a maintenance feed plus a broad-spectrum vitamin and mineral supplement could be fed to the old horse who is a good doer, and the specialist high-calorie veteran feed to the old horse who tends to lose weight. If an old, sedentary horse does not require any extra compound feed in addition to forage and grass, ensure that a broad-spectrum vitamin and mineral supplement is given to meet essential micronutrient requirements. Even if energy requirements drop, essential micronutrient requirements do not.

The most common feeding problem in old horses is weight loss, and this results, in most cases, from poor dental function rather than a systemic problem or absorption problems. Most adult horses receive most of their nutrients from forage, be that pasture or preserved forage, and if an old horse cannot physically eat these feeds, he will lose much of their nutrients (and calorie intake). This loss of nutrients will result in weight loss, which can be dramatic during winter when pasture grass is sparse. Many owners try to deal with such weight loss by feeding more compound feed, especially veteran coarse mixes, but this strategy often does not work and can make the problem worse. Many veteran mixes contain high levels of starch, which can cause digestive disturbance, especially if eaten with too little fibre. Horses who cannot eat forage need, most of all, a source of fibre, as explained in the section on dental function. Therefore dietary fibre should be replaced first, before any other type of feed is given. Most high-fibre feeds tend to be relatively low in calories and may not be the obvious choice for a thin horse, but a horse deficient in fibre will not put on weight and thrive until he is fed sufficient fibre. After fibre intake is resumed, conditioning feeds can be added – although in many cases these are not needed, and most old horses with little or no chewing ability will thrive on 2% of their bodyweight in high-fibre cubes, or a mix of cubes and sugar beet.

Old horses who are still chewing well but are prone to weight loss may have nutrient malabsorption problems. To these horses, high-quality forage such as leafy meadow grass hay or haylage should be offered ad lib, including in the pasture. Veteran feeds high in calories and protein can be given, along with other feeds such as sugar beet pulp and alfalfa, as recommended for weight gain in mature horses (see Chapter 8). Old horses with reduced liver and/or kidney function should be fed in a similar way to other horses with these problems (see Chapter 13).

In an old horse, being underweight should not be accepted as part of being old. The accompanying photograph of the old chestnut horse was taken when he was in his late thirties and his condition is excellent. Muscle wastage may occur in horses who have osteoarthritis and altered gait, but they should still have adequate body fat covering. If in doubt, condition scoring (see Chapter 8) should be used to assess body fat, and the assessor should be able to discriminate between body fat and other tissues, including muscle. If an old horse is underweight even after ad lib feeding of high-fibre feeds (soaked cubes if the horse cannot eat even chopped forage) along with moderate amounts of a conditioning or high-calorie

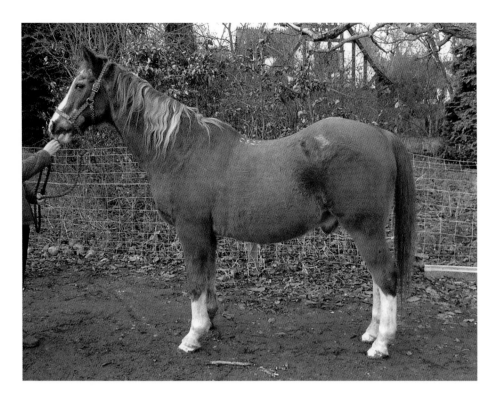

A dipped back is often a sign of age, but this old horse is in great condition.

veteran feed (e.g. 3–4 kg per day for a 500 kg horse, split into at least three meals per day), vegetable oil can be added to the diet, at a rate of up to 60 ml per 100 kg bodyweight (300 ml for a 500 kg horse). Introduce the oil gradually.

Probiotics are useful supplements for old horses, particularly those with reduced dental function and those who struggle to maintain weight. Live yeast products boost fibre and protein digestion and are ideal for old horses showing signs of ageing. Such products can be fed long term.

Dealing with infirmities

Joint mobility problems and osteoarthritis

Joint problems including osteoarthritis are common causes of lameness in older horses. It is important to maintain a healthy bodyweight and not allow an old, stiff horse to gain too much body fat. There are various supplements available that claim to help slow the progression of osteoarthritis and help general mobility, but there is little scientific evidence for their use in horses. However, research in humans and animals show that omega-3 fatty acids, glucosamine, chondroitin and some herbs do help, and there is plenty of anecdotal evidence for their usefulness in arthritic horses. Some old horses will benefit from the use of anti-inflammatory drugs.

Old, stiff horses should be encouraged to move around, which will help their mobility. Ideally, they should have free access to pasture and they may be able to live out permanently with adequate shelter and rugs. They should not be confined to a stable for long periods: in addition to causing them to stiffen up, they may be unwilling to lie down in such a confined space because getting back up can be difficult and they may require more space to do so. There is evidence to show that regular, low-intensity exercise is helpful in maintaining mobility in cases of osteoarthritis and, with care, horses in their late twenties and thirties can continue to be worked at a level suitable for the individual.

Cushing's syndrome

Cushing's syndrome, or hyperadrenocorticism, is a common condition in older horses, although it can occur at any age. It is caused by an abnormality of the pituitary gland (which may or may not involve a tumour) that results in the excess production of certain hormones. Signs include excess urination, excessive drinking, excessive hairiness (hirsutism) and retaining of the coat during the summer, sweating, lethargy, higher risk of infections and recurrent or chronic laminitis, although not all these signs may be present. Diagnosis should be carried out by the vet, and treatment options discussed. Treatment with drugs does not stop the progression of the disease but can help reduce the signs and improve the horse's quality of life. Although not registered in the UK for horses, drugs including trilostane and pergolide are available from the vet.

Horses with Cushing's syndrome often suffer from glucose intolerance, whereby they become less sensitive to the action of insulin and cannot cope well with dietary sugar and starch. Nutrition of horses with Cushing's syndrome should be considered according to each specific case, but in all cases diets high in sugar and starch (e.g., molasses, grain and coarse mix) should be avoided, to reduce the blood glucose load. A low-energy, high-fibre diet with adequate good-quality protein and micronutrients and extra antioxidants is recommended. Vegetable oil can be added for extra calories. The herb *Vitex agnus castus* (chasteberry) has been reputed to help in the treatment of Cushing's syndrome, but research studies to date have not been conclusive. Practically, the herb should be fed alongside other treatment.

Horses affected by Cushing's syndrome are at a higher risk of laminitis all year round (not just during summer) because of their hormone imbalances and glucose intolerance, and care must be taken to avoid triggering an attack (see Chapter 14). Grass intake should be restricted, and forage chosen with care. Affected horses often respond well to clipping, which helps to avoid sweating during the warmer months.

Excessive hairiness throughout the year is one of the common signs of Cushing's syndrome. This pony has been partially clipped to help him cope.

Supplements for support

Many old horses will benefit from dietary supplements. Live yeast products are particularly useful, especially for horses with reduced chewing ability. Probiotics (including live yeast) are useful for old horses prone to weight loss. Old horses not showing many signs of ageing and who do well on forage diets with some low-energy, high-fibre compound feed will benefit from a broad-spectrum vitamin and mineral supplement, particularly one with high levels of antioxidant nutrients (including vitamin E, vitamin A, zinc and selenium). Very old horses may benefit from herbs that support the organs, such as milk thistle for liver support. Various commercial products are available, but those should be fed as an extra and getting the basics of the diet right for the horse must be the priority. Antioxidant supplements, including those that contain a source of vitamin C, are useful for very old horses or those with chronic illnesses. Feed between 5 and 10 g per day to a 500 kg horse, preferably split into two doses. Various supplements are available to support mobility for old horses with arthritis (see Chapter 6).

chapter 12

Feeding more naturally

Keeping horses more naturally has become popular nowadays, and many owners and horses have gained benefits from this method of horse-keeping. The principle behind such management is to try to allow the horse to exhibit more natural behaviour patterns. The way to do this is to offer an environment and feeds that more closely mimic those the horse would encounter in the wild. Such an environment offers better welfare for the horse, and can have a wide range of benefits including a more tractable, trainable horse with fewer health problems.

Freedom and forage

In their natural environment, horses have free access to food and eat as they move around. In stables, horses do not have to search for food, and they are confined. Keeping horses at pasture is the most natural way of management, replacing the grass with preserved forage such as hay or haylage during the winter months when the grass stops growing. During the summer months, access to pasture may have to be restricted (perhaps by using strip grazing or bare paddocks with low-energy forage) to avoid excess weight gain.

Whenever it is necessary to supply additional forage to horses out at pasture, certain precautions should be taken. Forage should be fed in a safe area, and not around the gateway, where the ground could get poached. (Nevertheless, horses who do not come into stables every evening do not tend to wait around by the gateway – which is another major cause of poaching). Another cause of poaching is if forage is fed from permanent racks or troughs, in which case the surrounding area may become very poached, which could be dangerous. Ideally, therefore, racks or troughs should be moved regularly.

Herd hierarchy can cause problems during feeding in pasture-kept groups. Therefore, when forage is placed on the ground, if there are more than two horses, it should ideally be placed in triangular patterns, allowing each horse to observe the others.

Natural feeding necessitates offering forage ad lib so that the horse can choose to eat when he wants to. As explained in Chapter 3, horses choose to eat for about 70% of their time and a lack of forage can lead to a variety of physical and mental health problems. Horses who are stabled should always have forage on offer; preferably several different types of forage and fibre feeds. Research studies have shown that offering stable-kept horses a variety of different forages encourages them to spend more time foraging in the stable, thus reflecting a more natural eating pattern. Horses who are kept stabled would benefit from being offered a net of soaked hay or haylage, a trough of quick-dried grass or alfalfa, a bucket of root vegetables and a bucket of hay-replacement chaff or high-fibre cubes in a feed-decanting ball.

In cold weather, the best feed to increase for horses living out is forage. It helps to keep horses warm because of the fact it is digested via microbial fermentation, which produces heat. Therefore, from a body temperature point of view, fibrous feeds are the most 'heating'. Also, feeding a horse more naturally means supplying as many nutrients as possible from forage, the horse's natural diet. In this case, forages include quick-dried grass and alfalfa, which may be used as alternatives to compounds such as cubes and coarse mixes. If this is done, these forages should

Providing separate piles of forage minimizes the chances of squabbling.

be weighed, not simply scooped, to ensure an equal replacement. They are light and bulky, and a full water bucket of dried grass weighs about the same as one regular bowl-scoop (2.5 litres) of coarse mix.

Only if the various forages cannot supply enough nutrients should other feeds be added. Horses are not physically designed to be fed large meals of concentrate feed, and given the choice they will 'trickle feed', eating relatively small amounts of fibrous feeds throughout most of the day and night. Feeding moderate to large meals of concentrate feed has the following effects:

- Less time spent chewing, so more time for other behaviour (undesirable as well as desirable).

- Less saliva production, promoting a more acidic stomach.

- Faster emptying of the stomach and faster passage of food through the small intestine, increasing the risk of hindgut disturbance by undigested starch.

- Anticipation stress as the horse awaits the meal, especially in the meal if fed at the same time every day.

- Large fluxes in blood glucose and hormones, which may affect behaviour and causes insulin resistance in the long term.

Large meals of concentrate are very unhealthy and have no place in natural feeding regimes. If concentrate feed is offered, meals should be limited to half the general recommended amount (about 1 kg to a 500 kg horse) and ideally high-digestible fibre feeds and grain alternatives should be chosen (see next section).

Horses kept and fed more naturally are at reduced risk of abnormal behaviour (e.g. cribbing), colic, laminitis, tying up, acidic gut syndrome, over-exuberant 'fizzy' behaviour, gastric ulcers and allergic airway disease – in other words, all the common equine diseases and conditions.

Natural feeds and supplements

If a horse cannot obtain all his required nutrients from forage, and loses weight on ad lib forage, then other more calorific (higher-energy) feeds should be added to the diet. Sugar beet pulp is an ideal high-fibre food to help increase calorie intake, and unmolassed varieties are available, should the owner wish to avoid extra dietary sugar. Sugar beet should be weighed, or the amount to be fed calculated, before soaking, since adding water dilutes the product. Starchy grains are not natural feeds for horses, and none of the grasses or plants horses will chose in a feral situation are particularly rich in starch. However, of all the cereals, oats are the lowest in starch and highest in fibre, and are the best choice.

Avoiding artificial additives

Most commercial compound feeds contain artificial additives such as preservatives and synthetic vitamins. If a natural diet without artificial additives is preferred, there are good alternatives to compounds, but getting the balance of the micronutrients right may be challenging. First, feeding haylage rather than hay reduces the amount of extra feed required. Many horses at maintenance or in light work will hold their condition on ad lib haylage alone. If fed just haylage, a source of vitamin E is required for horses over the winter when grass intake is low. Feeding a couple of kilos of quick-dried alfalfa or grass per day and giving as much access to pasture as possible will help meet requirements. Forage-only diets may also be short of some microminerals, in particular copper, zinc, selenium, and iodine. The best natural source of these minerals is seaweed. It is a good source of minerals in their natural state, but has a particularly high content of iodine, which means that it should not be fed in large quantities. In order not to overfeed iodine, the maximum level of seaweed that can be fed is such that requirements for the other microminerals may not be met. Alternatively, some manufacturers produce natural vitamin and mineral supplements, usually based on seaweed. If in doubt, the forage should be analysed for minerals and an independent nutritionist contacted to run a dietary analysis and advise on how to balance the forage.

A vegetarian diet

Whether or not a horse eats a vegetarian diet is up to the owner, provided they have the information required to make the choice. It is not clear on some products that they contain animal and/or fish by-products. The problems of BSE in cattle have served as a warning for feeding mammalian products to herbivores and, in the author's opinion, horses should be fed vegetarian diets. Some manufacturers will state that horses pick up insects such as grubs while grazing, but anyone watching a horse pick out the pieces of coarse mix they like, leaving tiny pellets in the bottom of the feed bowl, will realize how dexterous the horse's muzzle is, and how skilled horses are at sorting out what they eat.

In some countries, animal fat is fed to horses, but it tends to be less palatable than vegetable oils. Fish meal and whole fish are fed to horses in Iceland over the winter, when they probably serve as a good source of minerals. Nowadays in the UK, animal, fish and shellfish by-products tend to be fed in compound feeds and supplements. Unfortunately it is not always clear which products contain such ingredients and, if in doubt, the manufacturer should be contacted. Many compound feeds and supplements contain vitamins that are coated in animal fat or gelatin. Some compounds are marketed as vegetarian, but if these cannot be found and a vegetarian diet is required, the guidelines given earlier for avoiding artificial additives should be followed.

Most joint support supplements contain either mammalian cartilage or cartilage by-products and/or shellfish by-products. Chondroitin is usually derived from cow, pig or shark cartilage, and glucosamine is usually derived from shellfish. To date, one manufacturer has launched a vegetarian glucosamine product for horses in the UK (www.equimore.co.uk). Hyaluronic acid (HA) is usually derived from chicken combs or cartilage – and there is absolutely no evidence that it helps joints when given orally.

Organic feeds

Organic forage and compound feeds (i.e. those free from artificial additives, herbicides, pesticides and other chemicals) are available for horses. It is important to ensure that no ragwort is present in organic forage, which will not have been sprayed with herbicides to kill weeds. Dried ragwort in hay is palatable and just as toxic as the fresh plant, and it can kill horses. Organic compound feeds tend to be more expensive but they may be necessary if horses are kept on farms with organic status. For more information on this subject, contact the Soil Association (see Useful Contacts).

General management

Living on permanent pasture provides horses with the most natural way of eating, but it does create some practical problems. In the first place, shelter is required. Mobile field shelters are ideal because they can be moved if the area around them becomes poached. Both traditional wooden mobile shelters and those made from scaffold-like frames and tarpaulin are available nowadays. Another option is having a barn or stable that opens out to the pasture so that horses can help themselves to shelter. Again, care should be taken that the entrances do not become very poached and muddy. With enough space, horses turned out permanently will not cause the muddiness associated with daytime turnout, but the extent of poaching will depend on the type of soil and turf, and the habits of the horses. Pasture near yards or homes, where horses tend to congregate by sections of a fence or a gate, will suffer more than those in different situations.

Horses are herd animals and giving them a more natural lifestyle includes allowing them to live with other horses, ideally in an established herd situation. Most horses can live out permanently, whatever their breed or age, provided they have adequate shelter and rugs. As explained earlier, horses use up calories to keep warm, but a forage-based diet will assist them because of the heat-producing

A field shelter offers shade in hot weather, as well as protection from the cold and damp.

process of microbial fermentation in the hindgut. Nevertheless, in cold conditions, rugs will help keep the horses dry, warm and comfortable. Thick, fully waterproof, but relatively lightweight rugs are available nowadays, and neck covers are integral or can be added. These provide adequate protection for clipped horses and even sensitive breeds such as Thoroughbreds. The type of clip carried out can also be adjusted, with less of the coat removed – just as much as is necessary to help the horse dry rapidly after heavy sweating.

Keeping horses without shoes

In the UK, horses tend to be shod whether or not they require shoes. However, some owners have chosen to have their horses' shoes removed, and keep them barefoot, also called barehoof. Ideally, the decision to have a horse shod or not should be made depending on whether or not the horse needs shoes – i.e. if the work the horse does wears down his hoof horn faster than it grows, the horse may need shoes. There are specialist hoof-trimming practitioners available nowadays, but check that they have suitable qualifications.

Horses who have been shod for some time may take many months for their hooves to become adapted to having no shoes, and for the sole to become tough and more resilient. Feeding a correctly balanced diet is important to support hoof horn production, perhaps adding a hoof supplement for horses with obvious problems. Hoof boots can be obtained to help the transitional period.

Minerals are particularly important for strong hooves, so these must be supplemented to horses on forage-only diets. Anecdotal evidence suggests that supplementary magnesium helps to promote the health of hooves, but this should be fed with regard to the total diet.

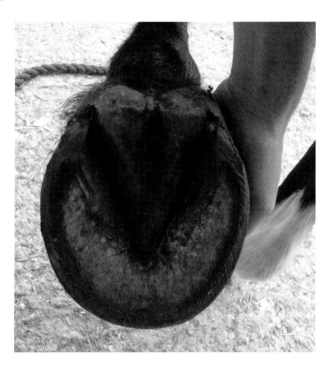

A healthy
unshod foot.

chapter 13

Clinical nutrition

M ANY VETERINARY PROBLEMS in horses are linked to feeding and nutrition. Colic is one of the most common health problems in horses, and one of the most frequent conditions requiring emergency treatment. Many cases are caused by digestive problems or inappropriate feeding regimes. Laminitis and tying up (rhabdomyolysis) are two conditions that can be caused by specific diets, and may be successfully managed with dietary strategies. Other diet-related health problems include diarrhoea, choke, gastric ulcers, poor skin, coat and hoof health, feed allergies, allergic respiratory disease, and nutrient deficiencies. Feeding inappropriate diets may also cause unseen symptoms, including acidic gut syndrome. Sick horses, those in confinement, starved horses and those with grass sickness need special dietary care, and horses with liver and kidney disease also need specialized diets. All are discussed in this chapter.

Colic

The term colic is used to describe any abdominal pain in the horse, which may have any cause. Signs include discomfort and pain, which are expressed as varying intensities of restlessness, pawing and rolling, looking around to the flanks, and loss of appetite. Pain is associated with increased heart and respiratory rates. Diarrhoea, or little or no droppings may be seen, depending on the type of colic. Colic tends to be caused by either the intestine wall being stretched by ingesta (e.g. impactions), gas or fluid; a lack of blood supply to the gut, usually arising from twisting or a piece of gut getting displaced and trapped, or a piece of gut telescoping in on itself (intussusception), and inflammation. It may also be a consequence of infection or have a variety of other causes, one of which is parasitic activity.

Rolling in discomfort, as opposed to rolling for pleasure, is one of the signs of colic.

Parasites, particularly large and small strongyles (redworms), roundworms and tapeworms, can cause colic in different ways. Large strongyles migrate through the arteries supplying the intestine and can cause inflammation and blood clots, disrupting the blood supply to the gut and causing spasmodic colic. Small strongyles have a dormant period when they are encysted in the gut wall and sometimes during winter their emergence is inhibited, resulting in large numbers of larvae emerging from the gut wall en mass in the spring, causing colic, diarrhoea, weight loss and even death. This condition is sometimes called 'cyathostomiasis'. Roundworms are a common cause of colic in foals, in whom they can physically block the intestine. Tapeworms tend to accumulate around the junction of the small and large intestines, the ileocaecal junction. The risk of colic in this area is increased when tapeworms are present, and they can cause both impaction colic and spasmodic colic. Refer to Chapter 8 for information on controlling parasites in horses.

Both parasitic worms and digesta can physically block the digestive tract with impactions, causing pain and, in some cases, a twisting of the gut. Large intakes of dry material without adequate access to water can cause impactions, and pasture-kept horses stabled suddenly on straw are susceptible. Fluid and gas accumulate and peristalsis is reduced, associated with reduced gut sounds. The flexures where the gut turns sharply are most susceptible to impactions. Sand colic is an accumulation of sandy soil eaten while grazing on bare pasture, and is more common in the USA than the UK. Eating hay helps to expel ingested sand, as does eating psyllium husks. In sandy areas, especially where there is little grass, concentrate feed should always be given in a bowl or trough, rather than on the ground.

Gas distention, which may accompany an impaction, is very painful, and may even cause rupture of the stomach or other affected area. Prompt veterinary attention is vital.

Certain feeding practices are associated with an increased risk of colic. Change of diet, including forage and concentrate feed, is one of them. The gut does adapt to dietary changes: bacterial populations will change, and the activity of enzymes that digest non-structural carbohydrates and fat is increased after these feeds are introduced, but all this happens slowly. Feeding high levels of concentrates increases the risk of colic, especially of the large intestine.

Stabled horses are more likely to get colic than those at grass, possibly because they are unable to move around naturally and are more likely to be fed more concentrates. Intensive exercise and changes in exercise level have been associated with increased colic risk, and this may be related to the changes in feed that usually accompany changes in exercise level. Lack of access to water increases the risk of colic, and transportation, which tends to cause dehydration, also increases the risk of impaction colic, probably as a consequence of this. Surgical colic cases at a UK veterinary hospital are much higher during winter, when horses are managed more intensively and fed more concentrates than in summer.

Overfeeding non-structural carbohydrate such as starch, which causes the hindgut environment to become more acidic, can cause colic. The horse's small intestine has a limited ability to digest starch, and if too much is fed at one time, undigested starch flows into the hindgut and cause a proliferation in the acid-producing bacteria, and a cascade of problems as explained in Chapter 4. If the acidity is not severe enough to cause colic or laminitis, it may still cause problems with the newly termed 'acidic gut syndrome' as explained in the next section.

Colic should always be taken seriously, and the vet contacted as soon as possible. Cases that require surgery have a much better chance if they are taken to hospital as early as possible. The level of pain will help the vet decide whether a colic case requires surgery. Colic cases that do not require surgery will be treated medically, i.e. with drugs. Painkillers will be given, often with liquid paraffin and electrolytes. The vet will advise on management – some colic cases will benefit from light exercise.

Prior to gut surgery, it is beneficial to reduce gut fill, but horses should never be fasted for longer than 24 hours. Horses who have undergone digestive tract surgery may have special feeding requirements: the vet should be able to advise on this matter. After part of the gut has been removed (intestinal resection), hay or soaked chopped hay should be offered as soon as possible after surgery. If the caecum or less than 50% of the small intestine is removed, no special requirements are necessary. However, if more major resection has occurred, the diet should reflect the remainder of the gut. For hindgut resection, feed high-quality grass hay or alfalfa/grass hay mix. Good pasture grass and concentrate feed plus vegetable oil may be necessary, as weight loss is common. B-complex vitamins should be supplemented. For small intestinal resection, feed high-fibre diets including sugar beet, and avoid concentrates and grain. Soft mash diets made from soaked high-fibre cubes (which can be fed as complete diets) with fresh green grass are useful. If the ileum (the last part of the small intestine) is unaffected, vegetable oil can be fed for extra calories. If the ileum is affected, vitamins A and E will need to be injected by the vet, and dietary calcium should be increased. Coarse forages such as mature stemmy hay should be avoided even after full recovery.

Acidic gut syndrome

It has been known for some time that overfeeding non-structural carbohydrates including starch to horses causes starch to flow indigested into the hindgut, causing a shift in the dominant microbial population and an increased acidity resulting from the production of large amounts of lactic acid. The acidity causes hindgut disturbance and, in severe cases, can lead to diarrhoea, laminitis and colic. What happens in severe cases is relatively well understood, but a vet and researcher in Australia has recently proposed a syndrome which involves gut acid levels that previously have not been considered harmful. Little is yet known about this acidic gut syndrome, but it has been proposed that it may be associated with behavioural changes, increased risk of gut disturbances and other problems that have, in the past, been put down to food allergies or stress. The adverse effects of acidic gut syndrome are believed to result from a breakdown in the integrity of the gut wall lining. Cells lining the gut wall are important for the absorption of nutrients, maintaining a barrier between digesta and the rest of the body, and for efficient immune function. Therefore acidic gut syndrome probably has an impact on the immune system, which may link it to other, secondary diseases. More research is necessary to improve knowledge and understanding of this syndrome, including at what level of non-structural carbohydrate intake it starts to become a problem. Current recommendations are that no more than 2 g starch per kilo of bodyweight (1 kg for a 500 kg horse) is fed in one meal. It is possible that, for some horses, less than this may cause acidic gut syndrome.

Diarrhoea

Any change in the consistency or frequency of droppings should be noted and the vet consulted if this is associated with weight loss or other health abnormalities. Diarrhoea is a term describing an increase in the frequency or volume of faeces or droppings, which is usually a result of increased water content. Normally, water in the gut is reabsorbed in the large intestine, leaving just enough to aid the passage of faeces. Diarrhoea not associated with other symptoms may be caused by intake of lush spring grass, which is high in water and non-structural carbohydrates (including fructans), low in fibre and can be eaten very quickly. The sloppy droppings that result are probably a combination of hindgut fermentation of the fructans, an overwhelming of the gut's water reabsorption capacity, and a more rapid passage rate. Adequate fibre should be fed along with the grass, and horses taken off the grazing for part of the day or night if they refuse the supplementary forage to continue eating the grass. (In such circumstances, care should be taken with horses and ponies susceptible to laminitis, and grass restricted if necessary.)

Horses with inefficient chewing ability or gut damage may have ongoing sloppy droppings and, again, if this is not associated with other symptoms, there is likely to be no further underlying problem. Probiotic supplements can be fed, and will help in some cases. As mentioned in Chapter 11, regular dental attention is important for all horses, and dental problems that cause a difficulty in fibrous-feed intake will cause diarrhoea through fibre deficiency and gut upset. Horses with such problems must have dental treatment and be provided with an alternative source of fibre, e.g. soaked high-fibre cubes. Horses with less severe chewing problems, who can cope with long forage, may have sloppy droppings because of the faster passage rate of larger pieces through the hindgut, which gives less time for water to be reabsorbed in the colon. Provided the horse has regular dental treatment, is maintaining condition, and is fed leafy early-cut forage, there is no additional problem, although the hind legs and the area under the tail may need to be washed regularly.

As explained in the previous section on colic, diarrhoea may result from overeating non-structural carbohydrates. The hindgut acidity and rapid production of lactic and other volatile fatty acids causes an osmotic influx of water into the gut, increasing the water content of the faeces. The changes in the hindgut environment may also damage the gut lining, causing toxin absorption and a 'leaky' gut, which also contribute to the diarrhoea.

Horses with diarrhoea that is associated with other symptoms should have veterinary attention. Their food should not be withdrawn, because fasting can itself cause diarrhoea in horses. The most common cause of pathogenic (disease-associated) diarrhoea in horses is cyathostomiasis, or small strongyle (redworm) infection (see Colic), especially in horses under 5 years of age. Large numbers of inhibited encysted small strongyle larvae emerge, generally in the spring, causing gut lining inflammation, which results in diarrhoea. Rapid weight loss is associated with this parasitic diarrhoea, and prompt veterinary attention in important.

Cases of starch overload and colitis should be fed grass or oat hay and should not be given non-structural carbohydrates such as starch and sugar. Psyllium husks may be supplemented as a good source of the short-chain fatty acid butyrate in the hindgut, which is reputed to have a healing effect on the gut lining.

Viral and bacterial infections cause diarrhoea through destruction of the cells lining the gut wall, which causes reduced nutrient and water absorption. Horses with diarrhoea caused by salmonella or clostridia infections should be fed forage and probiotics and a high-fibre cubed compound feed if necessary, split into several meals per day. Non-structural carbohydrates such as starch should be avoided. The vet may give fluid therapy orally or by nasogastric tube, and various drugs.

Choke

Choke, or impaction of the throat (oesophagus), can be caused by inefficient dental function, greediness and eating too fast, inadequate access to water, and the consumption of very coarse, or dry but soft, feed. Cases of choke often clear themselves, but veterinary attention may be required. Horses prone to choke should be given dampened feed and their consumption rate reduced by placing large, smooth stones in their feed bowl and/or by adding chaff to concentrate feed.

Gastric ulcers

The incidence of gastric (stomach) ulcers is very high, especially in performance horses and other horses managed intensively. Research trials investigating racehorses showed that up to 92% are affected, and trials investigating non-racing performance horses showed that about 60% of horses in that category are affected. When assessed at the end of 50 and 80 km rides, 67% of endurance horses in a study in the USA were found to have gastric ulceration. The condition, which can involve various degrees of stomach lesions and ulcers, has been called equine gastric ulcer syndrome (EGUS) by vets and researchers. Gastric ulcers used to be considered an inconsequential finding post mortem, but in the past decade vets have realized that they cause discomfort, pain and poor performance and, in some cases, rupture of the stomach. The diagnosis of gastric ulcers has been made easier since the mid-1980s with the use of endoscopes that allow vets to view the stomach directly.

Horses are particularly susceptible to gastric ulcers partly because of their stomach anatomy and physiology, and also because of the intensive way they are managed, and the stress of competition. In the horse, gastric acid production is not dependent on the presence of digesta or eating, but is continuous. Both food and saliva buffer the stomach environment, reducing acidity, but acid will build up in the stomach of a fasting horse. Thus feed deprivation leads to very acidic conditions in the stomach, which increase the risk of ulcers forming. The horse's stomach is comprised of two distinct areas, the upper part of which has no protection against acid, and this non-glandular (squamous) area is where most ulcers occur. Exactly why and how ulcers form is poorly understood, and it is likely to be more complicated than simply a consequence of excess acid. Exercise seems to exacerbate the problem, because cantering and galloping cause increased pressure within the abdomen, resulting in a rise in gastric acid, which exposes the unprotected non-glandular area to damage. It is known that the use of non-steroidal anti-inflammatory (NSAID) drugs such as phenylbutazone can induce gastric ulcers in horses of all ages.

Risk factors for gastric ulcers include periods of fasting, high-grain (high-starch) diets, low forage intakes, little access to pasture, intensive exercise, competition, the use of high levels of NSAID drugs, serious illness and transportation. Gastric ulcers are very rare in pasture-kept horses. Feeding large amounts of grain and little forage predisposes to ulcers because this type of regime is associated with hours of fasting between meals, and because grain meals cause changes in the stomach environment that increase the risk of ulcers. In addition, grain requires less chewing than fibrous forage, so produces less of the saliva that buffers stomach contents, reducing its acidity. It is easy to see why so many racehorses suffer from EGUS, if their lifestyles and diets are considered – high-grain diets, little forage, little or no access to pasture and intensive exercise (often after periods of fasting).

Signs of gastric ulceration in adult horses include poor appetite, dullness, grumpy attitude, poor performance, poor body condition, weight loss, rough coat and low-grade colic, but gastric ulcers may be present without external symptoms. Foals are also susceptible to gastric ulcers, and signs include intermittent colic, frequent lying down, diarrhoea, poor appetite, grinding teeth and salivation. Affected foals may also have an erratic suckling pattern, with interrupted bouts, probably because of discomfort. The syndrome in foals is likely to be caused by a lack of milk production in the mare, or inability of the foal to suckle often enough, and may be compounded by stress and/or infection in the foal.

The best treatment for gastric ulcers (not surprisingly) is pasture turnout, ad lib forage, withdrawal of grain and generally a more natural regime. Owners and managers of performance horses may not wish to adopt such a regime, and instead may use drug therapy. Drug treatment of gastric ulcers aims to inhibit acid production, and the drug omeprazole has been shown to be an effective treatment for gastric ulcers in horses. However, if no changes are made in the management of affected animals, the continuing regime will necessitate continuous treatment with drugs, which is expensive and may be harmful to the animal. Also, treating symptoms without any regard for the cause of a condition seems unwise. An alternative is to neutralize gastric acid with antacid compounds, and commercial preparations for this are available. There is no evidence of their effectiveness in healing ulcers, but they do appear to give some relief from the symptoms. Antacids should, however, be used in combination with changes in management and, where necessary, drug therapy.

Ideally, the regime of the affected horse should be scrutinized and adjusted where possible. The use of higher-energy forages, e.g. haylage, will reduce the need for concentrates and allow longer periods of chewing and eating; digestible fibre and oil feeds are an alternative to grain-based concentrates; the practice of fasting before exercise is unnecessary and access to some forage will not affect training or competition performance; some turnout should be provided every day, and forage offered where there is little or no grass; and periods of fasting should never exceed 2 hours. Ad lib forage should be provided if possible.

The use of electrolyte pastes prior to and during competition in endurance and eventing horses should be considered carefully, because research has shown that these may exacerbate gastric ulcers. Instead, horses should be trained to drink isotonic solutions and fed hypertonic pastes only when necessary, and mixed with feed such as chopped alfalfa. (Refer to Water and the Electrolyte Macrominerals in Chapter 10.)

Skin, coat and hoof problems

The most important nutritional factor for healthy skin, a shiny coat and strong, resilient hooves is a correctly balanced diet. There is no point in adding supplemental nutrients until the basic diet is balanced, and dietary analysis should be carried out as a first step. The skin and hooves are constantly being renewed, and they rely on nutrients to create new cells and, in the case of the skin, hairs and the secretions associated with them. The most important nutrients for skin and hooves are protein, lipids, vitamins and minerals. Dietary deficiencies of protein, zinc, copper, vitamins A, B complex and E could cause skin, coat and hoof problems. Management should be scrutinized to ensure that external factors are not having a detrimental effect, because not even a balanced diet can help badly trimmed, unbalanced hooves.

Healthy skin relies on adequate supplies of the essential fatty acids linolenic acid (an omega-3 fatty acid) and linoleic acid (an omega-6). In dogs, supplementing these fatty acids improves skin and coat condition. A similar effect has not yet been proven in horses, although one study showed positive results in horses supplemented with linseed, a rich source of linolenic acid. Horses' natural forage diets are relatively low in total lipids, and some people report that adding any vegetable oil to a horse's diet gives a shinier coat.

Research has shown that feeding megadoses of biotin (20 mg per day, in contrast to the 1 or 2 mg per day dietary requirement) helps hoof problems in some horses. These therapeutic doses need to be fed long term (for 2 years plus) for best effect. The minerals calcium and zinc and the sulphur-containing amino acid methionine are nutrients important for healthy hoof horn production, and are often included in hoof supplements. There is no evidence that levels of these substances above normal requirements help poor hoof horn, but supplementing them in reasonable amounts along with biotin will do no harm if added to a balanced diet. The hoof wall grows at a rate of about 8–10 mm per month, so 9–12 months are required for the whole hoof wall to be replaced and show the benefits of nutrient supplementation. The most important factor for hoof problems – in addition to a completely balanced diet – is good hoof balance from regular and appropriate trimming. The horse's hoof has an important biomechanical as well as a physical protective role, and an unbalanced hoof will not be able to dissipate forces efficiently, which could have a detrimental effect on hoof horn growth.

Food allergies

Many horse owners believe that their horses suffer from food allergies or intolerances, despite the fact that there have been few confirmed cases in veterinary literature. Allergies, or hypersensitivities, involve an inappropriate response by

the horse's body to a foreign substance (the allergen) that is inhaled, eaten or contacts the skin. Normally, the body protects itself against such foreign substances via the immune system in a controlled way, but in cases of hypersensitivity there is an excessive and harmful inflammatory response. Common non-food allergies in horses include sweet itch, which is hypersensitivity to the bite of the Culicoides midge, and allergic airway disease, which may be a response to mould and dust in hay and straw, and pollen in summer. Horses are also particularly susceptible to urticaria, a skin condition characterized by weals of different shapes and sizes, with or without itching. Urticaria can be caused by contact allergy, insect bites, reactions to drugs, allergies to inhaled mould, mites and pollen, or allergies to specific feeds. How-

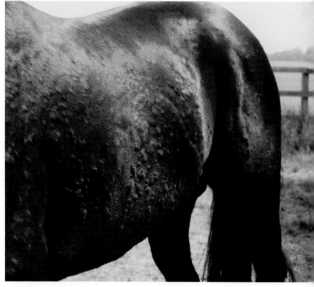

A horse with urticaria.

ever, as mentioned, true feed allergies are rarely confirmed. The affected horse's pasture should be investigated for possible contact irritants, which may be causing an irritant reaction rather than an allergy, despite the presence of weals on the skin. Look for irritant plants such as buttercup, treated wood and other possible irritants. Affected horses' rugs and clothing such as saddle cloths should be cleaned in simple soaps rather than washing powders. All possible skin irritants and allergens should be considered.

In order for a food allergy to be confirmed, the suspected food should be withdrawn from the diet for at least two weeks, then reintroduced and the horse monitored carefully. The reintroduction period is crucial in order to confirm the reaction. If an allergy or intolerance is suspected, but there is little knowledge of which food might be involved, a basic diet of grass and/or grass or oat hay can be given, and then single foods introduced in two-week spells. There are currently no blood tests available that have been validated for the diagnosis of food allergies in the horse. Skin tests can be carried out by a vet, but are not always reliable and must be interpreted with care.

There is no evidence that diets high in sugar or starch are connected to sweet itch, and control of the condition is based on preventing exposure to the biting Culicoides midges. Use of fly rugs and repellents, stabling during dawn and dusk, and fly fans in the stable are effective.

A horse wearing a fly rug.

Allergic respiratory disease

Allergic respiratory disease is very common in stabled horses, and can also occur during the summer in animals at pasture. The condition used to be called chronic obstructive pulmonary disease (COPD) but this has been replaced by the term recurrent airway obstruction (RAO), and is also sometimes called heaves. RAO is probably fundamentally an allergy to fungal spores in hay and straw, and the condition is further exacerbated by dust and other airborne particles. RAO causes exercise intolerance, coughing, excess mucus production and breathing difficulties.

Some researchers have found that up to half of stabled horses have RAO. Management is a crucial part of treatment, and ideally, affected horses should be kept outside. Even if this is done, care must be taken with the forage provided. Research has shown that all hay contains some dust and mould spores, which are a health risk to all horses, and must be avoided by horses with RAO. All hay should be soaked for half an hour prior to feeding to horses, to reduce airborne particles and mould spores – which swell and stick to the wet hay. The liquid left over after soaking hay is basically contaminated water that is a very strong pollutant; therefore it should be disposed of with care. Soaking hay causes leaching of nutrients and thus lowers the feed value of the forage, so the ration should be adjusted as necessary. Concentrate feeds and chaffs should be dampened before being fed.

Research has shown that the lungs of horses with RAO have lower levels of antioxidants than those of healthy horses. Vitamin C (ascorbic acid) is the most important antioxidant in the lungs and supplementary vitamin C in the form of ascorbyl palmitate, along with other antioxidant nutrients, has been shown to improve the antioxidant status and the function of the lungs of RAO-affected horses. Healthy horses do not have a dietary requirement for vitamin C, but horses with RAO or any other lung condition will benefit from increased dietary antioxidants and a source of vitamin C.

Practical aspects of clinical nutrient deficiencies

Although some horses may not be receiving adequate levels of nutrients for optimal health and performance, clinical nutrient deficiencies that cause disease are relatively uncommon in most horses. As explained in Chapter 4, the diets of most adult horses supply sufficient nutrients provided they are based on forage, with supplementary feed or vitamin and mineral supplements given to balance the forage. However, horses fed only grass may suffer from micromineral (trace element) and/or sodium deficiencies, depending on the content of the pasture. The microminerals most likely to be in short supply in grass include selenium, copper, iodine and zinc. Most pasture supplies adequate iron, manganese and cobalt. The macromineral supply of well-managed pasture should be adequate (with the exception of sodium, especially for working horses) although it may be short of magnesium for some horses who require abnormally large amounts.

Preserved forages lose much of their vitamin E and, in the case of most hay, provitamin A. A healthy horse out on good pasture all summer will store enough vitamin A (from ingested betacarotenes) in his liver to supply him through the first couple of months of winter. All horses fed preserved forage, with no access to grass, will require vitamin E as well as mineral supplementation.

Horses fed just grass (fresh or preserved) plus more than a moderate quantity (450–900 g) of grain (including wheat bran) per day will suffer from a deficiency of calcium, because of the high level of phosphorus in grain that inhibits calcium uptake. Calcium balance in the body must be kept strictly within specific limits, because of its importance in nerve conduction and muscle contraction. Calcium deficiency causes growth abnormalities in young horses, lameness and fractures in adult horses, and a swelling of the head ('big head') through replacement of hard bone with fibrous tissue.

Care should be taken with feeding single-nutrient supplements, particularly minerals (apart from sodium). Many nutrients have intricate interactions with each other, and adding too much of one can inhibit uptake or use of others. For example, excess phosphorus can cause a calcium deficiency, and large excesses of calcium will inhibit magnesium uptake, and in theory could cause a deficiency. In most cases, if in doubt about dietary nutrient supply, broad-spectrum supplements are the safest way of adding extra micronutrients. Ideally, a specific supplement for the horse should be found (e.g. a pasture or haylage balancing supplement) but in practice this may be difficult. Cases of suspected nutrient deficiency should be referred to the vet, who may be able to diagnose the problem. Unfortunately, nutrient status cannot be checked easily from a single test such as a blood test, and the most practical way of assessment is with detailed diet analysis. If a deficiency is diagnosed or recognized, a nutritionist should be contacted for help with the diet and to avoid future problems.

Obesity

Obesity, or excessive body fat, is a clinical problem. Ideally, horses and ponies should not be allowed to become obese; prevention is better than cure. Refer to Chapter 8 for strategies on feeding for weight loss.

Feeding horses on box rest

As well as meeting nutritional requirements, diets for box-rested horses must meet behavioural needs. Confined horses are at a higher risk of developing abnormal behaviour including crib-biting and wind-sucking. Horses naturally spend about 70% of their time eating, so this should be made possible by supplying forage of low enough nutritional quality to be fed ad lib to confined horses. Research has shown that stabled horses exhibit more normal behaviour if offered a choice of forages, so for example a choice of grass hay (soaked), hay-replacer chop, and some quick-dried alfalfa or grass can be fed. If haylage is included, it should be high in dry matter (> 65%) and fibre, and low in protein and energy.

Feed-decanting balls such as the Equiball or the Decahedron can be given, with high-fibre cubes in them, to encourage foraging behaviour, provided that such behaviour is appropriate to the horse's condition.

Care should be taken when feeding a horse who is not actually sick but is healing (e.g. post-injury) and needs to be confined to a stable, because it is easy to overfeed. Overfeeding confined horses increased the risk of obesity, abnormal and excitable behaviour, laminitis and colic. Because of the lack of activity, confined horses require only a maintenance level of nutrients or a little less and are usually best kept on an ad lib low-quality forage diet with vitamin and mineral supplementation (especially sodium, chloride, vitamin E, zinc, selenium, copper and iodine). Hay and haylage diets usually supply plenty of potassium, iron and manganese, and adequate calcium, energy and protein for maintenance.

Grain, coarse mixes and other starchy feeds, and cubes with medium or higher energy levels should be avoided. If the horse is under-eating or requires more calories, a higher quality forage (e.g. chopped dehydrated grass or alfalfa) could replace some of the current forage, or a medium-energy highly digestible

An injured horse on box rest; appropriate forage-based feed sustains basic health and helps to maintain normal behaviour.

fibre cubed feed and/or sugar beet pulp can be offered. A low-starch diet is particularly important for confined horses who are susceptible to tying up (rhabdomyolysis) caused by polysaccharide storage myopathy (PSSM) – see Chapter 15. The horse should be weighed and/or condition-scored once a week to monitor body fat and to help adjust dietary calorie intake in order to maintain weight.

Sick and anorexic horses

A sick horse who stops eating and fasts completely for a couple of days is at risk of gut disturbance and gastric ulcer formation. The body starts to break down lean tissue after 24 hours of food deprivation. Extended fasting of more than 2–3 days leads to shrinking of the gut cells, general weakness, depressed immune function, delayed healing and diarrhoea.

Loss of appetite can be self-perpetuating and if a horse is able to eat he should be encouraged to do so. It is important to offer sick, anorexic horses a variety of different feeds in a cafeteria style. A selection of forages is best, including fresh grass, alfalfa hay and a poor-quality grass hay, e.g. a late-cut stemmy hay. The selection should also include feeds the horse is familiar with. Although sick horses may have unusual feed preferences, fresh green grass is probably the most palatable feed. If the horse cannot be taken out to graze in hand, fresh grass can be cut and taken to the horse, but it must be fed immediately after cutting. Any uneaten grass must be removed after a few hours, because cut grass wilts and may begin to ferment, causing it to become dangerous if eaten.

Small meals should be offered frequently, with uneaten food removed after a few hours. A concentrated feed may be necessary to supply adequate nutrients, i.e. a feed balancer or a medium- to high-energy high-fibre and oil compound feed. Bran will not do any harm short term, but a source of calcium, i.e. calcium carbonate (limestone flour), should be added to balance the high-phosphorus, low-calcium content of bran. Either a bran mash or sugar beet pulp may be palatable to sick, anorexic horses, but a once-weekly bran mash should not be fed – all feeds should be given daily to reduce the risk of gut disturbance. Molasses, puréed apples or carrots (or apple juice), fenugreek, fennel and aniseeds and crushed polo mints can be added to the feed to try to tempt anorexic horses to eat. Place the feed where it is easiest for the horse; generally floor level is best, unless it is uncomfortable for the horse to lower his head. Drugs, given under veterinary supervision, may help with appetite – reducing pain and fever with non-steroidal anti-inflammatories can help; also appetite-stimulants such as diazepam. Feeding within the sight of another horse who is eating may also help stimulate the appetite. Always check for dental problems, which can cause eating discomfort and loss of food during chewing; pain in the mouth area can cause an unwillingness to even approach food.

Sick horses with poor appetites should be encouraged to eat any food, but the diet should be balanced as soon as the horse regains a normal appetite. Adequate nutrients are necessary for healing, especially the antioxidant nutrients. Supplementation of vitamin C (20–40 g ascorbyl palmitate daily) and vitamin E (an extra 500–1,000 mg daily) may help stressed, chronically ill horses. B-complex vitamins should also be supplemented in chronically ill horses, particularly if they are being given antibiotics or have hindgut disturbance, e.g. diarrhoea. Supplementation of iron is not useful, since it will not treat anaemia in most cases, and supplements containing it should be given with care. For patients with skeletal problems, special care should be taken to provide adequate macrominerals, a correct calcium to phosphorus ratio and adequate manganese and copper intake.

Feeding horses with grass sickness

Grass sickness in horses (equine dysautonomia) is a debilitating and often fatal disease that is characterized by nervous system damage, which causes gut paralysis. The cause is not proven, but the disease occurs in grazing horses and it is thought to involve some sort of toxin. The soil bacteria *Clostridium botulinum* is thought to be involved, and research is also investigating the cyanide-producing properties of white clover. Acute and sub-acute cases, in which the disease progresses rapidly, usually die or are euthanized, but many chronic cases can be nursed back to health.

Horses affected by grass sickness lose their appetite and are prone to choke and to diarrhoea. Nursing involves keeping the horse dry and warm in a stable with a deep bed, and offering a high-energy and high-protein diet. A wide choice of feeds should be offered as for sick, anorexic horses (see above). Nurses report that preferred feeds include cut grass, coarse mix, oats mixed with warm molasses, carrots and apples. Vegetable oil can be added to increase calorie intake and a probiotic supplement should be fed to help the disturbed gut microflora. Small amounts of feed should be offered as often as possible throughout the day and night. Horses should be taken out to graze in hand if they are strong enough, and turned out to graze within a few weeks of the onset of the disease, provided they are strong enough, although different pasture should be sought from that on which the horse became ill.

Re-introducing feed to the starved horse

Short-term complete fasting for as little as 2–3 days reduces immune function and causes shrinkage of the gut lining cells and decreased digestive enzyme production and activity. A chronically starved horse should have food introduced gradually, starting with palatable grass hay and water. After a few days, high-fibre 'concentrates' including sugar beet pulp and high-fibre low-energy compound feeds can be introduced gradually, as well as supplementary salt and vitamins. Small meals should be offered frequently. Overfeeding too soon – especially of starchy concentrate feeds – can cause diarrhoea, laminitis and colic and must therefore be avoided. A goal of at least 2–3 months should be given for re-establishing the normal bodyweight of horses who have lost up to 40% of their bodyweight.

Feeding the horse with liver disease

The liver has various metabolic, secretory, excretory and storage functions, and it also regulates the distribution of nutrients in the body. Chronic liver (hepatic) disorders are usually – but not always – associated with weight loss, which is caused by anorexia (a lack of appetite) and a lack of normal liver metabolism. Low blood sugar is often present, and body tissue insulin resistance is usual. Mental abnormalities are often seen in advanced cases of liver disease, and are thought to be caused by the accumulation of ammonia as a result of the liver's inability to metabolize it – ammonia is a by-product of amino acid catabolism (breakdown). In such cases, the vet will probably need to correct fluid and acid/base imbalances with intravenous fluids and glucose administration.

The aims in feeding horses with liver disease are to minimize further ammonia build up with a low-protein diet and to offer soluble carbohydrates that are easily utilized, and decrease the need for the liver to manufacture glucose. The branched-chain amino acids (BCAAs) should be high and aromatic amino acids (AAAs) low. Ideal diets include low-quality grass hay and 2 parts molassed sugar beet pulp to 1 part flaked maize, split into many small meals – ideally 6 or more feeds per day. Sugar beet is high in BCAAs, which may help with the neurological signs, because they are essential amino acids that are not extensively taken up by the liver. Wheatbran, linseed and maize also have a good BCAA to AAA ratio, but do need to be balanced because of their inappropriate calcium to phosphorus ratio. Horses should also be encouraged to graze.

Legumes such as alfalfa and soya should be avoided because they are protein-rich. Oil is also best avoided. However, meeting calorific requirements is the most important factor and if a horse is under-eating and can be tempted by some less suitable feed, this should be offered in small quantities. Extra B-complex vitamins (including folic acid) and vitamin K should be supplemented or administered, since, while the healthy liver usually processes these vitamins, the unhealthy liver may do so less effectively. Vitamin E is also recommended, particularly if the horse is eating a dry diet with no fortified feed (e.g. hay and grain) and has no access to grass. Zinc supplementation may also help – it is involved in the processing of amino acid breakdown products and deficiencies have been noted in humans with liver disease-associated mental abnormalities.

Hyperlipidaemia

High blood levels of triglyceride, leading to fatty infiltration of the liver, can occur in horses in negative energy balance (i.e. those taking in fewer calories than they are using) and/or under stress – e.g. late gestation, starvation and anorexia caused by other diseases. It is most common in ponies and donkeys and is often fatal. Affected animals should be encouraged to eat non-structural carbohydrates including molasses-coated grain or coarse mixes, and pasture grass and hay. Anorexic ponies may need to be given glucose intravenously, and fed via a stomach tube. Blood glucose concentrations should be monitored closely, especially in ponies with suspected insulin insensitivity.

Feeding the horse with kidney disease

The kidneys have essential functions in controlling body homoeostasis, in removing nitrogenous and organic waste products and controlling the body's water and ion content. Acute kidney (renal) failure is associated with disruption of the glomerular filtration rate and a failure to remove waste products, therefore leading to azotemia (presence of nitrogen compounds in the blood) and disruptions in fluid, electrolyte and acid/base balances.

Chronic renal failure (CRF) occurs most often in old horses and is usually associated with glomeruli injury, and symptoms may go unnoticed until late in the disease. Weight loss, lethargy and anorexia may be seen. There will be excessive loss of the electrolytes sodium, chloride, phosphate and bicarbonate, because they will not be conserved in the renal tubules. Also, since the renal system in the horse is an important route for calcium excretion (via urine crystals of calcium carbonate), blood calcium accumulation can be a problem in CRF.

For horses with kidney disease, the diet should be low protein (<10%) to reduce the degree of azotemia and reduce the load on the kidneys. However, adequate protein and calories should be fed (there should be a neutral nitrogen balance) because deficiencies have been associated with increased morbidity and mortality in human CRF patients. Adequate calories are necessary to avoid the breakdown of both dietary and bodily protein to supply energy. A highly palatable diet, fed in lots of small meals to encourage intake, is the most important factor. Supplementary B vitamins (especially thiamine or B_1) may help to boost appetite, and anabolic steroids may do the same. Supplementary B vitamins should also be fed to make up for the extra losses in urine. Extra antioxidant nutrients may help, although there is no evidence for them yet. If the patient has electrolyte imbalances, extra salt should be fed and free-choice salt is recommended, provided that the animal does not overeat this. Plenty of water intake should be encouraged, even if this means that water is replaced every few hours.

As is the case with liver disease, if the horse is under-eating then, generally speaking, anything the horse will eat should be offered. However, there are some constraints to this. Although some legumes such as alfalfa can be offered if the horse has an appetite for them, they should preferably be avoided because of their high protein and calcium contents. Adding oils and fats to the feed should definitely be avoided, especially if the horse also has hyperlipidaemia.

chapter 14

Laminitis

Call the vet!
Laminitis is a medical emergency and if it is suspected, a vet should be called without delay. Prompt treatment in the early stages could save a horse's life. If laminitis is diagnosed, the vet may administer drugs, provide mechanical support to the affected feet and advise the owner about management.

L AMINITIS IS A DREADED word, and rightly so. It is a debilitating and painful disease that can cause death, and once affected, horses and ponies are more susceptible to the disease in the future. Most (but not all) cases of laminitis are diet-related, and vets state that correct dietary management may prevent most cases. Many research studies have been carried out in recent years, investigating the mechanisms (i.e. what happens during the disease), with the aim of finding effective preventative and curative treatments. Unfortunately there is still much work to be done before a cure or guaranteed preventative is found.

What happens during laminitis

The word laminitis tends to conjure up a picture of a horse leaning back to take the weight off his painful forefeet as a result of over-indulgence in spring grass. Such a scenario simplifies what is actually a very complex disease.

In simple terms, laminitis involves a failure of the lamellae that attach the pedal bone of the foot to the inner hoof wall. The word 'lamellae' is used nowadays rather than 'laminae', because it is thought to be a more correct description of the complex folded membrane that holds the pedal bone within the hoof capsule. The trigger factors and what exactly causes the damage to the lamellae

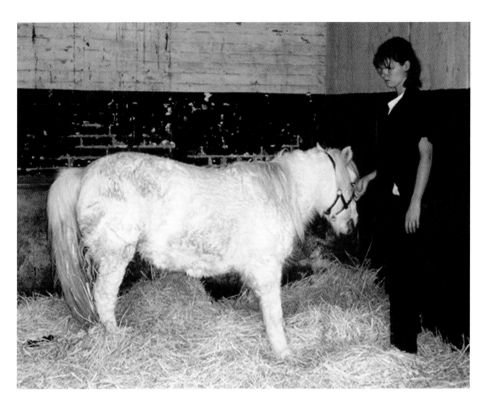

Typical posture of a laminitic pony.

are not fully understood, but there are several phases, including one when blood supply is increased in the very early developmental stages, then an ischaemic phase where the lamellae are starved of blood, then an inflammatory phase where the body tries to deal with the damaged tissues. Once the lamellae are damaged, their role of attaching the pedal bone to the hoof wall is impaired and the weight of the horse and the pull of the tendon on the pedal bone cause it to drop backwards and down towards the sole (a condition sometimes called founder). In severe cases, the pedal bone becomes detached and drops through the sole of the foot. Unfortunately the early developmental stages occur without any signs, so once the horse shows foot pain the disease is already in an advanced stage.

It was thought that laminitis was purely a vascular disease – that the hoof tissues were starved of blood because of a circulatory problem and this caused the lamellae to become inflamed and fail. A reperfusion of blood after the initial inflammation was then thought to cause further damage. Although this theory has not been completely disregarded, Australian vet and research scientist Dr Chris Pollitt showed that there was no inflammation in the very early developmental stages of laminitis, and initially there is an *increase* in blood flow to the hooves. Dr Pollitt proposed the involvement of MMPs (matrix metalloproteinases) as the initial activators of lamellar damage.

The hoof in an interesting structure because, in order for the wall to grow, it must constantly be detaching and reattaching the lamellar tissue that links the hoof wall and the pedal bone. This process takes place via the action of MMP enzymes. During laminitis the MMPs are thought to be activated by various 'trigger factors' that include substances released after hindgut disturbance, including bacterial endotoxins. However, endotoxins alone do not induce laminitis. British researcher Simon Bailey showed that high levels of amines, which affect blood flow, are produced in the hindgut after non-structural carbohydrate overload, and this might be the link between hindgut disturbance and the vascular changes seen in the hooves. Another contributory factor could be linked to the insulin resistance that many laminitic horses and ponies have. (Refer to Chapter 4 for more information on insulin resistance.) Some breeds of ponies, and overweight horses, are commonly insulin-insensitive (resistant), especially if they are not exercised regularly. There appears to be a genetic susceptibility to the development of insulin resistance and this may explain why some pony breeds are particularly at risk of laminitis. Insulin resistance is characterized by high blood glucose levels but low uptake into the tissues, because of the inefficient function of insulin. The hoof lamellae rely on glucose to maintain the strong bond between the hoof wall and the pedal bone and if these hoof tissues are starved of glucose, this could contribute towards the lamellar separation of laminitis.

In addition, whole-body metabolic stress that occurs with laminitis caused by non-structural carbohydrate overload or infection is associated with reduced use of glucose in peripheral tissue such as the hooves. High blood glucose levels have

Overweight horses who are not exercised may develop insulin resistance.

a variety of toxic effect in horses – as they do in human diabetics – and this could contribute to laminitis via disturbed blood flow and clotting mechanisms. Horses and ponies with Cushing's syndrome (see Chapter 11) usually develop insulin resistance, and this may be a contributory factor to their high risk of laminitis. Exactly how insulin resistance predisposes to laminitis is probably very complex, and further research is necessary in order to understand the link fully.

In reality, it is likely that a combination of factors are involved, because no one single theory appears to suit the wide variety of causes of laminitis (see below). From a practical point of view, hindgut disturbance is certainly one of the factors – if not the most important – that is involved in diet-induced laminitis, and for this reason the maintenance of hindgut stability should be paramount in the control of the condition.

Signs of laminitis

The earlier laminitis is suspected and the vet called, the better the chance of recovery. The following signs may be seen:

- A bounding pulse in the digital artery on the side and to the back of the fetlock.

- Reluctance to walk, or even lift the feet.

- Foot pain and lameness, which may be slight to very severe.

- A pitted area around the coronary band, resulting from pedal bone movement. *This is an emergency – call your vet.*

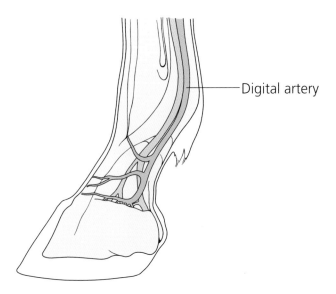

Digital artery

Figure 14.1 Diagram showing location of the digital artery.

Animals at Risk

Even before signs of foot pain or a bounding pulse are evident, the following factors put a horse at higher risk and such horses should be monitored carefully:

- Overweight horse or pony, particularly if a large, fatty crest is evident.

- Turnout to a large area of new spring grass, especially if the horse or pony is greedy or already overweight.

- Overeating of cereal grain or coarse mix.

- Infrequent trimming or shoeing and overgrown, unbalanced feet.

- Lameness in one leg, causing more weight to be taken on the opposite, unaffected leg, which makes it at risk of laminitis.

- A mare with retained placenta after foaling – *call your vet without delay.*

- A horse or pony with Cushing's disease (see Chapter 11).

- A horse or pony with a history of laminitis.

- A horse or pony given steroid drugs.

- Excess stress, e.g. long-distance travel, moving yard.

Diet-induced laminitis

As mentioned earlier, overeating non-structural carbohydrate causes laminitis because the horse has a relatively limited ability to digest such feed and absorb it from his small intestine. Therefore undigested carbohydrate reaches the hindgut where it is rapidly fermented by gut bacteria, which causes disturbance, a shift in acidity, release of toxins and other substances, and a leaky gut, allowing these substances to get into the circulation. Researchers have been working hard in recent years to try to understand the link between the hindgut disturbance and the disease process in the hoof but, despite the offer of various theories, there is as yet no obvious explanation. The problem is made worse by insulin resistance if the horse is overweight, relatively sedentary and/or fed high levels of non-structural carbohydrates long term. There is no link between dietary protein and laminitis.

Grass

Grass is the best-known trigger of laminitis and it is particularly dangerous because horses can eat a large quantity in a short space of time. The rate of eating is an important trigger factor as well as the type of feed, because the rate determines how much undigested non-structural carbohydrate reaches the hindgut. This is why greedy ponies are at much higher risk.

While it is the sugar in grass that was thought to be the trigger for laminitis, recent research has suggested that this may not be the case. Sugar is relatively well digested by the horse, and either very large amounts short term or moderate amounts long term would need to be fed to trigger laminitis. Research has confirmed that grass in the UK is richer in fructans than sugars, and these, rather than sugars, are now believed to be the dangerous carbohydrates. Fructans are not digested in the small intestine by the horse's own digestive enzymes but, like fibre, are fermented in the intestine by bacteria. Relatively small amounts of fructans are fine (and have beneficial effects on the gut), but a huge intake in a short time causes a massive proliferation of fructan-fermenting bacteria, leading to hindgut disturbance. The fructan concentration in grass varies as a result of changes in light, rainfall and temperature, but levels in young, growing grass can be high. Since fructans are the storage carbohydrate of the grass, levels are probably highest when the grass is active but cannot actually grow, i.e. on a cold, frosty, sunny morning.

Starchy cereals

These are another feed trigger for laminitis. Unlike fructans, starch can be digested in the small intestine, but the horse has a limited capacity to do so because of low production of amylase, the enzyme that breaks starch down. This, coupled with the fast flow rate through the small intestine, means that if large amounts of starch are eaten, dangerous levels may reach the hindgut undigested, leading to a proliferation of starch-loving bacteria that produce lactic acid, causing a shift in acidity and hindgut disturbance. More than 1 kg of starch in one meal to a 500 kg horse can overwhelm the small intestine and cause undigested starch to reach the hindgut.

Protein used to be blamed for laminitis, probably because fructan-rich grass is often rich in protein. Therefore horses eating protein-rich grass developed laminitis and owners made the link. However, protein overload does not cause the hindgut disturbance that is associated with the onset of laminitis, and there is no evidence that excess protein causes laminitis.

Feeding management of laminitics

Vets, researcher workers and experienced horse handlers all agree that management of a laminitic is everything. There is no cure, therefore avoiding the disease in the first place is important, and experts agree that careful management could drastically reduce the number of cases.

Most importantly, horses and ponies should never be overfed anything, including grass and concentrate feed, and should never allowed to become too fat. These are the two most important factors to help avoid laminitis. The horse's body condition should be continually assessed rather than reliance being placed on the amount of grass in the horse's pasture. As explained in Chapter 8, a weigh-tape and condition scoring should be used to monitor the horse. If necessary, concentrate feed should be withdrawn and replaced with a broad-spectrum vitamin and mineral supplement. Overweight horses should not be starved, but should be fed to ensure gradual weight loss. To avoid other problems such as wood-chewing, appetite should be satisfied with hard, stemmy hay and/or straw provided (but ensure good dental care). Plenty of fibre should be fed to support hindgut function, especially after a bout of laminitis and the associated gut disturbance. An absolute minimum of 1% bodyweight per day of forage, i.e. 5 kg for a 500 kg horse, should always be fed.

Other helpful hints:

- Monitor grass intake carefully, and restrict grazing with strip grazing, muzzles (with care and supervision) or even turnout on a bare paddock *with hay*. (Horses should not be turned out on large overgrazed paddocks without supplementary forage because stressed grass may contain relatively high levels of fructan.)

- Grass is thought to be at its safest during the very early morning hours before dawn, so consider turning out from dusk until dawn.

- Horses should not be turned out on frosty grass, particularly on a sunny morning, when fructan levels can soar.

- Do not allow horses or ponies to become overweight, particularly those who are not exercised – they are at risk of insulin resistance, which will increase their risk of laminitis.

- All dietary changes should be made gradually to avoid further hindgut disturbance, and several small meals per day should be given, rather than one or two larger feeds.

- Coarse mixes and cereals should be avoided and replaced with high-fibre cubes and vegetable oil if concentrate feed is necessary.

- For an underweight laminitic, the maximum recommended amount of high-fibre cubes (split between several meals), high-quality chaffs such as quick-dried alfalfa, and vegetable oil can be fed, as well as forage.

- With the vet's advice, an exercise regime should be maintained, particularly if the horse is overweight and/or in a restricted area. Exercise aids the circulation and boosts insulin sensitivity.

- Probiotic supplements can be useful after a bout of laminitis to help normalize gut function.

After a bout of laminitis, most horses and ponies will be on a restricted ration and therefore they may not receive optimal micronutrients to support the healing process. A broad-spectrum vitamin and mineral supplement should be fed, preferably one rich in antioxidants, particularly vitamin E and plant bioflavonoids to help tissue repair and regeneration.

To summarize, laminitis causes pain and suffering and can kill, so the risk factors should be considered at all times. Horses and ponies should go into spring in moderate to lean condition and access to pasture should be offered with care to horses with an unknown past. For horses who gain weight easily or are greedy, have had laminitis in the past or have any other risk factors, restrict grass intake. Keep horses at appropriate condition scores and never allow them to become overweight. Feed horses with their natural high-fibre diet in mind, and avoid starchy and sugary feeds. Finally, if laminitis is suspected, a vet should be called without delay.

chapter 15

'Tying-up' (rhabdomyolysis)

RHABDOMYOLYSIS MEANS 'disintegration of skeletal muscle' and is a term used to describe any condition that involves muscle breakdown. Affected horses have signs of muscular discomfort, stiffness, gait abnormalities and, in severe cases, reddish-brown coloured urine (myogloburina). Horse owners use the terms 'tying up', 'set fast', 'Monday morning disease' and 'azoturia' to describe all the conditions that include rhabdomyolysis as a symptom. Scientists often use the term 'equine rhabdomyolysis syndrome' or ERS. ERS is poorly understood, but sufferers have an underlying susceptibility to the problem, which can be triggered for a variety of reasons. In most cases, however, the muscular symptoms are associated with exercise. Unfortunately, there are no guaranteed methods of prevention for this syndrome, but specific management and nutritional strategies can reduce the likelihood of recurring episodes.

The disease process

The breakdown of muscle cells or fibres causes inflammation, pain and the release of cell contents including enzymes and the oxygen-carrying muscle pigment, myglobin, into the circulation. The condition tends to be diagnosed from a measurement of the muscle enzymes creatine kinase (CK) and aspartate aminotransferase (AST) in the blood plasma, the specific levels of which can help to determine the severity of the attack. The rate at which blood CK and AST levels fall is used to monitor the recovery from an attack. In severe cases, huge amounts of myoglobin are released and excreted via the kidneys, resulting in reddish-brown coloured urine. These severe cases may have kidney damage from the toxic effects of the myoglobin. Depending on the severity, signs in affected horses vary from a slight stiffness, usually in the hind limbs and hindquarters, to a complete inability to move, and even a recumbent horse.

Muscle enzyme	Plasma level (u/L)		
	Normal range	After acute episode of tying up	Several days after episode
CK	0–350	1,000–9,000	150
AST	150–425	1,000–1,500	2,000

Table 15.1 Typical blood plasma muscle enzyme levels.

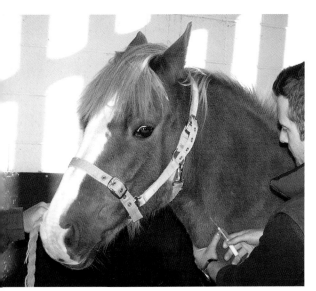
Taking a blood sample.

The underlying predisposition and trigger factors vary between sufferers, and this is why one treatment and means of control may be successful in one case but not in another. It used to be thought that lactic acid build-up in the muscles was the culprit, but this is now known to be completely untrue. Lactic acid accumulation from glycolysis in muscles does not occur in response to low-intensity exercise, and many cases of ERS have not had lactic acid in their muscles during an attack. In addition, lactic acid does not prevail in the blood or muscle long-term, but is transported relatively quickly to the liver and recycled.

ERS often occurs soon after the onset of exercise, particularly in fit horses fed high levels of concentrate feed, the day after a rest day, or after an inadequate warm-up. However, horses have been known to develop symptoms at grass, in the 10-minute box of a three-day event or during walking exercise. Many horses are prone to recurrent attacks and highly strung horses, especially mares, are often susceptible.

ERS affects the muscles of all types of horses of any age, breed or gender. However, certain types or breeds are more susceptible, and it is believed there is a hereditary basis for the condition. Recently, scientists have discovered two sub-groups of the syndrome, with different causes. One involves abnormal muscle glycogen storage and utilization and is called polysaccharide storage myopathy (PSSM) and the other involves muscle contractility abnormalities and is called recurrent exertional rhabdomyolysis (RER).

Polysaccharide storage myopathy (PSSM)

Horses affected with PSSM store and use glucose abnormally and have much larger muscle glycogen stores than normal horses. The breeds most commonly

ERS often occurs soon after the onset of exercise: an adequate warm-up period is essential for all horses.

The Quarter Horse is a breed susceptible to PSSM.

affected are Quarter Horses, Paint Horses and Appaloosas, but draught horses in general, Warmbloods, Arabs, Standardbreds and some Thoroughbreds can also be affected. It has been proposed that the condition is so prevalent in Quarter Horses because it may give them a performance advantage; therefore affected horses were more likely to be selected and bred from. Not all affected horses suffer bouts of muscle damage (tying up) regularly and the condition can be managed in many cases. Affected horses are often relatively calm – unlike many affected by

RER – and often in good physical condition. 'Monday morning disease' would be a classic description of PSSM because it is most likely to cause problems in a horse with packed-full muscle glycogen stores, who then goes out to exercise. A few days rest with a high-starch diet would cause a PSSM horse to accumulate very large muscle glycogen stores. Exactly why the large glycogen stores cause rhabdomyolysis is not yet understood and further research is needed. Other trigger factors include a change in exercise routine, infection and, in some cases, a high-starch diet coupled with a regular exercise routine. PSSM can be diagnosed with a muscle biopsy.

Recurrent exertional rhabdomyolysis (RER)

Horses affected with RER do not store abnormal levels of muscle glycogen, but instead have abnormalities in their muscle contraction. The breeds most commonly affected are Thoroughbreds, Standardbreds and Arabs, and the condition is often associated with nervous horses and particularly nervous young fillies. Like PSSM, there is thought to be a hereditary basis for RER. Trigger factors include intense exercise, exercise after a period of box rest, stress, and excitement. High-starch diets also seem to be linked to the condition. Diagnosis is more difficult than for PSSM and is rarely carried out.

Recognizing and treating the condition

If signs of ERS are seen or suspected, the horse should be stopped exercising, kept warm and taken to a stable quietly and slowly. If the horse is a significant distance from home, ideally he should be transported. The vet should be called. Treatment aims to limit further muscle damage, relieve pain and anxiety and restore fluid balance. Anxiety can make the condition worse, so the horse should be kept quiet and may need to be sedated. In the short term, the horse should be given hay and water plus drugs prescribed by the vet. Longer term and preventative feeding management is discussed below. The muscle breakdown involved in ERS does not seem to cause fibrous scar tissue in the muscle, which actually seems to heal well after an attack. Therefore, although attacks may be distressing for both horse and owner, there is usually no long-term damage.

Feeding management for affected horses

Feeding management for all types of ERS, including both sub-groups PSSM and RER, is similar. However, it is perhaps even more important to avoid dietary starch for horses with PSSM. All dietary changes should be made gradually; even changes in forage and time spent at pasture.

Forage

ERS sufferers should be turned out as much as possible, ideally on sparse or mixed grass pasture, but they must be kept warm. They should be allowed ad lib forage, and supplementary feed should only be added if forage alone cannot fulfil nutritional requirements. Rich spring grass, high-quality protein and energy-rich haylage should ideally be avoided, or at least intake-controlled, with another source of less nutritious forage offered. Alfalfa can be fed, but not in very large quantities (not over one-third of the total diet on a weight basis). If a forage-only diet maintains the horse's condition, this must be balanced with either a bespoke or a broad-spectrum vitamin and mineral supplement.

Electrolytes

All horses need balanced levels of electrolytes in their daily diet, and horses who sweat at exercise must have lost electrolytes replaced. However, electrolyte balance is particularly important for ERS sufferers because electrolytes are involved in muscle function, and imbalances could worsen their condition. It is possible that ERS sufferers have individual electrolyte absorption or utilization problems, and vet and nutritionist Dr Pat Harris has reported good results in reducing the frequency of attacks or preventing further attacks in such cases by appropriate electrolyte supplementation (along with good management). The selection of cases that may benefit from this needs to be done with the vet, via a fractional electrolyte excretion test after a high-fibre balanced diet is fed for 2 weeks.

Common salt (sodium chloride) provides two of the most important electrolytes and ERS sufferers should have supplementary salt added to their daily ration. Most forage and compound feeds do not supply sufficient salt and horses who sweat could have deficiencies. The precise amount of salt to add depends on the individual horse, so advice should be sought. As a general guide, for a 500 kg horse in very light work, add about a tablespoon (19 g) of salt per day and increase this up to 4 tablespoons (76 g) per day for a hard-working horse.

Supplementary feed

If a working horse does not maintain condition on forage alone, high-fibre supplementary feed should be given, including unmolassed sugar beet and compound feeds with high fibre and no, or little, starch. ERS sufferers should never be fed starchy feeds and dietary sugar levels should be kept low – so avoid molassed feeds. Also avoid wheatbran, which can be high in starch and has unbalanced mineral levels. Avoiding starchy feeds and supplementing feeds with oil (see below) may help maintain calmness in horses with RER, thereby reducing another trigger factor.

Low-energy, high-fibre cubes will be adequate for some horses, but others with higher energy requirements may benefit from the compound feeds with moderate energy levels, highly digestible fibre and low or no starch that are available nowadays. These also tend to be cubed and are sometimes marketed as suitable for endurance horses or for extra stamina. If there is doubt about the suitability of a compound feed, the manufacturer should be contacted and questions asked; most importantly about the starch content. Supplementary feed should be decreased if days of rest are expected, and extra feed for work added only *after* the work, not in anticipation of it.

Vegetable oil

Vegetable oil can be added to the diet to replace calories from grain and grain-based compound feeds. In fact some researchers believe that supplementary vegetable oil is helpful to horses with PSSM, and should be added to the diet of all sufferers. Fat reduces insulin sensitivity and this may be the mechanism for the beneficial effects of high-fat diets for PSSM sufferers. Good doers and resting horses should have their condition monitored carefully when fed extra oil, to avoid unwanted weight gain. Oil can be fed safely at rates of up to 300 ml per day for a 500 kg horse (equivalent in calories to 1 kg of competition feed), provided it is introduced gradually. Oil should be fed long-term for best effect, especially for working horses, because it seems to take a few months for the horse to adapt to getting the most from it. Corn oil is believed to be the most palatable, but blended vegetable oils, soya and linseed oil are also suitable.

Vitamin E and selenium

Deficiency of the antioxidant nutrients vitamin E and selenium causes muscle abnormalities and weakness and, although there is no evidence that deficiency causes ERS, careful consideration should be given to dietary levels. It is possible that the muscle damage and repair of ERS increases requirements for vitamin E and selenium, and dietary levels should be maintained relatively high rather than moderate. For a 500 kg horse in light to moderate work, eating 10 kg dry matter per day, aim for 3,000iu of vitamin E and 2–3 mg of selenium.

General management tips

In the long term, horses suffering from ERS should be turned out as much as possible, while being kept warm and encouraged to move around e.g. by placing feed or forage in various areas in the field. Adequate shelter and rugs are important.

Horses susceptible to PSSM should be exercised regularly to avoid excessive accumulation of muscle glycogen, and care should be taken with the exercise regime of all ERS-affected horses. Gradual increases in intensity and duration of exercise are important and, once in work, horses should be worked regularly.

Long, gradual warming up and cooling down periods should be carried out, and return to exercise after an attack should be gradual. Turn out on rest days is essential, especially for horses susceptible to PSSM.

Unnecessary stress should be avoided, especially for horses susceptible to RER. If a particular routine is unavoidable then it should be adhered to, and the horse's individual behaviour should be taken into account. For example, if the horse is calmer when travelled with a companion, ideally always ensure company.

chapter 16

Feeding Myths

IN THIS FINAL CHAPTER, I shall look at some of the common myths that have grown up around the subject of feeding horses – some of which have already been mentioned in passing – and explain how they are based on misconceptions.

I can't feed oats – they make all horses 'fizzy'

Oats are the cereal with the lowest energy and starch content and the highest fibre content. There is no obvious reason why oats, rather than any other cereal, would cause a horse to become excitable. It is the starch in cereals that may cause a susceptible horse to become more excitable. The starch in oats is more digestible than the starch in other cereals so perhaps, in some horses, the faster release of sugar into the blood as the starch is digested has something to do with a reaction to oats. However this would, in theory, probably only affect the horse within hours of feeding oats. Further research is necessary before we can understand the link – if there is one – between oats, other cereals and excitability in horses.

I can't feed my horse sugar – he's allergic to sugar

Sugar is the basic substance for life – a sugar compound is used to produce the energy that drives every bodily process, including muscle contraction. The body cannot function without sugar and it is a myth that a horse could be allergic to sugar. Nevertheless, large amounts of dietary refined sugar could be unhealthy for horses, just as it is for humans. Therefore overfeeding sugar is not to be recommended, especially to sedentary and overweight horse and ponies, but this is because of the results of overloading the blood with sugar rather than an actual allergic reaction. Sugar-free or sugar-intolerant compound feeds or supplements are pointless and are a marketing hype. A horse with any access to grass will ingest sugar.

Sugar beet shouldn't be fed during the summer

Sugar beet – both molassed and unmolassed – is a useful horse feed that contains high levels of fibre and relatively balanced supplies of nutrients as compared to cereal grains. Sugar beet can be fed all year round, although most people tend to feed it in the winter because, during the summer, their horses do not require the extra calories it provides. Because it is fed soaked it is a useful source of water in the typical dry winter diet of hay and compound feed. During the summer months care should be taken that soaked sugar beet does not ferment and go 'off', and only enough for the following day should be soaked.

Sugar beet contains too much sugar/protein

Sugar beet for horses is the by-product of sugar production; it is what is left from the beet root after sugar has been extracted. Therefore unmolassed sugar beet is relatively low in sugar (about 8% of the dry matter). Molassed sugar beet has molasses added after processing, and usually has around 20% added, which is equivalent to a total content of 30% sugar in the final dry product. Sugar beet also supplies around 10% protein. Compared with other feeds on an 'as fed' basis (i.e. soaked in water), sugar beet (molassed or not) is not particularly high in either sugar or protein. The actual amount of a feed constituent (in this case, sugar) that a horse receives depends on the amount of dry matter that is fed. Sugar beet tends to be soaked in about 4 times its weight of water, therefore 1 kg of soaked sugar beet supplies just 200 g of actual sugar beet. For fat horses, those prone to laminitis and those with insulin insensitivity, the unmolassed variety of sugar beet is more suitable if over 0.5 kg of dry weight beet is fed per day.

Vegetable oil is a good source of protein

Vegetable oils are extracted from relatively high-protein seeds that also have high oil contents, e.g. soya beans, sunflower seeds, rapeseeds, maize grains and linseeds. However, when vegetable oils are extracted, the end product is almost pure oil, i.e. 99% oil with no carbohydrates, fibre or protein. Therefore, vegetable oils are not a source of protein and only a good source of oil and calories, along with some vitamins.

You should feed less haylage than hay

Nowadays, the opposite is true – more weight of haylage than hay needs to be fed to supply the same amount of actual forage and fibre. Haylage contains more water than hay at around 30–45% compared to around 15% in hay. When haylage was first fed to horses years ago it was much higher in nutrients than the horse haylage fed nowadays, and was often fed in limited quantities. However, feeding such a rich forage in limited quantities will not fulfil the horse's requirement for dietary fibre or his need to chew, therefore such forage should be avoided. An ideal haylage is moderately high in fibre and has a dry matter of over 60%, and should be fed ad lib if possible.

Horses should not be allowed to graze on frosty grass

There is no reason not to allow a healthy horse to graze on frosty grass and there is no evidence that this causes colic or any other health problem. However, on a sunny day, frosty grass may contain very high levels of fructans during mid-morning, and could be risky for laminitis-prone horses or ponies. Supplementary low-energy forage is recommended as an alternative in these cases.

You should check the protein levels of supplements because some of them are very high

Protein levels are expressed as percentages on labels, but the actual amount of protein the horse receives depends on how much of the product is fed. For example, if 50 g of a supplement containing 40% protein is fed, the horse will receive 20 g of protein. If 2 kg of a feed containing 9% protein is fed, the horse will receive 180 g protein. Any supplement that is fed in quantities of anything up to a few hundred grams will not supply substantial amounts of protein to the diet.

Carrots are high in sugar and should not be fed to 'fizzy' horses or those prone to laminitis

Carrots are high in sugar on a dry matter basis, but very low in sugar on a fresh weight or 'as fed' basis. Fresh carrots contain about 80% water, which means for every 5 carrots you feed, 4 are, in effect, supplying water and 1 is supplying pure 'carrot'. A fresh carrot has a sugar content of about 7.5% so feeding 5 medium-size carrots supplies only about 37.5 g of sugar. There is absolutely no reason why you should not feed carrots to 'fizzy' horses or those prone to laminitis, provided the rest of the diet does not over-supply nutrients. Carrots are a good source of betacarotenes (vitamin A precursors) and are a useful winter succulent for horses on a dry diet, e.g. hay and compound feed.

Laminitis is caused by too much sugar in the diet

It is not known if an overload of sugar can cause laminitis in the same way as an overload of starch or fructans – but it is unlikely because sugar is well-digested by the horse and does not overflow into the hindgut, even if fed in large quantities. Nevertheless, the total non-structural carbohydrate (starch, sugar and fructans) content of the diet is believed to contribute to the risk of laminitis, so horses and ponies at risk should have all dietary non-structural carbohydrates minimized. On a slightly different note, overweight ponies susceptible to laminitis may also be insulin-resistant, and they should always be fed as little dietary sugar as possible.

My horse has a big belly so he needs to go on a diet

A large belly does not mean a horse is carrying too much body fat because body fat is laid down in other areas rather than the belly, such as the hindquarters, the neck and over the ribs and flanks. A large belly usually indicates a large amount of gut fill, caused by a high intake of fibrous forage. Having this forage belly is a natural, healthy state for a horse. The neck and the area over the ribs and flanks should be observed and felt to assess the horse's body fat covering, i.e. whether or not the horse needs to have his calorie intake restricted.

You should give different types of feed for morning and evening so your horse finds it more interesting

Owners often ascribe to their horses human attributes, e.g. they like a warm, clean stable, they like to have breakfast, lunch and tea. It is more respectful and healthy to consider the horse's actual needs, rather than transpose human needs onto him! Given the choice, horses do not eat single meals, but will graze and browse throughout the day and night. Furthermore, they do not seek out different types of feed and eat nothing but that for half an hour – they tend to pick and choose the tastiest sprouts of grass, buds on the hedge, plus the odd thistle and suchlike. Although they soon get used to being supplied with tasty meals, and will therefore anticipate their feeds keenly, it is healthier for horses to be fed the same blend of feeds in each meal and this supports a consistent balance of gut microflora.

Cubes or nuts contain nasty ingredients like floor sweepings and coarse mixes are better

The ingredients used in cubes (nuts, pellets) are mixed before being ground, then pelleted. Although, in theory, anything could be used in the mix, in practice there are strict laws about the ingredients that can be used in compound horse feed, so you will not find floor sweepings in cubes. All ingredients must now be included in a list on the label so they can be checked. Furthermore, coarse mixes themselves also contain cubes, which provide the ingredients necessary to balance nutrient shortfalls in grains and other ingredients. In practice, cubes may actually be better for horses than coarse mixes because, whereas the former are formulated just on a nutritional basic, the latter are formulated to look nice to horse owners as well as supplying nutrients to the horse.

Old horses should be fed a veteran feed

Horses 'grow old' physically at different ages and should be fed according to their individual needs and condition. Horses do not need specialist feeds as soon as they reach 16, or 20, or even 30. Healthy old horses with good body condition should be fed a similar ration to any mature horse, with slightly raised micronutrient levels. Many commercial veteran feeds are conditioning, i.e. high in energy, and are not suitable for old horses without digestive or dental problems. To date, one company has developed two different types of veteran feed; one conditioning and one lower in energy, which allows a more suitable choice to be made for an individual horse.

This veteran horse looks great, despite not being on 'veteran' feed.

Bran mashes once a week are a good laxative

Bran is not primarily a laxative for horses, but is a medium-energy feed that is well digested. However, it may act as a laxative if fed just once a week, simply by disturbing hindgut function. Any new feed introduced suddenly disturbs the hindgut microflora, which thrive on a consistent food supply. Bran mashes were traditionally given to hunters or other horses after an exhausting day's exercise –

probably because bran is so palatable that it tempts horses to eat. In addition, the water that bran absorbs will supply much-needed fluids, and it is a useful source of fibre. The practice of adding Epsom salts (magnesium sulphate) to a bran mash has the action of drawing water into the horse's gut from his body, thus helping to improve the flow of digesta, which slows down in an exhausted, dehydrated horse. Given in large quantity, it will also increase faecal water. If you wish to feed a bran mash, bran should be fed every day, to avoid digestive disturbance. A healthier alternative is to feed soaked molassed sugar beet every day, and a well-soaked large helping (with added electrolyte salts) after a hard day's work. Such a feed will supply sugar, salt, water and fibre… all ideal for a tired horse.

Horses should be travelled without forage

Horses should always have access to feed while being travelled for over an hour, and ideally should have access even for shorter journeys. It is unhealthy for horses to fast for long periods, and it is healthier to give them free access to forage. It is even more important to give horses access to forage in stressful situations because this helps maintain normal gut function. Perhaps this myth came about because long distance travelling causes dehydration in horses; therefore if this lost water is not replaced, in theory dry forage could increase the risk of an impacted colic. To ensure hydration is maintained during long journeys, give wet feeds such as soaked sugar beet pulp and dampened dried grass, and offer water at every opportunity. It is then safe to offer dry forage.

Under no circumstances should forage be placed in nets then hung outside the trailer or horsebox because it will become contaminated with pollutants from the road.

My horse needs more energy in his work – shall I give him more high-energy feed?

The energy in feed should not be confused with a horse's enthusiasm for work, because the two are not usually linked. Energy in feed is measured in terms of the calories it supplies the horse, which are utilized at cellular level. Behavioural energy reflects the horse's individual temperament, behavioural training and physical training or fitness. Fit (physically conditioned) horses tend to express more energy, whereas unfit and especially overweight horses tend to be more sluggish. Horses who have been poorly trained from a behavioural perspective may also express either more or less energy than required and ignore the rider's or handler's cues. Giving your horse more enthusiasm for his work is usually down to either getting him fitter or better trained to the rider's cues. There is anecdotal evidence that some horses seem susceptible to high-starch diets, which may make them more excitable, and therefore a high-starch feed such as oats or a grain-based racing feed, introduced with care, may be worth trying. However, in a horse not susceptible to the excitability inducing effects of starch, such a tactic will simply cause weight gain. Also, it should be stressed that any increase in energy needs to be matched by responsiveness to the rider's cues.

My horse is working so I am looking for a higher-protein feed

Working horses do not require significantly increased amounts of protein in their feed, and even hard-working horses require a maximum of about 12% protein in the total diet. It is energy supply that must be increased for working horses, not protein supply. This myth probably came about from production animal nutrition (for meat or milk animals), where high dietary protein is important. Rather than look for a '12%' or '14%' (protein) feed for a working horse, look for the digestible energy content – this is what matters most.

My horse is working now so I need to feed concentrates

In days gone by, most forage for horses was not particularly nutritious, and chaffs were generally made from chopped straw; therefore working horses often required concentrate feed to supplement their forage. Nowadays, there are other options. In addition, concentrate feeds include not just high-starch grain-based compounds, but also highly digestible fibre and compounds high in oil that supply equivalent nutrients but without the starch. Instead of adding a concentrate feed, sourcing more nutritious forage, e.g. haylage, and feeding a large bucket of quick-dried alfalfa or grass chaff overnight (perhaps with some vegetable oil and a broad-spectrum vitamin and mineral supplement mixed in) may well meet the increased requirements of the working horse. Regarding diet, horses should always be assessed individually – even some hard-working horses maintain condition and performance when fed just good-quality forage and low-energy compound cubes.

Racehorses should not be fed much forage

Racehorses are no different from any other horse in their basic physiological requirements, and this includes their dietary need for fibre. It is a myth that feeding forage to racehorses will slow them down, and feeding too little forage will increase the risk of colic, digestive disturbance, stomach ulcers, tying up and oral stereotypies such as cribbing, and will certainly will not lead to optimal performance. Work by researchers in Kentucky has shown that feeding racehorses 1% of their bodyweight in forage does not slow them down or affect their per-

Racehorses still have a need for dietary forage.

formance. Fasting horses for more than a few hours between hard feeds with no access to forage will lead to stomach erosion and may cause ulcers.

Horses must be fasted for an hour before exercise

For horses in general, this is a myth, but for performance horses it could be a useful strategy. Horses who are worked at low intensities do not need to have food withdrawn before exercise. Endurance horses, who ideally need to eat during their competition, should be encouraged to eat during exercise training so that they get used to this practice. Horses fed large meals of starchy concentrate would benefit from being fed such a meal several hours before intense exercise, but forage need not be withdrawn (see Chapter 10). However, most horses should not be fed large meals of starchy concentrate!

Horses must not be allowed to drink either during or just after exercise

This myth would cause disaster if endurance riders followed it! Horses should be allowed to drink at any time, including during a bout of exercise. For prolonged exercise, it is imperative that horses learn to drink at short rest stops, or whenever water is available, in order to prevent dehydration. There is no harm in allowing a horse to drink moderate amounts immediately after exercise, and this should be encouraged if the horse is dehydrated. However, the horse should, ideally, also have been allowed to drink during exercise so that he does not drink excessively after the exercise bout.

Appendix: Nutrient Requirements of Horses

Table A.1 Daily nutrient requirements of working, growing and breeding horses (500 kg mature bodyweight consuming 2% bodyweight in dry matter per day) (NRC,* 1989). Figures represent minimum levels to avoid deficiency from the NRC (1989); optimal levels may be higher and guidelines are given in brackets below the figure for minimum level.

	Weight (kg)	Gain (kg/day)	DE (MJ)	Crude protein (g)	Lysine (g)	Calcium (g)	Phos-phorus (g)	Mag-nesium (g)	Sodium (g)	Potass-ium (g)
Mature horses										
Maintenance	500		69	656	23	20	14	7.5 (8)	10 (15)	25
Stallions	500		86	820	29	25	18	9.4 (10)	10 (30)	31.2
Pregnant mares										
9 months	500		76	801	28	35	26	8.7 (10)	10 (20)	29.1
10 months	500		77	815	29	35	26	8.9 (10)	10 (20)	29.7
11 months	500		82	866	30	37	28	9.4 (12)	10 (20)	31.5
Lactating mares										
Foaling to 3 months	500		118	1,427	50	56	36	10.9 (12)	10 (30)	46
3 months to weaning	500		102	1,048	37	36	22	8.6 (9)	10 (20)	33
Working horses										
Light work	500		86	820	29	25 (30)	18	9.4 (10)	30	31.2
Moderate work	500		103	984	34	30 (50)	21	11.3 (17)	30 (50)	37.4
Strenuous work	500		137	1,312	46	40 (50)	29	15.1 (20)	30 (100)	49.9
Growing horses										
6 months	215	0.65	63	750	32	29	16	4 (5)	4.3 (8)	12.7
12 months	325	0.5	79	851	36	29 (36)	16	5.5 (7)	6.5 (12)	17.8
18 months	400	0.35	83	893	38	27 (39)	15	6.4 (9)	8 (15)	21.1
24 months	450	0.2	79	800	32	24 (38)	13	7 (10)	9 (16.8)	23.1

*National Research Council (NRC) (1989) Nutrient Requirements of Horses. Washington

Vitamin A (iu)	Vitamin D (iu)	Vitamin E (iu)	Copper (mg)	Iron (mg)	Zinc (mg)	Manga-nese (mg)	Selenium (mg)	Cobalt (mg)	Iodine (mg)
15,000 (20,000)	3,000 (1,500)	500	100	400	400 (500)	400	1	1	1–6
22,000	3,000	500 (2,000)	100	400	400 (500)	400	1 (2)	1	1.75–6
30,000	6,000	800 (2,000)	100 (200)	500	400 (550)	400 (500)	1 (2)	1	2–6
30,000	6,000	800 (2,000)	100 (200)	500	400 (550)	400 (500)	1 (2)	1	2–6
30,000	6,000	800 (2,000)	100 (200)	500	400 (550)	400 (500)	1	1	2–6
30,000	6,000	800 (2,000)	100 (150)	500	400 (500)	400 (500)	1 (2.5)	1	2–6
30,000	6,000	800 (2,000)	100 (150)	500	400 (500)	400 (500)	1 (2)	1	2–6
22,000 (30,000)	3,000	800 (2,000)	100 (150)	400 (500)	400 (625)	400	1 (2)	1 (1–2)	1.75–6
22,000 (35,000)	3000 (4,000)	800 (2,500)	100 (200)	400 (600)	400 (700)	400 (500)	1 (2)	1 (1–2)	2.5–6
22,000 (45,000)	3,000 (5,000)	800 (3,000)	100 (200)	400 (600)	400 (750)	400 (500)	1) (3)	1 (2)	3–6
10,000 (21,500)	4,000 (800)	215 (150)	43	250	172 (213)	200	0.43 (0.5)	0.43	0.43–2.58
15,000 (32,500)	6,000	325 (1,200)	65 (240)	375 (400)	260 (323)	300	0.65 (0.8)	0.65	0.65–3.9
18,000 (40,000)	7,200	400 (1,500)	80 (200)	450 (500)	320 (400)	360	0.8 (1)	0.8	0.8–4.8
20,000 (45,000)	8,000	450 (1,600)	90 (225)	500 (550)	360 (450)	400	0.9 (1.1)	0.9	0.9–5.4

Glossary

Acid detergent fibre (ADF): an analytical description of the fibre in a food (usually forage) sample, which consists of lignin, cellulose and also includes silica. The reading is taken by boiling the sample in sulphuric acid and a detergent called cetyl trimethyl ammonium bromide, and measuring the residue.

Ad lib feeding: offering food in a free choice manner. Feeding forage ad lib means that there is always some left when the next portion is fed.

Adipose tissue: fat is stored in the body mostly in adipose tissue, with a little in the muscles.

Amines: nitrogen-containing compounds, many of which are hormones. Amines are also produced by the bacteria in the hindgut, and are thought to be involved in laminitis because they leak through the gut wall into the circulation, where they act on body tissues, including blood vessels.

Amino acid: a building block of protein, of which there are 25. Ten of these are known as essential, because they must be supplied by the diet. The others (the non-essential) can be synthesized in the body from the essential.

Anthelmintic: a drug used to kill or paralyse worms; also called dewormer and wormer.

Antioxidant: see pro-oxidant.

As fed: describes a feed as it is fed rather than the dry matter state. For example, carrots contain about 80% water so, on an as fed basis, they are low in sugar; yet on a dry matter basis they are high in sugar. For every 5 carrots fed on an as fed basis, there is just one 'pure' carrot; the rest of the matter is water.

Ash: the residue of a food that is left after burning it at very high temperatures. Ash consists of various minerals including some silica.

Balanced diet: daily intake of food that supplies correct levels of all the essential nutrients, and results in no net gain or loss by the body.

Betacarotenes (β-carotenes): compounds present in plants that can be converted into vitamin A in the horse's gut; also called provitamin A.

Bolus: a chewed ball of food ready to be swallowed; also used to describe the ball of food as it travels through the gut.

Box-weaning: a traditional technique whereby a foal is separated from the dam and shut in a stable (box) until he becomes accustomed to being without his dam. An outdated method that is known to be stressful and inhumane.

Broad-spectrum vitamin and mineral supplement: a supplement that contains all or most of the essential vitamins and minerals in balanced proportions. Most branded compound feeds contain such supplements, but these feeds must be fed at the recommended rate for the horse to receive the full dose of vitamins and minerals.

Calorie: a unit of energy, which is the amount of heat required to raise the temperature of 1 g of water by 1 degree centigrade. The joule (J) tends to be used to describe the energy in horse feed (1 calorie = 4.184 J).

Colostrum: a thick yellowish substance that precedes milk production in the dam. It is produced prior to birth and for the first few days afterwards, and contains maternal antibodies (immunoglobulins) that are essential for the foal to acquire immunity. A foal must take in colostrum in the first couple of days because it is only during this time that the gut is permeable to the large antibodies.

Compound feed: a manufactured feed that contains a variety of ingredients. Could be a concentrate feed or a fibrous chaff-based feed.

Concentrate feed: a feed higher in calories and protein per given weight (i.e. per kilo) than the natural forage a horse has evolved to eat. Includes straight grains and blends, manufactured compound feeds, and is sometimes used to describe moderately high-energy fibre feeds such as sugar beet and quick-dried chopped forages.

Creep feed: a concentrate feed formulated for foals, to encourage the development of their digestive systems before weaning.

Crude fibre: an analytical term used to describe the residue left after treatment with ether extract, followed by successive boiling with acid and alkali of determined concentration. The value tends to be less than that ascertained via ADF or NDF.

Cubes: compounded feed that has been formed via a process forcing the ground (often cooked) mixture through the holes of a die. Versions formed by the same basic process are also (loosely depending on shape and size) called nuts, pellets and pencils.

Diffusion: the random mixing and spreading out of molecules.

Distal colon: the horse's colon has several bends or flexures, and each part is named according to where it lies in the abdomen. Dorsal means directed away from the belly surface, and is the opposite of ventral (see ventral colon). See Chapter 1, page 6 for an annotated diagram of the horse's digestive system.

Dry matter: describes feed without the natural water content, which is present in all feeds. Most compound feeds and hay are about 88% dry matter (DM) i.e. they contain 880 g of actual feed and 120 g of water per kilo of fresh weight.

Duodenum: the first part of the small intestine, which in the mature horse is about 1 m long.

Efficacy: the ability to produce a desired effect, e.g. how effective a treatment is.

Electrolytes: the macrominerals involved in body fluid balance, including sodium, potassium, chloride, and also magnesium and calcium.

Emulsify: to disperse a liquid in another liquid e.g. to disperse an oil into droplets throughout another liquid.

Enzyme hydrolysis: the division of a compound with the addition of water, via the action of an enzyme. Enzymes are proteins that act as catalysts in chemical reactions, increasing the rate of reaction. Animal bodies contain about 100,000 different enzymes.

Fibre: a term that describes the portion of foodstuff that cannot be broken down by digestive enzymes; therefore is available to the bacteria in the horse's gut. It consists mainly of the structural parts of plants (cellulose, hemicellulose and lignin), but also includes other more water-soluble fractions including pectins, gums and mucilages. Horses have a dietary requirement for fibre in order to maintain digestive health. High-fibre plant material also fulfils the horse's need to chew.

Forage: was used to describe all animal feed (also called fodder) but nowadays generally used to describe fibrous feeds or roughages.

Fortified: fortified compound concentrate feeds contain added vitamins and minerals to balance the entire diet (along with forage).

Glomerular filtration rate: the renal tubules of the kidneys absorb electrolytes to avoid losing them in the urine, and the rate of this activity depends on the diet.

Haemoglobin: the oxygen-carrying substance of the blood, which contains an iron pigment called haem and gives red blood cells (erythrocytes) their red colour.

Herbage: the green leafy parts of plants; usually includes stems as well.

Hindgut: the large intestine, or the caecum and both the large and small colon.

Ileum: the final part of the small intestine, which leads into the caecum.

Immunoglobulins: also called antibodies; specialized protein molecules that are involved in immune function. Different types exist, with IgG being the most abundant.

Ion: an atom that has an electrical charge, either positive or negative. Substances that form ions are called electrolytes.

Ischaemic phase (of laminitis): a phase that involves a lack of blood supply to the foot.

Isotonic: having the same osmotic pressure, e.g. a solution that is isotonic to the blood has the same concentration.

Jejunum: the middle part of the small intestine, extending from the duodenum to the ileum.

Legume: a family of plants, which includes forages such as alfalfa (also called lucerne) and clover, and seed crops including soya beans, peas and field beans.

Macrominerals: essential minerals required by the body in amounts measured in grams as opposed to milligrams per day. Include potassium, magnesium, calcium, phosphorus and sodium.

Macronutrients: essential nutrients required in relatively large amounts per day, e.g. protein, carbohydrates including fibre, and oils and fats.

Maintenance: describes a horse's nutrient requirements when not in work or reproducing.

Meconium: dark-coloured material that is contained in a foal's intestine prior to birth, which is passed soon after birth.

Microminerals: essential minerals required by the body in smaller amounts than macrominerals, measured in milligrams per day. Include iron, manganese, iodine, cobalt, copper, zinc and selenium. Also called trace elements.

Micronutrients: nutrients required in relatively smaller amounts, including vitamins and minerals.

Myoglobin: the oxygen-carrying substance of the muscles, which contains an iron pigment called haem. In cases of rhabdomyolysis (tying up), myoglobin is released and passed in the urine. In severe cases, a reddish-brown discolouration of the urine is seen, and such cases may suffer kidney damage as a result.

Neutral detergent fibre (NDF): an analytical description of the fibre in a food (usually forage) sample, which consists of lignin, cellulose and hemicellulose (primary the cell wall material). The reading is taken by extraction with boiling neutral solutions of the detergents sodium lauryl sulphate and ETDA.

Osmosis: the passage of a solvent from an area of lower concentration to an area of higher concentration, through a semi-permeable membrane.

Osteochondritis dissecans (OCD): inflammation of bone and cartilage that results in a splitting off of a piece of articular cartilage (called a 'chip' or a 'mouse'). OCD is classed as a developmental orthopaedic disease (DOD) and occurs as a result of osteochondrosis.

Osteochondrosis: a disease process of abnormal differentiation of growth cartilage. OC is classed as a developmental orthopaedic disease (DOD).

Peristalsis: the wave-like muscular movement of the gut wall, which propels partially digested food through it.

pH: describes the extent of acidity or alkalinity of a substance: pH 7 is neutral, lower than 7 is acidic and higher than 7 is alkaline. The measurement is of the hydrogen (H) ion concentration of a solution.

Poached (pasture): an area of pasture that has been trodden down by animal hooves, removing the grass and causing areas of mud to form.

Portal circulation: the circulation of blood from one organ to another; the term tends to be used for the blood vessels between the gut and the liver, which carry nutrient-rich blood for processing in the liver.

Prebiotics: carbohydrate substances used in animal feed that promote the health of the beneficial micro-organisms within the gut. Prebiotics are not affected by the horse's own digestive enzymes, and are available as a food source for the beneficial bacteria within the gut.

Probiotics: live feed additives that promote the health of the beneficial micro-organisms within the gut. Usually describes live bacterial or yeast products. Live bacterial products are thought to recolonize the gut, helping to exclude the proliferation of pathogenic (disease-causing) bacteria. Live yeast products are thought to create a more favourable environment for the beneficial bacteria residing in the gut.

Protein quality: a reflection of the amount of essential amino acids a protein contains. A higher-quality protein contains higher amounts of essential amino acids.

Pro-oxidant: a substance that has a promoting effect on oxidative processes in the body. Too much oxidation results in oxidative stress, which is harmful to the body tissues. Antioxidants help minimize the harmful effects of oxidative stress.

Ration: the total amount of feed a horse takes in per day.

Reperfusion: after a period of reduced blood supply (ischaemia), the affected area is reperfused with blood, which can cause injury.

Roughage: used to describe fibrous feeds, usually long-fibre feeds such as hay, haylage and straw; also called forages.

Straights: single foods, usually grains such as oats, barley and grain by-products such as bran.

Supplements: usually describes extra feeds that are added in small quantities to the daily diet, e.g. vitamins and minerals, probiotics, nutraceuticals such as glucosamine, and herbs. Manufactured supplements made from a mixture of ingredients, which may include additives, are classed as complementary feedstuffs.

Sward: a description of the mat of grass on turf.

Ventral colon: the horse's colon has several bends or flexures, and each part is named according to where it lies in the abdomen. Ventral means directed towards or situated on the belly surface, and is the opposite of dorsal (see dorsal colon). See Chapter 1, page 6 for an annotated diagram of the horse's digestive system.

Useful contacts

Australian Equine Laminitis Research Unit
School of Veterinary Science,
Faculty of Natural Resources, Agriculture and Veterinary Science,
The University of Queensland,
St Lucia, Brisbane, Qld 4072,
Australia.
Web: www.laminitisresearch.org

British Association of Equine Dental Technicians
The Bungalow,
Bonehill Road,
Mile Oak,
Tamworth,
Staffordshire B78 3PS.
Tel: 01827 284718.
Web: www.equinedentistry.org.uk

British Equestrian Federation
Stoneleigh Park,
Kenilworth,
Warwickshire CV8 2RH.
Tel: 02476 698871
Fax: 02476 696484
Web: www.bef.co.uk

British Equestrian Trade Association
Stockeld Park,
Wetherby,
West Yorkshire LS22 4AW.
Tel: 01937 587062
Web: www.beta-uk.org

British Equine Veterinary Association
Wakefield House,
46 High Street,
Sawston,
Cambridgeshire CB2 4BG.
Tel: 01223 836970
Fax: 01223 835287
Web: www.beva.org.uk

The British Horse Society
Stoneleigh Deer Park,
Kenilworth,
Warwickshire CV8 2XZ.
Tel: 01926 707700
Fax: 01926 707800
Web: www.bhs.org.uk

The British Nutrition Foundation
High Holborn House,
52–54 High Holborn,
London WC1V 6RQ.
Tel: 020 7404 6504
Fax: 020 7404 6747
Web: www.nutrition.org.uk

British Veterinary Dental Association
Rahlea, 525 Woodham Lane,
Woking,
Surrey GU21 5SR.
Tel: 07831 286961
Web: www.bvda.co.uk

Department for Environment, Food & Rural Affairs
Nobel House,
17 Smith Square,
London SW1P 3JR.
Helpline Tel: 0845 9335577
Web: www.defra.gov.uk

Direct Laboratories (food and forage analysis)
Woodthorne,
Wergs Road,
Wolverhampton, WV6 8TQ.
Tel: 01902 743222
Fax: 01902 746183
Web: www.directlabs.co.uk

Donkey Sanctuary
Sidmouth,
Devon EX10 0NU.
Tel: 01395 578222
Fax: 01395 579266
Web: www.thedonkeysanctuary.org.uk

Equine Grass Sickness Fund
www.grasssickness.org.uk

Farriers Registration Council
Sefton House,
Adam Court,
Newark Road,
Peterborough PE1 5PP.
Tel:01733 319911
Fax: 01733 319910
Web: www.farrier-reg.gov.uk

National Equine Welfare Council
Stanton,
10 Wales Street,
Kings Sutton,
Banbury,
Oxfordshire OX17 3RR.
Tel/Fax: 01295 810060
Web: www.newc.co.uk

National Foaling Bank
Meretown Stud,
Newport,
Shropshire TF10 8BX.
Tel: 01952 811234
Fax: 01952 811202

National Office of Animal Health
3 Crossfield Chambers,
Gladbeck Way,
Enfield EN2 7HF.
Tel: 020 8367 3131
Fax 020 8363 1155
Web: www.noah.co.uk

Natural Hoofcare Practitioners (UK)
Web: www.uknhcp.org

The Nutrition Society
10 Cambridge Court,
210 Shepherd's Bush Road,
London W6 7NJ.
Tel: 020 7602 0228
Fax: 020 7602 1756
Web: www.nutritionsociety.org

Sarcoid information from the University of Liverpool
http://pcwww.liv.ac.uk/sarcoid/

Society of Master Saddlers (UK) Ltd
Greenlane Farm,
Stonham,
Stowmarket,
Suffolk IP14 5DS.
Tel/Fax: 01449 711642
Web: www.mastersaddlers.co.uk

The Soil Association (promotes organic farming)
Bristol House,
40–56 Victoria Street,
Bristol BS1 6BY.
Tel: 0117 314 5000
Fax: 0117 314 5001
Web: www.soilassociation.org

Veterinary Medicines Directorate
Woodham Lane,
New Haw,
Addlestone,
Surrey KT15 3LS.
Tel: 01932 336911
Fax: 01932 336618
Web: www.vmd.gov.uk

Index

Note: Page numbers in *italic* refer to tables in the text

absorption *see* nutrient absorption
acetic acid 62, 175
acidic gut syndrome 211, 212
acidity
    hindgut 12–13, *14*, 32, 212, 232
    stomach 9, 20
ad lib feeding 141–2
additives (artificial) 97, 205
    labelling of feeds 66
adenosine diphosphate (ADP) 172, 173
adenosine triphosphate (ATP) 172, 173
adipose (fat) tissue 18, 34, 37, 39
aerobic energy production 173–4
aflatoxin 87
alfalfa 195, 226
    chopped/chaff 76–8
    feeding rates 195
    fibre constituents *60*
    hay 72, *79*, *94*
    quick-dried 203–4, 205
allergies
    food 217–18, 242
    respiratory 218–19
amines 32, 229
amino acids 35
    essential 35
    'limiting' 35
    sulphur-containing 45, 217
    synthesis 36
amylases 8, 11, *12*, 32
amylopectin 32
amylose 32
anaemia *42*, 55, 102, *103*, 181–2, 223
    iron supplementation for 47, 223
anaerobic energy production 173
analytical constituents 67, *68*
animal-derived products 37, 96, *103*, 205–6

labelling of feed stuffs 66
antacids 20, 104, 215–16
anthelmintics (wormers) 127–31
antinutritional factors (ANF) 85, 87
antioxidants 50–2, 54, 183, 195, 201
    plant 104–5
    respiratory disease 219
    rhabdomyolysis 240
    supplements *103*
    working/performance horse 180
appetite 17–18
    and diet 32
    and exercise 190
    loss of 222–3
    vitamin B_{12} supplements 55
apples 58, 197
Arab horse
    growth 166
    racing 189
ascorbic acid *see* vitamin C
ascorbyl palmitate 53, 183
ash values 67, *68*
aspartate aminotransferase (AST) 235, 236

Bailey, Simon 229
bakery waste 90
balanced diet 24
'balancers' 93, 95
balls, feed-decanting 220
barefoot horse 207–8
barley 82, *94*
    boiling 82
    in compound feeds 96
    fibre content/constituents *60*
    nutrient composition 80, *80*
barley straw *60*, 76
beans *see* peas and beans
behaviour, normal time budgets 15–16
behavioural problems 15, 19–22

feeding-related 22–3, 62, 92, 155, 242
    risk in youngstock 22, 162, 163
    supplements for *103*
belly, forage/hay 245
bentonite 105
benzimidazole *128*
betacarotenes *51*, 52, 183
bifido bacteria 105
'big head' 220
bile 11, 13, 39
bioflavonoids 104
biotin 54, *103*, 216–17
'blood boosting' supplements *103*
blood glucose/sugar 32–4, 204, 229–30
blood loss 182
body condition
    broodmare 157, 159
    endurance/racehorse 187–9
    ideal for job/breed of horse 137
    older horses 197–9
    performance horse 187–8
    scoring 132, 134–7, 198
    stallion 160
body temperature
    and fibrous feeds 203, 206–7
    regulation 26, 178
bomb calorimeter 28
bone cysts, subchondral 166–7
bots 125, 126–7
botulism 74–5
box rest 220–2
bran (wheatbran) 58, 62, 84, 222, 239
    mashes 84, 246–7
brewing by-products 85
British Equestrian Federation (BEF) 192–3
broodmare
    conception 157–8
    condition scoring 136

lactating 26, 106, *138*, 148, 149, 159–60, *250*
   nutritional requirements 49, 148, *250*
   pregnant 136, *138*, 148, 150, 250
Brunner's glands 11
buckets, feed 153–4
butyric acid 62, 75, 175, 214
by-products 65, 84–5, *94*, 95

caecum 13
caffeine 193
calcitriol 53
calcium 40, *41*, 43, 101, 181, 217
   absorption *14*, 40, 43
   in cereals 80
   deficiency 43, 219–20
   dietary requirements *41*, *250*
   pasture grass *113*
   role in body 40, *41*
   in sweat 178
calcium carbonate 85, 96
calcium:phosphorus ratio 43, 44, 80, 84, 88, 219–20
calmative supplements 23, *103*
'calories' 27
canine teeth 7
capillary refill 27
carbohydrases *12*
carbohydrates 29–34
   classification 30
   digestion and absorption 11
   energy production from 174–6
   fate in body 30–1
   non-structural 29, 231
   overfeeding of non-structural 32, 62, 80, 212, 213–14, 231
   water soluble (WSC) 112
carboxypeptidases *12*
cardiac sphincter 9
carotenoids 52, 183
carrots 87–8, 195, 197, 244
   water/dry matter content *26*, 88, *139*
cartilage 46
cattle 5, 115
cellulose 30, 31, 58, 61
cereal grains 79–83, *94*, 204
   and behaviour of horse 22–3
   by-products 84–5, *94*
   calcium content 80
   in compound feeds 96
   digestion 11
   dry matter content *139*

fatty acids 38
   glycaemic index 80
   husk/hulls 65
   nutrient balancing 85, 93
   processing 83–4
   types of 81–3
cereal hay 72, *94*
cereal mite 152
chaffs 18–19, 63, 68, 76–8, *94*, 196–7
   blends 95
   intake rate 18–19
   molassed 196–7
changes to diet 62–3, 154, 211, 233
chasteberry (*Vitex agnus castus*) *103*, 200
chewing 5, 8, 9, 204
   concentrate foods *17*
   forage 16, *17*
   problems 18, 63, 124, 213
   wood 19, 20
chloride 40, 42, 45, 178
choke 9, 214
chondroitin *103*, 206
chromium *43*, 48
chronic obstructive pulmonary disease (COPD) *see* recurrent airway obstruction (RAO)
chronic renal failure 225–6
chylomicrons 39, 53
chymotrypsin *12*
cider apple vinegar *103*
citrus pulp 90
clipping 207
clostridia bacteria 74–5
clostridial infections 214
Clostridium botulinum 223
clover 118, 120, 223
coarse mixes 83, 91, *95*
   dry matter content *26*
   formulation of 245–6
   ingredients *95*, 96
   low-energy 92
cobalamin (vitamin B_{12}) *43*, 49, 54–5, 182, 190
cobalt 49, 182
   dietary requirements *43*, 251
   functions in body *43*, 49, 54, 55, 182
   in pasture grass *113*
coconut meal 87
cod liver oil *103*, 107–8, 183
colic 209–12
   causes 21, 32, 62, 80, 209–11
   management 211–12

colitis 213–14
collar, crib-biting/wind-sucking 21
colon 13
colostrum 159, 161–2
   replacement 162
competition, feeding prior to 154–5, 190–1, 249
competition mix *185*
competition rules *103*, 104, 107
compound feeds 90–1, *95*, 141
   dry matter content *139*
   ingredients 93, *95*, 96–7
   low-energy/calorie 92, *95*
   performance horse 185
   types of 91–3
   vitamin and mineral content 91, 99, 100
   for weight gain 144
concentrates
   chewing rate *17*
   feeding before/during competition 154–5
   feeding rates 154, 204
   forage to concentrate ratios *139*, 140–2
   intake rate 19
   reasons for feeding 64–5
   for weight gain 144
   working horse 92, 248
   youngstock 162–3, 164–5
   see also types of concentrates
condition *see* body condition
contaminants 193
conversions (metric/imperial) 4
copper 46–7, 167, 182, 205
   deficiency *42*, 46
   dietary requirements *42*, 182, 251
   excess intake *42*, 46–7
   functions in body *42*, 182
   in pasture grass *113*
   supplementation *103*, 182
copper:zinc ratio *42*, 167
coprophagy 18
corn (maize) oil 38, 107, 240
creatine kinase 235, 236
creep feed 162–3
crib-biting 19, 20
   causes 22, 162, 163
   control 21
cubes (nuts) 90–1, *95*, 96
   dry matter content *26*
   ingredients 91, 245–6
Culicoides midge 217, 218

Cushing's syndrome 33, 200, 230
cyathostomiasis (small redworm
     infestation) 125–6, 213

dehydration 177–8, 211, 249
     fluid replacement 27, 179, 189
     signs of 26–7
dental formula 6–7
dental health 7–8, 122–4, 213
dental technician 123
developmental orthopaedic disease
     (DOD) 41, *42*, 43, 46, 80, 165,
     166–7, 182
DHA *see* docosahexaenoic acid
diarrhoea 212–14
     causes 26, 32, 62, 80
diet formulation 131–2
     see also ration formulation
dietary changes 62–3, 154, 211, 233
digestible energy (DE) 28, 29
     calculation of feed content 29
     calculation of requirements 147–50
     in cereals *80*
     requirements in classes of horse 250
          digestion
     enzymes 11, *12*, 32
     fibre 5, 61–2
     oils and fats 13, *14*, 39, 174
     older horse 194
     protein 11, *14*, 36
     sugar and starch 11, 31–2
digestive tract
     infections 214
     structure and function 5–6
digital artery pulse 230
docks 118
docosahexaenoic acid (DHA) 38,
     107–8
dressage horses 187
droppings *see* faeces
dry matter (DM) *26*, 138–9
     carrots *26*, 88, 139
     concentrates *26*, 139
     forage *26*, 73, 74, 138, *139*
     sugar beet *26*, *36*, *139*
duodenum 10
dust, hay 69, 219

eating *see* chewing; food intake
echinacea *103*
eicosanoids 37
eicosapentaenoic acid (EPA) 38, 107–8
electric fencing 120–1

electrolytes *14*, 40, 44, 45, 177–8
     oral rehydration solution 27, 179,
          189
     pastes 189, 216
     rhabdomyolysis 239
     supplements 100–1
     in sweat 178
endotoxins 32, 229
endurance horse 92, 187–8
     body condition 187–9
     feeding before/during competition
          154–5, 191, 249
     salt/electrolyte pastes 189, 216
energy 27–9, 47
     currency of 172
     depletion 176–7
     extraction from feed 170–1
     in grass 112–13
     in horse's work 247–8
     'metabolizable' 28
     in oils/fats 37–8, 107, 174
     pathways of production 172–6
     storage in body 171, 186
     see also digestible energy (DE)
energy requirements 18, 28
     calculations 147–50
     and exercise 169–70
     and food intake 18
     youngstock 164–5
enterocytes 36, 39
enzymes, digestive 11, *12*, 32
EPA *see* eicosapentaenoic acid
equine dysautonomia *see* grass sickness
equine metabolic syndrome 34
eventer 150, 187, 191
excitable behaviour 22–3, 33, 92, 242
excretion, waste nitrogen 36
exercise
     and appetite 190
     and colic 211
     dehydration 26, 179
     and developmental orthopaedic
          disease 167
     and drinking 249
     energy supply 169–70
     and feeding 154, 187, 214–15, 249
     laminitic horse/pony 233
     older horse 197
     overweight horse 147
     and rhabdomyolysis 236, 240–1

faeces (droppings) 13
     analysis 115, 130

diarrhoea 212–14
     eating 18, 168
     removal from pasture 114–16, 127
fasting
     before exercise/competition 187,
          214–15, 249
     overweight horse 146, 225
     re-introduction of feed 223–4
fat (adipose) tissue 18, 34, 37, 39
fatigue 176–7
fats 22–3, 37–9
     animal sources 37, 96, 205
     digestion, absorption and use 13,
          14, 39, 174
     feeding to horses 37–8, 107, 174–5,
          186
fatty acids 216
     essential (EFA) 37, *103*
     omega-3 38, 107–8
     omega-6 38, 113
     volatile (VFAs) 12, *14*, 38, 61, 62,
          175, 190
feed 'balancers' 93, 95
feed ball 16
feed blocks 100
feed containers 153–4
feed storage 152–3
The Feeding Stuffs
     (England/Scotland/Wales)
     Regulations 2005 (TSO) 66–7
feeds
     anticipation stress 155, 204
     timing of 154–5, 190–2
     see also ration formulation
FEI (International Equestrian
Federation) 192–3
fenbendazole *128*, *130*
fencing 120–1
fermentation
     haylage 75
     hindgut 12, 13, 31, 38, 61, 62
fertility
     broodmare 157–8, 159
     stallion 161
fertilization, pasture 119–20
fibre 20, 30, 56
     absorption and use *14*, 62
     acid-detergent (ADF) 59, 60
     analysis 59–60
     in compound feeds 96
     crude *68*
     deficiency 62–3
     definition 31, 56–7

digestion 5, 61–2
energy from 27, 175
neutral-detergent (NDF) 59, *60*
soluble 59, 60
'superfibres' 61–2, 184–5
types of 58–9
fish meal 205
fish oils 37, 38, 107–8
fitness 23, 247
flavour of foods 6, 17
flaxseed *see* linseed
fluid balance 25, 40
fluid replacement 27, 179, 189
foal 61
    colic 210
    gastric ulcers 162, 215
    gut microflora 61, 168
    newborn 161–2
    orphaned 167–8
    risk of abnormal behaviours 22, 163
    roundworm 127
    suckling 159–60, 162–3
    weaning 163–4
foetus, development 158–9
folic acid 55
food allergies 217–18
food intake, rate 18–19
food selection 17
forage 68, *94*
    access to 15–16, 20, 203, 216
    ad lib feeding 141–2, 143
    chewing and intake rate 16, *17*, 18–19
    chopped 18–19, 63, 68, 76–8, *94*, *95*, 196–7
    definition 68
    dry matter content *26*, 138, 139
    feeding at pasture 153–4, 202–4
    feeding during transport 156, 247
    feeding in rhabdomyolysis 239
    feeding for weight loss 145–6
    heating (body temperature) 203, 206–7
    laminitic horse 233
    minerals 205, 207
    nutrient analyses 78–9, 100
    older horse 196–7
    performance horse 155, 184, 248–9
    quick-dried *26*, *60*, 76–7, 78, 195, 203–4, 205
    variety 16, 203
forage replacers 197
forage to concentrates ratio *139*, 140–2

'founder' 228
free radicals 50, 180, 182
fructans *14*, 29–30, 57–8, 112, 213, 232, 244
fructo-oligosaccharides (FOS) 105
fructose 32
fruit *95*
fuller's earth 105

garlic 96, 107
gastric ulcers 9, 20, 62, 187, 189, 190, 214–16
    causes 62, 214–15
    foals 162, 215
    incidence of 214
    signs of 215
    treatment/management 215–16
gastrin 10
gelatin 96
glucosamine *103*, 104
    sources of 206
glucose 30, 32–3
    blood levels 32–4, 204, 229–30
glucose intolerance 200
glucose tolerance factor (GTF) 48
glutamine *103*
glutathione peroxidase 52
glycaemic index (GI) 33, 34, 80, 167, 186
glycogen 29, 30, 32
    muscles 174, 175–6, 177, 186, 191
glycogenesis 33
glycolysis 173
goitre *43*, 48
grass 68–9
    dry matter *26*, *139*
    feeding value *79*, 112–13, 146
    fibre constituents 58–9, *60*
    fructans *14*, 29–30, 57–8, 112, 213, 232, 244
    growth 111
    and laminitis 231–2
    lipids 38, 113
    quick-dried *26*, *60*, 76–7, 195, 203–4, 205
    species for permanent pastures 110
    spring *26*, 59, 112, 213
    vitamins 52, 55, 113
    water content 25, *26*
    see also pasture
grass meal *60*
grass sickness 223
grazing

non-equine species 115
    restriction of 112, 117, 146, 202, 233
    selectivity of horses 112, 115
    see also grass; pasture
grazing muzzle 146
groundnuts 87
growth 46
    nutrient requirements *250–1*
    patterns in youngstock 164, 165–6
gums 59, 61

haemoglobin 47
hair analysis 40
Harris, Dr Pat 239
harrowing 116
hawthorn 111
hay 69–72, *94*
    dry matter content *26*, 138, 139
    dust and mould spores 69, 219
    feeding 71, 153–4
    fibre content and constituents 60, *60*
    for horse on weight loss regime 145
    non-grass 69, 72, *79*, *94*
    nutrient content 69, *79*
    soaking before feeding 69, 71, 153, 219
    types of grass hay 69, 70
hay belly 245
hay cubes/wafers 71
hay replacer chaffs 78
haylage 72–6, 184, 185, 205, 220
    dry matter content *26*, 73, 74, 138, 139
    feeding rates 243–4
    nutritional values 74, 75–6, *79*, 94
    production of 72–3, 75
    safety of 74–5
haynets 71, 154
'heating' feeds
    body temperature 203, 206–7
    excitability 22–3, 33, 92, 242
hemicellulose 58, 61
herbicides 118
herbs 200, 201
    anthelmintics 131
    compound feeds 96
    in pasture 110
    supplements 102, *103*, 106–7
hindgut (large intestine) 5, 6, *10*, 12–13
    acidity 32, 212, 231, 232
    foal 61, 168
    resection in colic 211–12
    wall lining 212

hindgut (large intestines), resection in colic 211–12
hoof
    balance of 217
    changes in laminitis 227–8
    problems *103*, 216–17
    supplements for 208
    unshod 207–8
hormones 36, *103*
    thyroid *43*, 48
Horseracing Regulatory Authority 192
humans
    dietary fat 37
    energy requirements 18
    muscle glycogen loading 177
husks/hulls 62, 65
hyaluronic acid (HA) *103*, 206
hyperlipidaemia 146, 225
hypokalaemia 44

ileum 10
    resection in colic 212
immune system 36, 52, *103*, 195
immunoglobulins, colostrum 159, 161–2
imperial measurements 4
infections, digestive tract 214
insulin 33, 34, 186
insulin resistance 33–4, 80, 146–7, 200, 204, 230, 231, 243
internal parasites 55, 124–7
    bots 126–7
    causing colic 210
    causing diarrhoea 213
    control in pasture 114–16, 127
    drug treatment 127–31
    faecal egg counts 115, 130
    large redworm 126, 210
    roundworms 125, 127, 210
    small redworm 114, 125–6, 210, 213
    tapeworm 126
intestines *see* hindgut (large intestine); small intestine
inulin 105
iodine *43*, 48–9, *113*, 182, 205
iron 47, 181–2
    deficiency *42*, 47, 181–2
    dietary requirements *42*, 251
    functions in body *42*, 47
    in pasture grass *113*
    supplementation 47, 102, *103*, 223
    toxicity 47
ivermectin 127, *128*, 130

jejunum 10
joint problems 199–200
    see also developmental orthopaedic disease (DOD)
joint supplements *103*, 104, 206
joules 28

kidney disease 225–6
kidneys 25, 36, 53, 235
Krebs cycle 174

labelling
    feedstuffs 65–8
    supplements 98–9
lactase *12*
lactic acid 12–13, *14*, 32, 62, 212
    in haylage 74
    hindgut 212, 232
lactose 96
lamellae, hoof 227–8
lameness 199–200
laminitis
    causes/triggers *14*, 32, 58, 62, 80, 231–2, 244–5
    disease process 227–30
    feeding management 75, 232–4
    risk factors 34, 109, 137, 200, 231
    signs of 230
    supplements for *103*
latherin 178
laxatives 246–7
lazy horses 23
legumes 226
    hay 69, 72, *79*, 94
    in pasture 118, 120, 223
    seeds 87, 93, *95*, 96
leptin 18, 37
lignin 58–9, *60*
limb deformities 166, 167
limestone flour 85
linoleic acid 37, 38, 216
α-linolenic acid 37, 38, 107, *113*, 216
linseed (flaxseed) 35, 38, 39, 59, 85, 87
linseed meal 93
linseed oil 107
lipases 39
lipids 37–9, *113*, 216
    animal sources 37, 96, 205
    digestion, absorption and use 13, *14*, 39, 174
    feeding supplementary 37–8, 107, 145, 174–5, 186, 240
    in pasture grass 38, 113

lipoproteins 39
lite salt 179
liver 13
    copper levels 47
    functions 32, 33, 35, 36, 39, 53
    support 201
liver disease 36, 224–5
locust beans 90
lucerne *see* alfalfa
lysine 35, 85, 87
    in cereal grains 80
    dietary requirements 149–50, *250*

magnesite, calcined 96
magnesium 44, 96, 101, 181, 208
    deficiency *41*, 44
    dietary requirements *41*, 250
    excess 40
    functions in body *41*, 44
    in pasture grass *113*
    in sweat 178
maize 80, *80*, 83, 96
maize gluten feed 85
maltase *12*
manganese *43*, 49, *103*, 182, 251
mannanoligosaccharides (MOS) 105
manure, farmyard 120
mare see broodmare
margo plicatus 9
mashes, bran 84, 246–7
matrix metalloproteinases (MMPs) 228–9
meals/cakes (seed) 35, 85, 87, 93, 95
meconium 162
megajoules 28
metabolic syndrome 34
methionine 35, 45, 86, *103*, 217
metric measurements 4
micelles 39
microbes (gut) 12–13, 80, 105, 212
    fibre-degrading 31, 61, 62–3
    fluctuations in 61
    foal 61, 168
    lactic acid production 32, 62
microminerals (trace elements) 45–9
'middlings' 84
midge, Culicoides 217, 218
milk powder 96, 168
milk replacers 168
millet 83
minerals 40–9
    absorption 11
    compound feeds 91, 96

dietary requirements *41–3*, 180–2, *250–1*
  forage-only diet 205, 207
  hoof support 208
  in pasture 113, 219
  in sweat 178
  youngstock 167
mites, cereal 152
MMPs (matrix metalloproteinases) 228–9
molasses 76, 77–8, *95*, 96–7, 196–7
molybdenum 49
monosaccharides 30
moulds
  hay 69, 219
  haylage 75
mouth 6
  see also teeth
moxidectin *128*, *130*, 131
MSM (methylsulphonylmethane) *103*
mucilages 59, 87
mucous membranes, dehydration 27
muscle enzymes 235, 236
muscle glycogen 174, 175–6, 177, 186, 191
muzzle, grazing 146
myoglobin 47, 235
myths, feeding 242–9

National Research Council (USA) 24–5
natural diet of horse 64, 202
natural feeding 202–4
natural feeds 204–6
Nicol, Professor Christine 22
nitrogen excretion 36
non-starch polysaccharides (NSP) 30, 56–7, 60
nutraceuticals 104
nutrient absorption 11–12, 13, *14*
  calcium *14*, 40, 43
  carbohydrates 11, *14*, 32–3
  fibre *14*, 62
  lipids 39
  older horse 198
  proteins 11, *14*, 36
nutrient declarations
  feeds 65–7, *68*
  supplements 98–9
nutrient deficiencies 219–20
  see also under named nutrients
nutrients
  essential 24
  interactions 220

nutritional requirements 24–5
  broodmare 49, 148, *250*
  older horse 194–6
  ration formulation 147–51
  stallion 148, *250–1*
  working/performance horse 177–83, 248, *250–1*
  youngstock 149, 150, *250–1*

oat hay 72
oatfeed 84
oats 81, *94*, 96, 204
  and excitable behaviour 22, 242
  husk/hull 65, 81
  'naked' *80*, 81, 82
  nutrient composition 80, *80*, 81, 82
obesity *see* overweight horse
oesophagus 9
oils 20, 37–9, 107
  analysis in feeds *68*, *80*
  digestion, absorption and use 39
  feeding supplementary 37–8, 107, 145, 174–5, 186, 240
  fish 37, 38, 107–8
  see also fats
oilseeds 85, 93, *95*
  by-products 87, *95*
older horse
  Cushing's syndrome 200
  joint problems 199–200
  maintaining health weight 197–9
  nutritional requirements 194–6
  supplements 199, 201
  teeth 7, 18, 196–7
  veteran feeds 92, 197–8, 246
oligosaccharides 30
olive pulp 90
omega-3 fatty acids 38–9
omega-6 fatty acids 38, 113
omeprazole 215
oral rehydration solutions 27, 179, 189
organic feeds 206
osteoarthritis 199–200
osteochondrosis 167
osteochrondritis dissecans (OCD) 166–7
overweight horse 18, 34, *136*, 137
  exercise 147
  feeding for weight loss 145–7
  insulin resistance 34, 229
  restriction of grazing 112, 117, 146, 202, 233
oxalates 40

oxidative stress 180, 195
oxygen consumption 180

palm kernel meal 87
pancreas 11, 13, 36
pancreatic juice 11, 13
parasites, internal *see* internal parasites
parotid salivary glands 9
pasture 114–21
  area required 110
  control of worms 114–16, 127
  feed value of 112–13, 146
  fencing 120–1
  irritant plants 217
  maintenance 114–18
  management 114–20, 206–7
  mineral deficiencies 48, 49
  poaching 120, 202, 206
  poisonous plants 17, 118–19
  re-seeding 110
  shelter 120, 121, 206, 207
  supplementary feeding 153–4, 155, 202–4
  types 109–10
  water supply 121
  see also grass
peas and beans 87, 93, *95*, 96
pectin 58, 61, 88
pedal bone, rotation 228
pepsin 9, 10, *12*, 36
performance enhancers 104
performance horse 184
  forage 155, 184, 216, 248–9
  gastric ulcers 214, 214–16
  nutritional requirements 177–83, 248, *250–1*
  practical feeding 184–9
  prohibited substances 191–3
  timing of feeds 154–5, 190–1, 249
peristalsis 13
pharynx 9
phosphocreatine 173
phosphorus 40, *41*, 43–4, 85, 167, 181
  absorption *14*
  deficiency *41*
  dietary requirements *41*, *250–1*
  functions in body *41*
  in pasture grass *113*
  ratio to calcium 43, 44, *80*, 84, 88, 219–20
physitis 166, 167
phytates 40
pigs 5

pinocytosis 11
plants
    antioxidants 104–5
    fibre constituents 58–9
    irritant 217
    poisonous 17, 118–19
    selection by horses 17
poaching, of pasture 120, 202, 206
poisonous plants 17, 118–19
Pollitt, Dr Chris 228
polysaccharide storage myopathy
    (PSSM) 236–8
polysaccharides 30
    'non-starch' 30, 56–7, 60
ponies 8, 33, 166
potassium 44, 96
    deficiency *41*, 44
    dietary requirements *41*, 250
    functions in body 40, *41*, 44
    in pasture grass *113*
    in sweat 178
praziquantel 128, *130*
prebiotics 105–6
probiotics 105–6, 199, 201, 213, 234
prohibited substances *103*, 104, 107,
    191–3
    manufacturer's guarantees 193
propionic acid 32, 55, 62, 175, 182, 190
proteases *12*
protein 35–6
    calculation of requirements 149–50
    in cereal grains 80
    crude *68*
    dietary requirements 164–5, 180,
        248, *250*
    digestion and absorption 11, *14*, 36
    energy source 27
    excess 180
    in forage *79*
    functions in body 35–6
    and laminitis 232
    quality of 35
    in supplements 244
psyllium husks 211, 214
pyrantel *128*, *130*, 131
pyruvate 173

Quarter Horse 166, 237
quick-dried forage *26*, *60*, 76–7, 78,
    195, 203–4, 205
quidding 124, 196

racehorses 187
    body condition 187, 189
    forage intake 155, 184, 248–9
    gastric ulcers 190, 214, 215
    timing/restriction feeds 155, 191,
        249
ragwort (*Senecio jacobea*) 117, 118,
    119, 206
rapeseed oil 38
rapeseeds 87
ration formulation
    simple method 138–43
    using nutrient requirements 147–51
    for weight gain 143–5
    for weight loss 145–7
reactive oxygen species 180
rectum 13
recurrent airway obstruction (RAO)
    53, 218–19
    supplements for 102, *103*, 219
red blood cells 47, 55, 102, 107, 182
redworms
    large 126, 210
    small 114, 125–6, 210, 213
    treatment/control 127–31
rehydration 27, 179, 189
respiratory disease 53, 69, 183, 218–19
    risk factors 153
    supplements for 102, *103*
rhabdomyolysis (tying-up) 80, 92, 107
    disease process 235–6
    general management 240–1
    recognition and treatment 238–40
    recurrent 238
rice 83
rice bran 84
root vegetables 16, 87–8, 95
rosehips 111
roundworms 125, 127, 210
rugs 207, 217, 218
ruminants 5, 46–7
    see also cattle; sheep

saccus caecus 9
saliva 8–9, 16, 20, 26, 204, 215
salivary glands 9
salmonella infections 214
salt (sodium chloride) 17, 45, 100–1
    kidney disease 225–6
    rehydration solutions 179
    rhabdomyolysis 239
salt/electrolyte pastes 189, 216
sand ingestion 210–11

scoop, feed 142
seaweed 43, 49, 59
    calcified 119
    feeding 205
seeds 59, 85–7
selenium 47–8, 52, 102, 159, 182, 205,
    240
    deficiency *42*, 48
    dietary requirements *42*, 182, 251
    functions in body *42*, 47
    in pasture 48, *113*
    toxicity *42*, 48
sheep 5, 115, 118, 120
shelter, field 120, 121, 206, 207
shoes, keeping horse without 207–8
sick horse 222–6
silage *94*
skin pinch test 26–7
skin problems 216–17
skin supplements *103*
small intestines 10–11, 61
    nutrient absorption *14*
    resection in colic 212
    starch and sugar digestion 31–2
sodium 40, *41*, 45
    deficiency 41, 45
    dietary requirements *41*, 250
    excess 45
    in sweat 178
sodium chloride *see* salt
soil
    in haylage 75
    mineral deficiencies 48
Soil Association 206
sorghum 83
soya beans 85–6
    hulls 62, 65, 86, *95*, 96
    meal 35, 93
sperm quality 161
stable door, banging 155
stabled horse
    access to forage 203
    box rest 220–2
    respiratory disease 69, 183
stallion 157, 160–1
    nutritional requirements 148, *250–1*
starch 20, 22–3, 30, 31, 204
    absorption and use *14*, 32–3
    digestion 11, 31–2
    and laminitis 232
    maximum feeding rate 80, 144, 154,
        186, 212
    overfeeding of 32, 62, 80, 212,

213–14, 231
performance horse intake 185–6
structure 31
starved horse *see* fasting
statutory statement 65–8
stereotypies, oral 19–22, 62
stomach 9–10, 36, 61
emptying 204
ulcers *see* gastric ulcers
volume of 10
storage of feedstuffs 152–3
'straights' *see* cereal grains
straw 76, *94*, 145–6
feeding 18
fibre 59, 60, *60*
in molassed chaffs 77–8, 196–7
nutrient analysis *79*
stress
feed anticipation 155, 204
weaning 164
strip grazing 146
subchondral bone cysts 166–7
sucrase *12*
sugar *30*, 31
absorption and use *14*, 32–3
allergy 242
blood levels 32–4, 204, 229–30
in carrots 244
digestion 11, 31–2
in grass 232
and laminitis 244–5
performance horse intake 185–6
sugar beet 58, 62, *95*, 145, 197, 204, 243
dry matter content *26*, *36*, *139*
fibre constituents *60*
forms of 88, 89
nutritional value 88
soaking 88
sulphur 40, *42*, 45, *113*
sunflower meal 93
sunflower oil 38
sunflower seeds 35, 86
'superfibres' 61–2, 184–5
supplements 97–8
broad-spectrum vitamin/mineral 91, 99–100, 113, 234
calmative 23, *103*
herbal 106–7
joint support *103*, 104, 206
labelling 98–9
nutraceuticals 104
older horse 199, 201
plant antioxidants 104–5

probiotics/prebiotics 105–6
protein levels 244
respiratory disease 219
salt and electrolyte 100–1
specific nutrients 102
for specific problems 102–4
weight loss regimes 147
surgery, colic 211–12
swallowing 9
sweat, composition 178
sweating 44, 101, 178
sweet itch *103*, 217, 218

tapeworm 125, 126
causing colic 210
control 127–31
diagnosis 130
taste 6, 17
teeth 6–8
age at eruption 7
dental formula 6–7
examination and care 7–8, 122–4, 213
older horse 7, 18, 196–7
wear 8, 122
theobromine 193
thermoregulation 26, 178
thiamine (vitamin B_1) *51*, 54, 190
thirst mechanism 179
Thoroughbreds
growth patterns 166
see also racehorse
threonine 35
thyroid hormones *43*, 48
time budgets 15–16
trace elements (microminerals) 45–9
transamination 35
transport (nutrients) 11
transport (of horses) 154, 155–6, 211, 247
treats, horse 108
triacylglyceride 37
tricarboxylic acid (TCA/Krebs) cycle 174
trypsin *12*
tryptophan *103*
tushes (canine teeth) 7
tying-up *see* rhabdomyolysis

urea 36
urine 28, 36
urticaria 217

valerian 103, 107
vegetable oils 38, 107, 145, 240, 243
vegetables 16, 87–8, *95*
vegetarian diet 37, 96, 205–6
veteran feeds 92, 197–8, 246
'vices' *see* behavioural problems
vitamin(s) 49–50
absorption 11–12, *14*
broodmare 159
in compound feeds 91, 96, 99–100
deficiencies *51*, 54
excess *51*, 183
fat-soluble 50–3
in grass 52, 55, 113
labelling of feedstuffs 66
older horse 195
recommended daily amounts *51*, 251
sick/anorexic horse 223
synthesis in hindgut 12
water-soluble 53–5
working horse 182–3
vitamin A 46, *51*, 52, 108, 162, 183
vitamin B-complex 12, *14*, *51*, 54–5, *103*, 182–3, 190, 225
B_1 (thiamine) *51*, 54, 190
B_{12} (cobalamin) *43*, 49, 54–5, 182, 190
biotin 54, 103, 216–17
folic acid 55
vitamin C *51*, 53–4, 104, 183, 195, 219
supplementation 183, 219, 223
vitamin D 40, *51*, 52–3, 108, 113, 183
vitamin E 50–2, 54, 102, 159, 183, 205, 240
vitamin K 12, *14*, *51*, 53
Vitex agnus castus 103, 200
volatile fatty acids (VFAs) 12, *14*, 38, 61, 62, 175, 190

water 25–7, 151–2
access to 151–2, 211
consumption rates 151
content of feeds 25, *26*
deprivation 26–7
during transport 155
and exercise 249
loss from body 177–8
performance horse 177–8
requirements/drinking rates 25, *26*, 151, 249
role in body 25
supply at pasture 121

weaning 163–4
weed control 117–18
weighbridge 132
weight 23
    determination of 132–4
    see also body condition; overweight
horse
weight gain
    energy requirement calculation 149
    feeding for 143–5
    in youngstock 163, 165–6
weight loss
    energy requirement calculation 149
    feeding for 92, *138*, 145–7
    in older horse 198–9
weigh tape 132–4
welfare issues 21
wheat 65, 80, *80*, 83, 84
wheatbran (bran) 58, 62, 84, 222, 239,
    246–7

wheatfeed 84, 96
whey powder 96
wind-sucking 19, 21, 22
wood-chewing 19, 20
working horse 22
    concentrates 92, 248
    fat supplementation 174–5, 186
    forage 155, 184–5, 248–9
    nutritional requirements 177–83,
        250–1
    ration formulation 148–50, 187–9
    salt and electrolytes 101
    starch and sugar intake 185–6
    timing of feeds 154–5, 190–1, 249
worming
    drugs 127–31
    herbal agents 131
    strategic plan *130*
worms *see* internal parasites

yeast *103*, 105, 106, 199, 201
youngstock 161–8
    concentrate feeds 93, 162–3, 164–5
    developmental problems 166–7
    growth patterns 165–6
    nutritional requirements 149, 150,
        250–1
    see also foal

zinc 46, *103*, 181, 205, 217
    deficiency *42*, 46
    excess *42*
    functions in body *42*, 46
    in pasture grass *113*
    requirements *42*, 251
zinc:copper ratio *42*, 167